MAUDE (1883 - 1993):

SHE GREW UP WITH THE COUNTRY

By her son, Mardo Williams

Erma Gebhart!   3-1-96
with best wishes from mom!
you'll like reading about the
life and times of my 110-year-old
cousin. The author thinks
you will enjoy the humor and pathos.

Mardo Williams

Calliope Press

Publisher's Cataloging-in-Publication
(Prepared by Quality Books Inc.)

Williams, Mardo.
    Maude (1883-1993) : she grew up with the country / by her son, Mardo Williams.
    p. cm.
    Includes bibliographical references and index.
    ISBN 0-9649241-2-9
    LCCN: 95-71983

    1. Williams, Maude Allen. 2. Women--Ohio--Biography. I. Title.

CT254.W55 1996   305.4'09771'092
                                         QBI95-20609

First Calliope Press Hard Cover Printing June 1996

Printed in the U.S.A.

CONTENTS

*PRETTY BOY FLOYD

By Woody Guthrie

© Copyright 1958 (renewed) by FALL RIVER MUSIC INC.

All Rights Reserved   Used by Permission

Book II: Maude Leaves Rush Creek
*She missed her porch, bowered with honeysuckle,
the colorful sunsets, and the spectacular
storms that gave unpredictable drama to the
quiet harmony of rural life*

FOREWORD

---

*M*y mother's family, the Allens, arrived in Massachusetts from England in 1632, just 12 years after the Pilgrims landed at Plymouth Rock. Samuel Allen and his wife, Ann, were among the first settlers of Windsor, Connecticut.

My father's great-great-great-great-grandfather, George Williams, arrived in Philadelphia from Wales in 1690 with other Quakers (Friends) like himself. He received a land grant from King Charles II and settled in Prince Georges County, Maryland.

Those early Allens and Williamses left England because of hunger, overpopulation, religious tensions, trade ambitions, or civic aspirations and helped shape the future of a large part of the New World. My mother was a distant cousin of Revolutionary War hero, General Ethan Allen. In my father's line of descent was Levi Coffin, Jr., the famed anti-slavery leader and one of the founders of the Underground Railway.

Between wars and battles with the Indians, expansion of the country continued. All the early settlers had to do was pack their clothing on the back of the horse, or load their meager furnishings in the wagon and move on to settle new wildernesses, seek new neighbors or find a more tolerant religious atmosphere.

When a likely spot was reached, a temporary shelter was fashioned on the bank of a small stream. The man and his mate, and children, if there were any, began clearing a spot for the log cabin they would build. After that, land would be prepared for the crops that would sustain them.

They were tenacious souls, ready to cope with hardships,

uncertainties and danger in their search for a better life. They had nothing to lose--they had lost every material thing when they left the homeland.

In the early 1800s, many took their religions and moralities with them in helping settle the Ohio Territory. My father's branch of the Williamses, Quakers, came to Ohio, to start over, leaving their prosperous lands in North Carolina because of their opposition to slavery. My mother's great-grandfather, Adam Allen, left Massachusetts in his early twenties, entered the Army of Washington in Pennsylvania, fought in the battles of Brandywine and Monmouth. After the Revolutionary War, he set out on horseback for the Western territories. He finally settled in Ohio with his second wife, Nancy Gardner, my mother's great-grandmother.

Some crossed the Mississippi River to become part of the untrammeled West and Northwest. When the times changed, they left the farm (which once accounted for 95% of the population) to become artisans, educators, ministers, and politicians.

Many had a restlessness that forced them to move on, leaving behind them their friends and any semblance of civilization. They helped settle the nation, give it a texture of courage and initiative, and produce a populace from the original Williamses and Allens that must by now have reached the millions.

My mother lived for 110 years, from 1883 to 1993, establishing a record of longevity among the Allens, a hardy, long-lived people. Her life extended from the industrial revolution, through the inventive frenzy, and the early part of the Space Age. During her 57 years on the farm, she went without many things that are considered necessities today. She lived simply, endured hardships, took in her stride the time-consuming hand labor of the early 1900s--and left us, at age 110, with an enduring memory of her patience, her quiet acceptance of the conditions over which she had no control, and the exemplary standards by which she lived.

I thought she would live always. It wasn't until she had passed her 106th birthday that I began to think of the historical significance of the changes she had witnessed. During the next four years, I questioned her about her memories, marking down those events that happened before I was born or too young to understand, making notes on those daily tasks that she performed so laboriously--churning butter, making bread, canning vegetables and fruits, doing the laundry on the washboard while she cared for her husband and four small children. She had to be cook and servant, seamstress and teacher, friend and advisor.

She was our champion and, when we disappointed her, our severest critic. She was very understanding, always approachable, and the most "extraordinarily" ordinary woman I ever met (and I was 88 years old when she died). Her life, her approach to it, and the times through which she lived, I thought, would be of interest to everyone, from older persons whose relatives may have gone through similar experiences, and eventually to the youngest children (like her great-great-great-granddaughter, born eight months before Grandmother Maude passed away) and to everyone in between those two extremes.

Mother gave quiet support to Dad as both grieved at the violent deaths of his brother, sister-in-law and brother-in-law. They jointly celebrated their little victories--savored the almost daily incidents as their four small children fashioned their own entertainment in a home life that boasted of no modern conveniences. They had no electricity, no plumbing. Kerosene lamps provided the light; galvanized buckets contained the water.

The true story, as it unfolds, tells of life as it perhaps will never be lived again; of the circumstances that made for both happiness and sorrow; of the way my mother and my dad met their trials and tribulations on the scenic Rush Creek farm, and how she coped alone when she became a widow at a youthful 73 years of age.

Mardo Williams,
Columbus, Ohio
October 1995

ACKNOWLEDGMENTS

*T*his book is for my mother, father, and sisters who, I think, would be pleased with this account. And for my wife, Geneva, who died before she could enjoy reading this chronicle of the woman with whom she shared so many of the same traits

Many thanks to Albert Ashforth, P.M. Carlson, Ralph Gardner, Jr., Joanna Wolper, and Eileen Wyman for their encouragement and insightful comments.

Thanks also to Doris Barnhart for information about her father Harry Marmon and to Isabel Perry for her invaluable memories of Mildred, Maude and Lee. Isabel's comments about Gene Perry's World War II exploits were very important. We are grateful to the widow of Robert Hall for permission to reprint his poem, "The Tiger."

My daughters, Jerri Lawrence and Kay Williams, insisted the story of Maude Allen Williams be told. Their suggestions for adding to, cutting, and shaping of the narrative were invaluable. They traced and compiled the Allen and Williams genealogies. This story would have foundered without them. In particular, Kay's many contacts and her knowledge of the publishing world made what at first seemed a formidable task possible.

Genealogical and historical materials about the Allen and Williams families were gathered from the New York Genealogical and Biographical Society Library, New York Public Library, Family History Library of the Church of Jesus Christ of Latter Day Saints, Ohio Historical Library-Genealogy Division, Carnegie Public Library (Washington Court House, Ohio, with help from Jane Rankin), Society of Friends Library at Guilford College, Greensboro, North Carolina (with help from Carol Treadway, Librarian, and Ruth Maynard, Volunteer). Additional reference materials were *American Chronicle: Six Decades in American Life, 1920-1980,* by Lois and Alan Gordon, Atheneum, New York, 1987; and *The New York Public Library Book of Chronologies*, First Edition, 1990 by Bruce Wetterau, The Stonesong Press and the New York Public Library, Simon & Schuster, New York.

The 32-page photo insert was designed by Kara Glasgold.

The Williamses

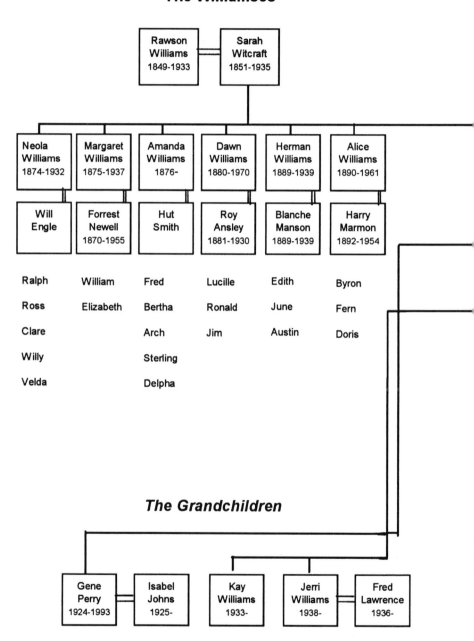

Rawson Williams 1849-1933	Sarah Witcraft 1851-1935				

Neola Williams 1874-1932	Margaret Williams 1875-1937	Amanda Williams 1876-	Dawn Williams 1880-1970	Herman Williams 1889-1939	Alice Williams 1890-1961
Will Engle	Forrest Newell 1870-1955	Hut Smith	Roy Ansley 1881-1930	Blanche Manson 1889-1939	Harry Marmon 1892-1954
Ralph	William	Fred	Lucille	Edith	Byron
Ross	Elizabeth	Bertha	Ronald	June	Fern
Clare		Arch	Jim	Austin	Doris
Willy		Sterling			
Velda		Delpha			

The Grandchildren

Gene Perry 1924-1993	Isabel Johns 1925-	Kay Williams 1933-	Jerri Williams 1938-	Fred Lawrence 1936-

The Allens

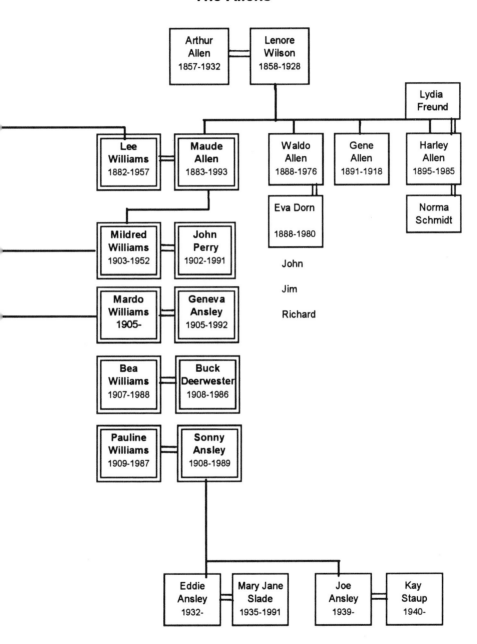

In October 1883, near the day of Maude's birth,
the *Old Farmers Almanack* noted that
"life is at its best now. The mild, sweet days with their bracing air
send a thrill of joy bounding through every vein, while the myriad
tints of gold and gray, red and green--mixed in endless profusion
through the forests--delight the eye and cheer the heart."

PROLOGUE

*N*o bells rang. No whistles blew when, on October 23, 1883, a little girl was born in the rural reaches of Fayette County, Ohio. The birth warranted a line in the *Washington Courthouse Herald*--"a daughter to Arthur and Lenore Wilson Allen."

The parents were farm people. The child was normal, with no unusual attributes. And no one could know that it was the start of a 110-year lifetime during which Maude B. Allen would witness the most amazing transformation of civilization in history--affecting every area of communications, transportation, manufacturing, retailing, farming and financing.

Inventions would make necessities of conveniences, conveniences of luxuries, and open new areas of inconceivable opportunities. As Maude marveled, new processes, new products and dynamic thinking swept the world from the horse and buggy days to the space age.

During her lifetime would come the telephone, radio and television, the automobile, airplane, jet planes, rockets and space vehicles, the typewriter, cash register and computer, all part of the industrial revolution which transformed home and work place. Candles and coal oil lamps became obsolete; new water services added to comfort and health (and in so doing eliminated the historic outhouse), and oil/natural gas explorations expanded the quality of life by making attainable both clean heat and efficient power.

Maude would read but not understand that an intricate mechanism called a computer was making possible automated manufacturing processes, continuous control of inventories and solution of space age technology that eventually would place a man on the moon and touch off a series of manned and unmanned space explorations.

On that autumn day in 1883, there was no hint of what was to come. The midwife gave little Maude a slap on the rump, listened to her cry, then pronounced her fit and healthy.

When the child was four years of age, the Allens moved to a small farm in central-western Ohio, three miles northwest of the village of Ridgeway. Her three brothers--Waldo, Eugene and Harold--were born there. She attended rural one-room schools and then completed the upper elementary grades at the more pretentious Ridgeway school.

The year Maude became 16 her horizons expanded. In order to attain a high school education, she had to go to the Mt. Victory, Ohio school, five miles from home. Arthur and Nora concluded that their little girl, if she were to become the first Allen in more than six generations to complete a high school education, would need a bicycle. So for four years, Maude bravely pedaled her bike to and from classes daily, except for those winter days when she was forced by snow and rain to stay overnight with an aunt and uncle in Mt. Victory.

She was graduated in 1902, with no job, no hobby and a wholesome bias against spending the rest of her life with her parents and three brothers. The combination of her 19th birthday, a golden harvest moon and the unexpected return from college of her favored boy friend combined to effectively seal her future.

They celebrated not wisely but too well. So when Lee Williams told her he wanted to quit Ohio Wesleyan University and return to the home farm, she was interested. They decided to get married just as soon as they could make arrangements.

Book I

100 Acres on Rush Creek

At the beginning of the 20th century, the farmer of 100 acres earned about $750 a year.

Part I: The Wedding, the Belling, and the Unknown

ONE

*M*aude B. Allen became Mrs. Lee Williams on February 25, 1903. She said later she didn't sleep a wink the night before. Lee, who also spent a sleepless night, was up at daybreak on his wedding day. Before he retired, he would drive his horse and buggy more than 30 miles--to obtain the signature of his bride on the marriage application, pick up the license at the probate court in Kenton, 12 miles distant, meet Maude at the minister's home in Mt. Victory, then take her in the open buggy to their new home (another three miles). The weather was chilly but luckily it wasn't snowing.

They were married by the Rev. J. J. Richards shortly after 2 P.M. on that February 25. The only attendant was the minister's secretary. There was no reception but as the newlyweds climbed into the buggy, they were greeted by loud shouts, words of congratulation and the clapping of hands. Several passersby had congregated, bent on embarrassing the popular young couple.

Slapping the reins against Old Topsy, Lee hurriedly drove away. During the 45-minute drive, Lee and Maude huddled under a lap robe, clutching each other's hands. They talked about the stress of the day and their plans for the future.

At last the house came into view, a rambling story-and-a half, 10-room dwelling, built by Lee's grandfather, William I. Witcraft, in 1854 (vacant now because Mrs. Witcraft had died and he had moved to town). The horse and buggy crossed the bridge over Rush Creek, swollen with runoff from the winter storms. Old Topsy turned into the graveled lane toward the place Maude would call home for over 57 years.

Attached to the east end of the house was a combined woodhouse and smokehouse, where the family's home-butchered meats would be cured. Located between the house and a huge bank-barn was the granary where corn was stored, where farm machinery was kept out of the weather, and where chickens roosted. A wind mill whirred quietly at one side, pumping water to the livestock supply tank 300 feet away.

An encouraging factor on this gloomy February day was the sight of the roomy porch which extended along more than three-fourths of the south side. Maude later admitted to being overwhelmed by the sprawling wooden structure, painted an off-white with a light green trim. She had been accustomed to sharing a modest home with her parents and three brothers, and the thought of keeping her new home clean was almost frightening.

Inside were kitchen, pantry, living-dining room, the seldom-used parlor and three bedrooms on the ground floor. Upstairs were two rooms separated by a 12-foot-square study. Unfinished rooms under the eaves were used for storage of unused furnishings. They extended from end to end on either side of the upstairs residence area.

The interior was sparsely furnished. Lee's parents had donated some of their furniture. The woodwork was scraped and gouged. Repairing and repainting it would be her first project, Maude decided. And she would need to add both furnishings and cook-dinner wares. Only one bedroom was furnished, she noted, and there were no closets. Clothing was hung on hooks attached to moldings along one side of the room. A wardrobe or some sort of storage receptacle would be mandatory. She was glad to see that a chamber pot rested on the floor at the side of the bed. There would be no necessity of a cold, late night trek to the outhouse.

There was no honeymoon for Maude and Lee. They ate the light meal his parents, Ross and Sarah Williams, had left on the kitchen table--apple pie and milk, with bread and butter if they were still hungry. Then they prepared for guests. No newlyweds were safe from the dreaded "belling" which was sure to materialize about the time they were ready for bed. During that era, every young couple in a rural community had to endure it. It was an initiation into married life.

Maude hoped she wouldn't be separated from Lee and subjected to endless teasing and words of advice.

As the wind howled and snow flurries whipped past the window, the five feet, six inch, 120-pound brunette wondered if her future would be as bleak as her wedding day. She had good reason to fear that problems would not be long delayed--problems of money and the challenge of raising a family. Her husband, although likable and fun-loving, had yet to prove that he could be steady, serious and a good provider.

Later, much later, she admitted that her qualms were unwarranted. She and Leonidas (Lee) Witcraft Williams enjoyed an almost friction-free and happy life for more than 54 years.

Lee and Maude were the same height within a fraction of an inch. He was 30 to 35 pounds heavier--at a trim 155. His father Ross, by comparison, always tipped the scales at 185 to 190 pounds. Ross had a bushy mustache that was permitted to grow without points, peaks, or curleycues. Lee was always clean shaven. Ross was a gruff man, not given much to smiling, unlike his son who was full of jokes and teasing.

Lee had light brown eyes, with a sort of cast or slant in the right one. Partial loss of sight was due to a friendly battle with Beryl Wallace when both were young. "We were having a corn cob fight when Beryl hurled one that hit me directly in the right eye. I couldn't see for awhile so we discarded the remaining cobs and conveniently forgot to tell our parents what had happened."

Both Lee and Maude were better educated than most rural residents in the early 1900s. After completing the eighth grade, each took the Boxwell Examination (required of all students from the non-accredited rural schools) at the county seat town of Kenton. He entered Mt. Victory High School in 1896; she in the fall of 1898. When she graduated in May, 1902, she became the first member of the Allen clan to obtain a high school education. He was the first of his family.

Lee was the extrovert--the practical joker, the party-goer, the goodwill ambassador. She was the diplomat, the example-setter, the quiet voice of reason. And after Lee died in 1957, she continued alone to set the standards for relatives and friends--a living testimonial to the traits of love, sympathy, charity, goodwill and consideration of others. And she did it even as she entered her 111th year.

But this is about the wedding day, the belling, and the early life of Maude and Lee Williams, the hardships they endured (as did all farm people of that era), their satisfactions, amusements, work and recreation.

Her recollection of the dreaded "belling"--the first incident of married life--was vivid. "It was exciting rather than terrifying," she recalled. There was a lot of noise--the beating of tin pans, loud shouts and desultory firing of shotguns. Looking out from their new home, Lee and Maude found the front yard overflowing with a hundred or more laughing men, women and children.

When the revelers broke into the house, they promptly separated bride and groom. Maude was taken aside by the women and, from their superior knowledge and experience, given instructions on how to cope with her new status. She was warned of possible arguments, the certain conflict of wills, the necessity of maintaining a low profile, a quiet temperament and a worry-free attitude.

Maude sorted out the worthwhile suggestions and applied them to her life, setting a sterling example for all who would come in contact with her during the next 90-plus years. She always lived quietly, modestly, uncomplainingly, thankful for little blessings, refusing to worry about life's setbacks and uncritical of those who didn't live up to her expectations.

Lee, by contrast, was subjected to an entirely different kind of ordeal by the men. Their comments were often crude. He was advised to see that his wife be taught to harness the horses, do some of the plowing, take over the twice daily milking chores, mow the lawn when needed and, in her spare time, cultivate a large garden, then do the canning, cooking and all household duties--meanwhile caring for the children!

The tormentors dallied with the idea of keeping bride and groom in separate places during that first night but were dissuaded by their wives who had learned that the bride was "in a delicate condition." Their first child was to arrive five months later.

It was rumored at the time that the pregnancy was intentional. Maude and Lee Williams were in love. She wanted to get away from her parents and three brothers (about to move to Toledo, Ohio), and he wanted to leave Ohio Wesleyan University.

The young couple hadn't let anyone know (including their parents) about their prospective parenthood until their wedding day. Maude was slender, had not suffered the morning sickness so common in early stages of pregnancy, and had not been tempted to tell all to a friend (who might have violated a secrecy promise by confiding it to a friend or two).

Despite the fact that Lee's folks were Quakers and Maude's parents frowned on card playing and dancing because they felt these practices led to lewdness, there was no censure of the young couple at a time when out-of-wedlock pregnancies were frowned on--when babies born without benefit of the wedding ceremony were called bastards or woods colts.

The "bellers," already well off their normal dusk-to-dawn sleep routine, took pity on the newlyweds by leaving after refreshments of cookies, milk and coffee. Lee's parents, Ross and Sarah, and his closest neighbors, Charles and Lizzie Marmon, served the snack, then shepherded the group out. It was 11 P.M. when the couple bade the last guest good-bye, decided they would let the cleaning-up process go to the next day and shuffled off to bed.

But, tired as she was, the belling wasn't over for Maude. She had no sooner closed her eyes than she felt the coverlet sliding toward the foot of the bed, exposing her to the chill of the unheated room. She kept pulling the blanket back in place until she was fully awake. Practical-joking hubby broke into a guffaw. He had attached a cord to the top of the cover, passed the string through the brass bed rail at the foot and was pulling on his end of the string whenever Maude closed her eyes. She gave him a stiff poke in the shoulder and told him what she would do to him if he didn't quit his tomfoolery.

That was the end--or was it? The next confrontation, which almost broke up their marriage on their wedding night, came when she got up to use the chamber pot rather than brave the outside cold to use the outhouse a hundred feet away. She tumbled to the floor as a cord pulled the vessel out from under her. It was Lee's last effort to instill his own brand of humor in serious marriage. Hereafter, he would be a little more tactful about both the type of joke and the victim. No one was told what Maude said but it was effective.

When she awoke the next morning, Lee was gone. Their cows needed milking.

The honeymoon was over. Through the bedroom window, she saw snow was falling steadily. The muddy flood waters rolled bank-full down the nearby creek. She was 19, four months pregnant, and already missing her parents and three brothers. She wondered what the future would hold with her likable, fun-loving 20-year-old husband.

The house contributed to Maude's nervousness. At least her husband thought so. He had been born a stone's throw away and his grandfather, William I. Witcraft, had contracted for the house to be built on a 100-acre Congressional tract acquired by him in the early 1850s. When completed in 1854, it became somewhat of a tourist attraction.

People came from miles around to see the sprawling, 10-room house that was the first non-log cabin in the area. It utilized clapboard siding and laths and plaster in interior walls.

Hand-hewn, load-bearing beams of ash and oak, some of them 40 feet long and 14 inches on a side, formed the framework. The flooring was of maple, woodwork was black walnut and the remainder, including the doors, was solid oak. Replacing the usual exterior logs were overlapping shakes that had been laboriously shaped by hand and sanded smooth. It was painted white and, from its perch on a knoll a short distance from Rush Creek, was a landmark for years. It is gone now, razed by Amish carpenters for the valuable timber.

It was a monstrous home for a young bride. And it was the worse for wear. It stood vacant after Lee's grandfather moved out. The roof--now 50 years old--was leaking. The wind blew at will under doors and through the window frames.

But Maude put somber thoughts aside on that first morning as a married woman. Her spirits picked up when she realized Lee had taken time to start the fire in the wood-burning kitchen range before he left to do the chores.

He is going to be considerate and we are going to be happy, she thought. She had known Lee for almost five years--or since her first day at Mt. Victory High School. He had been outgoing, more so than she, but was almost always kind and considerate, with occasional lapses into rough teasing and practical jokes. They had gone on a few dates before he was graduated in May, 1900, and continued to date after he enrolled at Ohio Wesleyan (under pressure from his parents Ross and Sarah who felt that, as the elder son, he should go to college).

Maude and Lee became more serious after she got her high school diploma in 1902. Both wanted to get married but their parents frowned on it because of their youth. "Wait a year--or two years," they advised. But Lee was disillusioned with college. He was taking a liberal arts course and decided he'd rather be a farmer. In those days, farmers were considered the best people--independent, reliable, hard working--as opposed to the fast-talking city dwellers.

Lee had few happy memories of OWU. In later years, only two events were worthy of recall. He remembered playing football against a team from the Columbus Deaf and Dumb school who, of course, had to rely on gestures to determine when a play had ended. Those with their backs to the referees continued to play each time after the whistle had blown. "We poor OWU freshmen got battered relentlessly," Lee said, "since officials were always a few seconds late in stopping the action."

The other noteworthy memory was credited to an upper classman named Hefner. It seems he had answered the call of nature and left a huge turd--variously estimated up to two inches in diameter and a foot long--in the toilet bowl. His classmates had declared that toilet off limits and installed a placard above it, "Here's where Hefner died!" According to Lee, students and faculty came from all over the campus to marvel--even some coeds were granted admission--until the janitors regained control.

TWO

On a sunny March day two weeks after her wedding day, Maude watched from the window as her husband plowed the east field. The sun, a burnished yellow, was barely over the horizon but already he'd done the milking and fed the livestock. Now he steered the team of horses back and forth across the tract, turning over one strip of soil (or furrow) at a time. It would take him 10 hours--with a 40-minute break at noon to eat and water the horses--to prepare two acres for cultivation. And that one field contained 18 acres, or nine days of dawn-to-dusk work.

She and Lee had discussed their separate work duties. She had told him that she was prepared to do all housewifely chores. "I will not mow the lawn, milk the cows or help you in the fields," she'd insisted. For his part, Lee agreed to do all he could to lighten her tasks, employ temporary help during peak cultivating and harvest periods, even do some of the menial jobs around the house to make life easier for his pregnant bride.

As she turned away from the window, the young housewife decided to perfect a schedule for herself.

On the agenda of the next few days or weeks, in addition to repainting of kitchen chairs and table, would be renovation of the corner cupboard, transformation of damaged woodwork in both kitchen and living areas by application of putty and paint, fashioning of baby clothes for the infant's arrival in July, and, when weather permitted, the planting of flowers and shrubs.

Also she would make time on the daily worksheet for the preparation of oil lamps, their only means of illumination. That duty entailed the cleaning of the chimneys, trimming of wicks and filling the base of each lamp with kerosene.

And what about the three bountiful meals a day the active working man required? When the days became longer, she was sure she could keep busy with the planting, picking, cleaning and canning of the garden produce. Where would she find the time for all the things she wanted to do?

She asked her husband to purchase some bright white and yellow paints and a brush. She was busy repairing the badly pitted baseboard in the kitchen one morning when she heard someone in the vacant upstairs room. The "clomp, clomp, clomp" was so loud that she became frightened and ran to the barn, 300 feet distant, to get her husband.

Armed with a club, he investigated, searching rooms upstairs and down, even the attic rooms under the roof. He reassured Maude there was no intruder and was preparing to return to the barn when a resounding "thump, thump, thump" sounded overhead.

"Something's on the roof," Lee said. They dashed outside. A wild turkey, attracted by the warmth emanating from the flue, was attempting to roost on the side of the chimney. As the gobbler scrambled for a foothold, bricks were dislodged and came tumbling end over end down the roof.

The mystery was solved. But the newlyweds were presented with another problem. Before the next winter arrived, they would have to rebuild the chimney with new bricks and mortar--it was too much of a fire hazard in its present form.

Part II: Daylight to Dark Demands

Underneath the drudgery was the satisfaction of surviving, the pleasure in what you created--the home-churned butter, the vegetable garden, the field of corn.

ONE

*B*y hit and miss, the couple found their way into a happy family relationship that provided shared work and pleasure, arguments that ended in lovemaking, and long talks that brought to each a new awareness of the other. They had plenty of opportunities for conversation--there was no radio or television to interfere. Lighting was dim so long periods of reading were impractical.

The principal barrier to social evenings, however, were the arduous work days. After arising before daylight, working through the daylight hours and finishing the milking and feeding chores after dark, neither felt like delaying their appointment with Morpheus. Five o'clock the next morning came all too soon.

For most of her farm life, Maude experienced what most people today would term real hardship--a life-style that was emulated for a time by the flower children and dropouts of the 1960s. She graduated from a washboard to a hand-propelled washing machine in the 1920s, got a hand-cranked Victrola in 1930, electric lighting in the 1940s and a radio shortly thereafter. But there was no indoor plumbing so she continued to use the outhouse (100 feet from the back door) for the entire 57 years she lived on the farm.

"The most drastic change in our life," she commented when she observed her 110th birthday with friends and relatives, "came when the house was wired for electricity."

From the earliest days of marriage, Maude said, Lee practiced the basic acts of kindness and consideration. He filled the bucket with drinking water from the well before setting the windmill in motion to pump water to the livestock storage tank. He saw that the stack of wood at the side of the kitchen range was ample for her needs during the day. He brought in the can of kerosene from which she would fill the "coal oil" lamps after cleaning the chimneys.

And he gave her a hug with the admonition that she ring the dinner bell, hanging from a post at the front of the house, in event of an emergency or if she needed him at once. Then he left her to her self-assigned duties.

Both said they adhered to their agreed-upon duties without fail-- except for rare instances. That May, she helped him plant the 1903 corn crop. She was drafted because the neighbor boy failed to show up. The corn planter, a comparatively new piece of equipment, mechanized the placement of seeds.

Maude sat on a spring seat at the rear of the horses and, while the planter was in motion, pulled a lever that deposited the corn, hill by hill--a slow and tedious job. The field of 18 acres took the better part of two days to plant. Lee tried to spell her as often as he could, but the jouncing in the hard seat, the sun boring down, and seven months pregnant--it must have been an ordeal.

The couple's first child, born at home, arrived kicking and squalling in the late afternoon on July 20th. Mildred was tiny, little more than six pounds, with straight black hair and brown eyes. And she demanded so much attention during those early weeks that her mother helped in the fields only part of one day, and that under protest when the neighbor boy again failed to appear, leaving Lee with no one to help get the cured hay off the wagon and into the mow.

Maude, four weeks after Mildred's birth, aching and hot under the summer sun, led the horse that pulled the hay fork, saving the day and getting all the crop safely under the roof of the huge barn before the threatened rainfall came.

Getting the hay off the wagon was a simple procedure made more involved by a series of pulleys used in the operation. Lee pressed a six-pronged grappling hook (called a hay fork) into the forage on the wagon bed, locked the contrivance and signaled the go-ahead.

Maude led the animal a required distance from the barn. The horse was hitched to a singletree (a pivotal horizontal crossbar) which in turn was attached to a one-inch rope threaded through pulleys. As the horse plodded forward, it pulled the loaded hay fork upward until it locked on a steel track immediately under the roof. Maude stopped the horse and Lee pulled on a long cord which he'd held in his hand all the while. This tripped the catch which held the grappling hook closed, and the hay dropped into place in the mow.

Interlaced with the farming activities were the just-as-important housewifely duties. Many chores were done "the hard way," by hand. Present day housewives can't visualize the monotonous detail involved in normal tasks, the additional time required and the expertise needed, for example, just to bake a cake. Mixing it wasn't too difficult (flour, baking powder, eggs, milk, lard, flavorings). Baking it was another matter.

Maude's stove took up about 12 square feet of the kitchen floor and most of that portion of the east wall between the porch entrance and the window. With its full length warming closets above the cooking surface, and its water reservoir at one end, it weighed between 350 and 400 pounds. "It was never moved," she said.

It was a "Kalamazoo" with six removable lids, two of them directly over the flames. The warming closet had hinged covers which, when closed, could keep the cooked food warm for 30 minutes or more. The reservoir held about 2 1/2 gallons of water. It was warmed by heat from the cooking fire of coal or wood (whichever fuel was available) and water could be withdrawn a cupful or panful at a time through the hinged lid. Water from the reservoir was used to wash dishes, face and hands, and to shampoo hair. It came from the cistern and, because of the inflow of surface pollutants, was unsuitable for cooking or drinking.

When Maude first started using the stove, she said she had difficulty maintaining the proper oven heat. One part of it might be too hot (next to the fire box) and another (at the rear or at the side next to the water reservoir) might be too cold. So she had to watch closely, and when one side of the cake or pie seemed to be cooking faster than the other, she shifted its position.

Maude also heated her irons on the temperamental stove. Called sadirons, they were made of cast iron and had flat bottoms and holes in the top for the patented handle to lift each off the stove and guide the heated object over the fabric.

The flat surface of the iron had to be kept clean and free of rust. It had to be hot enough to erase wrinkles in the cloth, cool enough to prevent scorching. And the only way to approach a semblance of the desired temperature was to moisten an index finger and strike it lightly against the heated surface. A low hiss-s-s meant the heat was right; a low scream meant you had burned your finger, Maude said.

She had four irons on the stove at the start, then alternated them so as to always be using a hot one. The flat surface had to be cleaned frequently so she had a wiping cloth at the ready. When one of the sadirons came in contact with food that had been spilled on the stove, it might require polishing with a fine sandpaper, and perhaps washing with soap and water too.

Nora Allen had told her daughter not to worry about not knowing how to cook and bake. "Just get a good cook book and follow the directions," she said. Maude became one of the best cooks around, but she learned early not to add a little more of this and that to the recipe. She followed the recipes religiously and if the cook book said "beat the mixture briskly 100 times," she counted out 100 sweeping strokes.

She became so adept with that southpaw stroke--she was left handed --that every tablespoon in the house was worn down a half and was sloped to indicate the friction between spoon point and surface of mixing bowl in what became millions of stirrings over the years.

Maude relied on the staple "meat and potatoes" meals routinely but also fashioned her own menus and special dishes. She said no one liked liver when it was prepared normally so she dressed it up by stewing it in milk and adding more seasonings than usual. At the last, she put in stir fried onions to cover the liver flavor and served it with a thin milk-enriched gravy. "Lee told me I'd surpassed myself," she recalled, "that liver prepared this way took on a unique flavor."

Maude baked her own bread. When it became stale, she sliced the whole loaf and put it in the oven. It dried out and became a light brown. Each slice was spread with her home-churned butter, sprinkled with sugar, and covered with sweet, hot milk. Lee wasn't as enthusiastic about her milk toast as about the liver. He couldn't envision bread as a main dish. Lee liked heartier fare.

"We didn't have much money," Maude said, "especially the first 15 years. I saved pennies in a glass in the cupboard. Pennies were worth something then. But no matter how lean the times were, we always had food because we had a garden and I canned a lot."

Maude said she relied on home grown vegetables and fruits, home-butchered meats, milk from the Williams' six cows, eggs from the hens, and bulk foods (bought from the store in Mt. Victory) like rolled oats, rice and beans to assure variety.

She prepared delicacies such as rice pudding (with raisins), a bread pudding using stale bread, filled pies and cakes of every kind, doughy noodles rich with egg yolks. One summer, she remembered, Lee concocted a dessert he said was better than strawberries and cream. He sliced plump tomatoes in a bowl, covered them with milk and sugar.

Making butter wasn't arduous, Maude said, just time-consuming. First, she dumped the crock of cream into the wooden receptacle--a tall, slightly pear-shaped container with a tightly closing lid through which a rod protruded. She had to grasp the rod with both hands to pump it up and down. A paddle, attached to the bottom of the rod, agitated the sour cream and eventually separated the butter fat from the liquid. She salvaged the butter in the final phase, gently rolled it to remove as much moisture as possible and pressed it into a mold. Lee and, later, the children drank the fresh buttermilk, with the surplus becoming slop for the hogs.

Obtaining cream was a problem during summer days when milk would often sour before the cream could rise to the top. The milk, direct from the cows, would be stored in as cool a spot as possible, then the butter fat gently skimmed from the surface. It was churned only after a sufficient supply of cream had been obtained.

To make a pumpkin pie, Maude said, "We had to bring in a medium-sized pumpkin (8-10 pounds) from the field, cut it into sections and remove the inner pulp." It was boiled, drained, crushed and forced through a screen mesh or colander. Lumps were removed and the puree measured and flavored with milk, eggs, sugar, nutmeg and cinnamon. The crust was fashioned from flour, water and lard, kneaded, rolled out and placed in a nine or ten-inch pan.

Residents of the Rush Creek neighborhood shared in the recipes, as well as the adventures, disappointments, embarrassments and tragedies of every individual in the area, Maude recalled. If one didn't know the person, a friend or acquaintance did. Stories were welcomed that added color of any kind to every-day life. It wasn't gossip so much as healthy interest.

One day Lee came home from visiting a neighbor, eager to tell Maude of the latest tale going the rounds. It was told as the truth, but he may have exaggerated a little.

A young mother was dashing frantically about the kitchen, looking after two young children and a baby while trying to put together a pumpkin pie for supper. Her baby started crying as if he were being stuck with a safety pin (customary fastener for the hand-laundered buttocks cover of the day). She grabbed him up, plopped him down on the cabinet top to change the diaper and started wiping the light yellow substance from his bottom.

Too late she realized that the baby's poop was extremely close to the pumpkin she had just processed through the colander, and may even have mingled to some extent. What to do? The pumpkin was ready-cooked, strained, and seasoned. No other pumpkin was available. And she'd promised her husband a freshly baked pie for supper.

She studied the alternatives and decided to go ahead with the baking. When her husband came into the kitchen for a glass of cold water, he found her sorting through what he thought was pumpkin mix for the pie. But he was mystified by her behavior. She would lift a spoonful to her nose, sniff, and declare either "That's pumpkin," and toss it into a bowl; or "That's not," and toss it into a paper sack. The conclusion of the story was left up in the air. Lee never said if the family had pie that night for supper or if the husband convinced his wife he wasn't hungry for pie after all.

TWO

Maude was introduced to Pal, an intelligent collie dog, during her first year of marriage. She took over his care and training. Within a few weeks Pal had learned simple commands and was being sent to the woods and pasture lands to bring in the cows at milking time. No other dog--and there were several in later years--would command the friendship and affection she felt for Pal who lived with them for nine years.

She forgot the names of the next few dogs, but Major was memorable for being the most boisterous, as well as the most headstrong of them all. He brought in the cows as instructed but could not be kept from nipping at the heels of the horses. He was kicked in the ribs in November, 1934, during one of his onslaughts against the horses and suffered internal injuries. Refusing to give up, Major followed a hunter through the fields the next day. He collapsed and died overnight, perhaps dreaming of the rabbits he had flushed from their snowy lairs.

The collies that followed became shepherds only. Maude said she couldn't remember the name of the last one. They left it with a neighbor when she and Lee made their second trip to Arizona in the fall of 1949. Efforts to lure the dog home failed. They had been away too long--or the neighbor had fed it too well.

THREE

Throughout those early years on the farm, Maude retained the same basic hair arrangement. The style was called "a la concierge," she said. Long strands were pulled to the top of her head and pinned in a knot. Later, she found the care of her hair was taking too much time, so she cut off the waist-length tresses and wore her hair loosely, tied in at the back with barrette or ribbon when cooking and baking.

Maude dressed with the fashion trends, preferred the dress styles of the 1890s--long skirts and fitted waists, but not the Mother Hubbard, which, she said, "covers everything and touches nothing."

The youthful mother established a routine for baby-caring, housework, cooking and the ever-developing new chores. With Mildred by her side, she allowed herself a little free time to walk--to the barn, to the orchard. She strolled along the creek which ran through the front pasture, walked to neighbors and friends, to the wooded 30 acres at the back of the farm, where she gathered wildflowers, listened to the caroling of the birds, and wondered if she was hearing a robin, a meadow lark or a red bird. She decided to learn the various bird calls. She started to absorb farm knowledge.

Pulling Mildred in a small wagon, she walked to the back field where Lee was planting corn. She noted the process had been simplified since last year when she'd been called into emergency service. The knotted wire had been added. It speeded the operation and eliminated the monotonous job she'd performed when pregnant with Mildred, that of pulling the lever by hand and depositing the seeds.

Lee unrolled a spool of knotted wire across the field and staked it solidly at each end. As the corn planter advanced and the slotted arm on the seed box struck a knot in the wire, three or four kernels of grain at a time were deposited in the shallow trench made by blades attached to the planter.

The knots usually were 42 inches apart in those early days so the hills of corn were uniformly 3 1/2 feet apart in each row. When the planter reached the other end of the field, Lee moved the stake anchoring the wire the required distance and the planter straddled the groove marked on the previous cross-field trip. The route was traced by a disc on the end of a rod attached to the planter. If the horses were allowed to wander, the groove became more and more crooked and the planter deposited its grain in an increasingly meandering row.

When Lee's father Ross first started farming, he planted corn laboriously with a hand tool which was jabbed into the soil, its jaws opened by a wrist movement, and the predetermined amount of grain deposited in each individual hill.

Weeding the crop was tedious, starting when the plants were less than four inches high. Lee would drive the two-horse team across the field, straddling a row so that his foot-operated spans of shallow plows would pass on each side of the plants--tearing out the weeds but leaving the corn plants unharmed.

The cultivating of the corn crop would be repeated two or three times before the plants were large enough to shade the ground and effectively control the weeds. Lee quoted an old farm rule of "knee high by the Fourth of July," and plowing ordinarily would be completed by the first of August, in time for the start of the hay harvest.

Plowing the fields one furrow at a time, behind a slowly moving team of horses was even more monotonous than cultivating the corn. Lee said he might pause on a corner and listen to the song of the meadowlark. He welcomed the sudden showers which left him sodden but refreshed in the oppressive heat. And frequently he would look up to see his wife walking down the fence row to confide she just wanted to see him.

When Lee trudged up the lane to the farmhouse, or drove the team of horses into the barn after his dawn to dusk labor in the fields, he was cheered by the conviction that he would be met with a smile from his mate--and perhaps a glass of lemonade--before he washed away the grime of dust and sweat at the cistern pump. He would have a brief rest, then supper, and finally he would milk the cows before falling in bed about 9:30. When he rose at 5:00 A.M., Maude fixed him a hearty breakfast of oatmeal or boiled rice with milk and sugar, ham, eggs, toast, and coffee. For variety, she might serve pancakes or fried mush with syrup. Lee was out in the field again by 6:00 A.M.

FOUR

Lee considered haying a demanding chore, due to a combination of mid-summer heat and the strenuous labor involved. It was a multiple action project, the first part of it comparatively painless. Lee drove his team of horses, Daisy and Bell, hitched to a mowing machine along the edge of the standing clover. One end of the five-foot long cutter blade was attached to cogs that caused the blade to move back and forth as the machine moved, severing the plants about three inches above the ground.

After the hay was cut, it lay on the ground overnight before being raked into rows. A horse-pulled contrivance, with closely spaced wire tines, gathered up the individual straws and deposited them in a continuous windrow across the field.

When the hay was sufficiently cured, the mechanized hayloader (which replaced the man with the pitchfork) moved into the field. This piece of equipment (now almost obsolete) was attached to the rear of the wagon and, as the horses walked on either side of the windrow, its tines raked the ground and conveyors lifted the hay onto the wagon. A workman then rearranged the hay to ensure a maximum load. If improperly placed, a part of the towering load could slide off or, in extreme cases, cause the wagon to topple over on its way to the barn.

Lee considered the proper curing of hay (usually seven to ten days) a matter of concern. If left in the field too long, the blades would dry out, losing much of their nutrition. But if too moist when stored, the hay would mold or heat would build up and destroy both barn and crop in spontaneous combustion. After a neighbor lost his barn in a fire of this sort, Lee became even more careful. He checked the stored hay for days after the harvest. If he found evidence of mildew or a heat buildup, he took immediate action, tearing the clumps apart to aerate the trouble spots.

Lee labored alone during the early years of his marriage (except for occasional help from neighbors whom he would help in turn). He eventually was able to hire a teenage farm youth on a regular basis during the summers. The lad worked for 75 cents a day at those times when he was needed, and provided his own lunch!

"I now had help, except when the boy went fishing," Lee said. Maude noticed the change in her husband's temperament--he became more cheerful when he had help--and she insisted that he hire a farmhand on a seasonal if not a year-around basis, so they set aside a spare bedroom off the parlor and started budgeting their meager funds.

In 1907, Enoch Spain became the first of a series of live-in, hired hands. He was paid $20 per month plus board and room and had Sundays off. During his first year, he lightened Lee's work in the plowing, cultivating and harvesting; took part in all the barnyard farm chores except the milking; cut down trees and sawed them in lengths for the cooking and heating stoves; and made himself available for corn husking, machinery repair and all the sundry winter activities.

In 1908, "I raised his pay to $30 per month and made a horse and buggy available for his personal use," Lee said. "When he left at the end of the 1910 harvest season to operate his own farm, we felt we had lost a member of the family." Thirty dollars became the standard pay for the succeeding workers.

Alfalfa, legumes, and red and white clover were forage crops, and used as feed for the livestock. Alfalfa and clover could be cut two or more times, but the first harvest was considered in those days to be the most nutritious. Sometimes Lee cut the second crop of red clover to process through the clover huller for the seeds, which then were used to establish a forage crop in another field.

One hot summer day the mowing machine was eating its way steadily through the standing clover when Lee heard frightened squealing. The five-foot long cutting bar had passed over a rabbit's nest, leaving one small rabbit badly mutilated, the other three scampering madly for cover. The mother rabbit had escaped. He believed she would be back. He restored the nest as best he could. In it, he placed the three little survivors and marked the spot so it would be bypassed by rake and loader. He knew the hawks, owls or foxes would wipe them out unless mother rabbit could move them to a better concealed location.

He watched closely as he resumed mowing but realized he would never be able to see another hidden nest in time to avert a similar tragedy. He had become a factor in nature's pattern of survival of the fittest.

FIVE

As Maude became more proficient in housework and mothering, she canned and preserved more and more of the family foods. She picked, shelled or snapped, cored and quartered or otherwise prepared peas, beans, apples, berries, tomatoes, peaches, cherries and other products for the family larder. Produce was cooked thoroughly before being placed in containers that had been sterilized in boiling water.

Tomatoes were more susceptible to spoiling in the can, she said, so she labored more carefully with them. Tin cans were used in those early days. And the lids had to be placed carefully in the grooves before the hot sealing wax was poured around the top. When spoilage occurred, as demonstrated by a bulge in the tin, the entire can was thrown away.

Botulism was just as prevalent then, and just as fatal.

Apples came from the family orchard just west of the house. Cherries also were available for the picking. But blackberries and black raspberries were a little more difficult to obtain. Maude, and sometimes Lee, braved the hordes of mosquitoes, the thorns and the August heat to pick wild berries growing in the brushy part of the woods. Each picker donned the most substantial garb to ward off mosquitoes. But, more often than not, all returned home with a mass of red welts and itches that kept them scratching for a week.

In addition to the berries, the harvest frequently included chiggers. Nothing seemed to repel the little insects which dropped from twigs and leaves to lodge against the body at every spot where clothing was tight enough to hold them. Each year, the couple agreed that berry picking was too much trouble and too irritating. Then, in each succeeding year, they concluded that maybe the delicious pies and other pastries were worth it.

Maude liked the flowers and the vegetable garden, so much of her free time during summer months was spent outdoors. She had old-fashioned yellow and pink roses along the front yard picket fence during those early years. And she contrived a bower of wild morning glory and other flowering vines at both ends of the spacious porch.

A grape arbor, under which went the walkway to the well and barnyard, added its touch of scenery. Cherry and pear trees were on the fringes of the lawn. Holly hocks, the one-trunk type with a row of bell-like flowers down the side, were a staple.

And the 80-foot long clothes line of No. 9 wire, on which were hung the weekly washing and, in springtime, the carpets for their yearly beating, was strung clear across the side yard between a pine tree and a black walnut tree. The wire was embedded deeper and deeper as the years passed and made each tree unsuitable for harvesting as lumber even as they became large enough.

At the southwest corner of the house stood a giant sweet pear tree. In its prime, it was 30 feet high and was prone to drop its fruit day after day during August and September--littering the lawn with the juicy debris that attracted both bees and flies. Maude spent endless hours trying to clear up that mess and keep the porch safe from the free-stinging insects.

The garden, at the back side of the house, proceeded predictably. Lee fertilized it in late winter, using manure from the livestock. After the plowing and cultivating came the tedious work of marking out the rows with a hand-propelled appliance for shallow indentations and a rounded horse-pulled plow for deeper trenches (in which potatoes or similar underground-growing vegetables would be planted). Lee and Maude then planted each variety of seed or plant in the assigned area.

It was important to plant "under the sign"--a reference to stages of the moon. Potatoes would be planted by St. Patrick's Day, if at all possible. If the condition of the soil or the weather made that impossible, then planting should be delayed a full month until the moon again was full, new or in the right phase. Sweet corn, as an above-ground crop, was planted in another aspect of the moon. Peas were an early crop; beans came later.

Tomatoes were grown from both seeds and plants. Lee liked to plant the seeds early in a sheltered place, then replant in rows the right distance apart. He covered each tender plant with a burdock leaf to shade it from the hot sun, then removed the leaf a day after re-planting. Weeds were curbed by hand hoeing.

By the end of her first year of married life, as Maude dragged herself from bed in the dark each morning, she decided she liked the farm routine. She liked the idea of being her own boss, of not having to keep up with the Joneses (everyone outwardly lived the same, had the same basic possessions) and of having simple solutions for every problem.

SIX

In mid-July, Lee moved on to the next task, the cutting and shocking of the wheat and oats. In the early 1900s, he used a recently improved binder which cut the plants and tied them into bundles while the contrivance was being pulled by horses across the field. A reel, on which long slats were mounted, revolved to guide the swath of waving grain toward the cutting bar (a device similar to that on the mowing machine).

Workmen following the binder assembled the sheaves, placed each seeded end upright, capped the shock with other sheaves. Threshing was scheduled only after the grain was dry, normally in late August or early

September. That was a frenzied time in the Williams household. Lee was kept busy operating the threshing outfit which he pulled with his steam engine from farm to farm until the last member of the 10-to-12 farm threshing ring was served.

Maude, when theirs was the host farm, was responsible for feeding 20 to 25 harvest hands after they left their stations at the grain separator or came in from the fields. Big tubs of water were placed in the yard so they could slap it on their face and hands, wash away the sweat and grime.

Lee's mother and two or three neighbor women helped prepare the meal, always more elaborate at Maude's than at the other farms. The men ate fried chicken or steak, mashed potatoes and gravy, coconut cream or apple pie, coffee, tea, and milk. The kids would eat after the farm hands finished.

Children of farm families developed a certain excitement when threshing time arrived. The smaller ones--including the early teen-age group--fought for places on the steam engine platform. Lee said he had trouble keeping them from trying to climb aboard while the vehicle was steaming down the road, its cumbersome grain separator behind.

"They seemed to think it was a cousin to the calliope which sounded its musical theme at fairs and circuses," he commented. "And when I blew the whistle, they went mad. They fought for a seat on the tool box at the left side of the platform even after the equipment was anchored in place." Lee operated the controls from the right side and needed the platform for shoveling coal into the firebox.

The equipment was owned by Lee's father, Ross Williams, but the son was responsible for its upkeep and operation. Every day during the threshing season, Lee fired up the steam engine, dragged the separator to the next farm, leveled it, attached the drive belt and started the separator mechanism which ate the plants at one end and spewed out a stream of grain and mountains of chaff at the other.

Each sheaf was tossed into the maw of the separator so that the grain end entered the mechanism first. This was supposed to assure greater efficiency and reduce the amount of grain being discharged in the chaff.

Members of the threshing ring--and there were 10 to 12 farms in the group each year--followed Lee and his steam engine from farm to farm and shared the work. Some took horse-drawn wagons into the field.

Others tossed the golden sheaves to the man on the wagon who, upon arriving at the threshing site with his load, tossed a bundle at a time onto the conveyor which led to the slashing knives. It was a team effort--a sort of assembly line procedure that utilized man and beast to the best advantage.

The host farmer at each stop had responsibility for seeing that the grain was stored in sacks or bins as it flowed down the outflow chute. He also provided the team of horses to haul the grain from the site and perhaps a second wagon to help bring the sheaves from the field.

With the invention of the harvester, the process would be simplified, since both the cutting and the threshing, which separates the grain from the chaff, would be done in one operation, in the field. This development was years in the future.

When the dinner bell sounded, the entire threshing operation halted. Those men at the separator ate first. The men in the field completed loading the wagons and when they had washed themselves at the washtubs in the yard, the second sitting was ready.

"The men ate as if they hadn't had a meal in days," Maude said. And from the conversation at the table, the threshing dinners were the finest most would have until the next season. For the housewives competed with each other to place their most delicious foods on the table, and relished comments that Mrs. Bird, or Mrs. McMahon, or Mrs. Early, or Mrs. Williams, or Mrs. Marmon served the best meal, the most delectable pie or the finest, moistest cake on the circuit.

Farmers welcomed threshing time as a chance for sociability as well as work, and a chance to tell jokes and tall tales--since for most of the year their farm chores were done alone. Lee was well known for his jokes. If he heard one, he remembered it for re-telling. He told stories about Jews, blacks, the Irish, labor organizers, salesmen, farmers, and the clergy-- with a gleam in his eye and no malice in his heart.

One of the many of varying vulgarity told during those rural days were recalled by friends long after Lee had died.

This Irishman lived in Mt. Victory (Lee liked to give his jokes verisimilitude by using real names; Mt. Victory was just a few miles away). He was a rough, ungainly, whiskery lout--sunburned a deep brown from working six days a week on the railroad right-of-way. He awoke one morning in deep pain after a celebration of someone's birthday (he couldn't remember whose).

So he dashed into the nearby office of Dr. M.B. Hunt, where the waiting room was filled with the town's most genteel women. The doctor came for another patient, recognized him, and called out: "Why, Pat, what brings you here?"

"Begorra, Doc, and my cock is awful sore." Dr. Hunt, with an apology to the waiting women, rushed Pat into the examining room and prescribed the necessary medicine. Pat was instructed to report back in three days.

The doctor, in an effort to shorten Pat's visit since the waiting room was nearly always full, suggested that he stand near the back door. Doc would ask him how his foot (or some body part) was doing. The answer would determine if he needed different medication.

Pat made his appearance at the back door as instructed, also on another busy day. And Dr. Hunt used the agreed-on code. "Well, Pat, how is your arm today?" The reply: "Faith and begorra, Doc, it still hurts to piss through it!"

Lee was a born performer (his Welsh heritage), acted out his jokes with gusto, making them funnier than they were.

SEVEN

When the haying and the threshing of wheat and oats were completed, the still growing corn became Lee's last major concern of the season. Two or three inches of rainfall during August would be sufficient for the corn to mature. With too little rain, the ear would be small and the grains shriveled. Too much rain would cause the roots to rot. Wide-spreading blades would catch and hoard every drop of moisture in times of drought.

Normally, kernels hardened on the ear and the blades turned light yellow in mid-September, signaling the start of what many considered the most time-consuming and disagreeable task on the farming cycle--the cutting, shocking and husking that separated corn from fodder.

Lee really suffered during the corn harvest. He was allergic to the dust or mold that settled on his skin and was breathed into his lungs. From the time he took a corn knife in his hand until he laid aside his husking peg--he coughed and scratched.

Maude did everything she could to ease the terrible itching. She bathed the irritated skin with cooling cloths soaked in salt or baking soda or the astringent obtained from doctor and druggist. She applied compresses that had been coated with the prescribed ointments and when that failed made up her own mixtures of lard, or butter or kerosene, enhanced by calamine lotion and baking powder.

Nothing helped for long and Lee's fingers continued scratching legs, arms, chest, stomach--even in his sleep. His skin became so raw he had to shelter it from clothing with poultices.

His ordeal began in mid-September with the first downward slash of the corn cutter (an 18-inch knife with a six-inch wooden handle) on that first unoffending stalk. It was necessary in the early 1900s to open the field for passage of the corn binder. That was done by hand, cutting six rows across the field and carrying the cut corn in one arm before dragging it to a gallus, where the loose stalks were arranged into a shock.

The gallus was formed by using two hills of corn from one row and two hills directly opposite them to form a support, twining the tops of all plants together. Loose plants were braced together in this gallus and another stalk was looped around the top to hold the shock together. Each row of shocks was usually 12 hills from the next row. This distance between shocks could be shortened if the density of the stalks and weight of the corn presented an undue burden on the farmer.

Lee admitted that during his first year on the farm he was overwhelmed by the sight of the endless rows of proudly waving corn. The stalks were eight feet high and the thought of cutting six rows across the field by himself, dragging armload after armload between shocks, and doing it shock after shock until the entire field was ready for the mechanical binder was demoralizing. He was thankful he was able to hire a helper.

He glanced down at the long knife which would be slashing through hundreds of plants before day end and hoped that its edge would remain keen for the task. The tool required some practice for efficient operation.

For speed and safety, the right-handed worker would walk at the inner side of the plant, reach across with the left arm and pull the hill (usually three or four plants) in front of his body while powerfully slashing downward along his right side. He added to the effort and lost time if he had to make more than one cut at each hill. If the blade glanced off the target, he could end up with a badly cut leg, a broken knife or a dulled tool. The procedure was the same, in reverse, for the left-handed person. There were no right and left-handed knives.

After the binder (a machine pulled by two horses) had cut the remaining corn one row at a time and tied it in bundles, workmen gathered them and placed them, tassel-end up, at the nearest shock. They were tied together with twine or with two or three stalks spliced together. The corn was left to dry out a month or so before being shucked in the field or hauled to the barn where the fodder (corn stalks) was fed to cattle after the ears of corn had been removed.

Lee used a corn shredder during the first few years. The sheaves were loaded on wagons and hauled to the side of the shredder beside a farm building. Plants were steered into a set of blades, in a procedure reminiscent of the threshing operation for small grains. Ears of corn rolled out on a conveyor into a wagon bed and the shredded corn stalks were blown onto the floor of the barn. From there, the shredded plants became cattle feed; the grain became corn meal, cereals, or animal feed.

The corn harvest sometimes extended throughout the fall and early winter, into the new year. Weather and the availability of help were factors in completion of this heavily work-loaded operation.

Over the years, Maude grew to appreciate how each season had its own traits and inflicted its demands upon farm people. She learned to cherish the moments of beauty, watch for the threats of climatic changes and prepare for the ever-recurring crisis.

She learned that spring was a time of preparation--getting the soil ready. Summer was for the cultivation of newly planted crops and for the harvest of small grains. Fall became a beehive of activity as farmers began an onslaught on the corn crop--three months were devoted to cutting, husking and processing the flood of yellow gold.

Winter was almost as busy for the successful farmer. The shortened daylight hours were devoted to repairing and lubricating the machinery needed during the other three seasons, for fattening cattle and hogs for the marketplace, and preparing for the arrival of little animals--the births of pigs and calves were scheduled for February and March.

And the plowing, which had been started between stints with the corn last fall, now must be pushed so the soil would be ready for spring planting. The wheat crop had been sowed in late September. Plants already were four inches high when the first cold blasts swept the land in November. They would survive the winter if there was sufficient snow cover.

Maude, who would spend more than 57 years on that farm, said she never felt lonely, even after her husband of 54 years died. That was due as much to her temperament as to her early resolve to look for her solace in the beauties of sunrises and sunsets, in the songs of birds and the smell of rain on the parched earth. She took things as they came. She never worried. She spelled out her philosophy: "If you can't change it, don't worry about it."

EIGHT

In 1904, Maude asked her husband to remind his father about repairing the house, as he'd promised. In 1905, pregnant with her second child, she said she definitely needed some place to keep the butter and milk cool. In 1906, renovations began to happen. Mildred was three, son Mardo (named after a hero in a book) was one, and Maude was pregnant with Bea. Between the demands of the children and the cleaning up after the carpenters, she had no time for complaints of any kind.

She'd needed a cooler of some kind from that first summer on, she said. One day, after throwing out a crock of soured milk, she gave the question some serious thought. She could ask Lee to excavate a small area in the garden, near the back door as an underground cellar, or get her one of the popular iceboxes of the time. It had a compartment on the top for the ice and a food storage compartment on the bottom.

She acquired both during the next year or two. Lee purchased a used icebox at a farm sale. It was used for one entire summer and part of the next one. Both Maude and Lee found so much fault with it that when it rusted out there were no regrets. Maude said that the two feet by three feet by 16-inch storage space held a limited amount of perishables and those foods frequently were little cooler than lukewarm.

Lee had to hitch up the horse and go to Mt. Victory twice a week for ice (three miles and about an hour each way)--usually on days when he should be busy with farm work. Also the icebox took up space in the kitchen which already contained the massive kitchen range, a dining table and six chairs, and the china cabinet.

The two were seriously discussing plans for excavating a cellar when Maude came up with another plan. Why not use the water-cooled area that was in place already? She referred to the eight feet by eight feet, six-foot-deep area under the outside well--where all their drinking water came from.

Water spilling from the pump at every use would trickle through the wooden platform, keeping the impromptu icebox at 45 degrees, Lee estimated. The major drawback, both agreed, would be climbing in and out of the subterranean area with an arm full of perishable foods.

It was worth a try. Lee painted the brick walls beneath the well and scrubbed the concrete floor. He placed a section of the wooden platform on hinges and dropped a two-step stool under the opening. He attached a rope to the leg of the windmill.

The person descending into the well could grasp it as he or she groped with one foot for the crosspiece three feet down. From there, one could reach the stool. It was tricky. Maude said Lee or one of the children--when they were big enough--would fetch and carry for her, especially at those times when she was pregnant.

The under-well cooler served them the remainder of their lives on the farm. Insulated from both heat and cold by the six feet of earth in which it was sunk, the compartment became a storage area for perishables other than foods. Lee found it convenient to keep his beer there--at an average 47 degrees in summer and 36 degrees in winter.

And while they were busy solving their food storage problems, workmen razed the historic icehouse that had been used by Grandma and Grandpa Witcraft when they lived on the farm. It stood at the northeast corner of the house for almost half a century. It was a windowless structure with a wide opening on the north side so a loaded wagon or sled could be backed partially inside for unloading slabs of ice. Grandpa Witcraft, years earlier, had carved his ice from Rush Creek during the coldest days of winter.

The ice chunks were carefully packed in sawdust upon arrival. The last of the ice would be used in August, after particles clinging to it were washed away. None of it went into beverages--there were too many impurities--but it was used to keep perishables cold and was packed around the metal container in the hand cranked freezer when home made ice cream was made.

Lee and Maude never used the icehouse. There were too many uncertainties--the coldness of the winter, availability of a new supply of sawdust and needed equipment to cut and haul the ice from the creek--as well as too few uses for ice that would be impure.

The under-well "icebox" had barely been placed in use when Lee's father Ross authorized widespread improvements on the house. He said the shake roof, a fire hazard, would be replaced, the two fireplaces removed, a chimney rebuilt, the stairway relocated and damaged walls made like new.

Forrest Newell, Ross Williams's son-in-law and Lee's brother-in-law, was hired as general contractor. It took him and his one employee--a black man who, like Forrest, was skilled in the building trades--most of the summer of 1907 to complete the project.

They tore off the shakes and unrolled the strips of galvanized roofing, crimping each strip to the next one so water wouldn't leak into the house. They tore down the chimney below the roof line and covered the hole with tar paper before moving inside to remove the twin fireplaces in the parlor and dining/sitting room.

The fireplaces had not been used since the time they flooded the house with smoke because of a clogged-up flue. The facade bricks were crumbling and dangerous. Winter winds blew down through the chimney and out the fireplaces, making the house even more drafty.

The fireplace-chimney work seemed to last forever, Maude said. Dirt, soot, and mortar dust spread everywhere. When the massive fireplaces came out, so did a large portion of that wall separating living room and parlor. Ornate mantels in each room had been formed from the same three-inch thick slab of black walnut lumber. It was three feet wide and six feet long. It came out in one piece and left the entire wall in shambles--the chimney base exposed.

The chimney was rebuilt to provide sufficient draft for two heating stoves, one in the parlor and one in the dining/sitting room, each with a separate flue. So far, Forrest and his helper had been laborers, tinners, and brick masons--now they would become carpenters.

The stairway to the upstairs rooms was diverted from Maude's and Lee's bedroom to the living room. Their bedroom previously had four door openings, three on that same inside wall (to the living room, parlor, and the upstairs).

By adjusting the stairway to enter the living room, Lee and Maude obtained space for a wardrobe along the wall, and the assurance of greater privacy. No longer would a child--or a visitor--trek down the stairway and make an unannounced entry into their bedroom.

The change also gave Forrest and his helper the opportunity to fashion a rough storage place in the stairwell, for canned produce or packages, plus the challenge of rebuilding the partition which became the west wall of the living room and the east wall of the parlor.

Maude was forced to seek the comfort of the porch and her reed rocking chair as the craftsmen sawed and pounded--creating a din and raising clouds of dust.

Maude used that rocking chair many times over the years and always on that roomy, partly shaded porch, from spring to fall. She did her thinking there, her planning there, and her needlework there. She was sitting there on that day in late summer, 1907, when Forrest packed up his tools and suggested she now could complete the cleaning up without fear that he would mess things up again--he was finished!

As she checked the improvements, her gaze kept returning to all the outside doorways. Four were in the front, two in the rear; two of the six led into the living room from the porch, one from porch to parlor, and two into the kitchen (one from the porch, one from the back stoop). "We should have had two or three of those doorways closed," she told Lee.

But Forrest already was reporting to a new job. He would not do the work as part of his original contract, and Ross was not willing to pay more. "We'll have to put up with the snow and dust blowing in, and the rag rugs bunched in front of the cracks under the doors," she lamented.

That summer may have brought her more cleaning, scrubbing, and washing--to remove the grime and soot--than any before or since. But it also brought her the realization that in times of turmoil she could find relief by simply sitting on her porch in her reed rocking chair, listening to the bird concerts and staring at the far horizon.

NINE

In the farm life of the early 1900s, everyone used the primitive, also referred to as the privy. The Williamses was a two-holer equipped with a sack of lime, a Sears Roebuck catalog (The Wish Book), and, during the summer, a fly swatter.

The Sears catalog, in its heyday, was 1,500 pages, weighed six pounds, and featured 100,000 products. The Williamses perused the listed bargains and dreamed, then tore out pages for toilet paper. Lime was scooped into the hole after each visitation--for sanitation and to repel the flies.

The structure was approximately five feet by seven feet, with a shingled roof and a hinged door in which had been carved a crescent-shaped aperture. The crescent not only identified the building's purpose but provided ventilation. The door swung outward but could be latched from the inside.

A wide shelf extended the length of the rear wall at a height of approximately 22 inches. Two circular openings in it assured accommodations for as many persons, if needed. One was smaller than the other and was designed to prevent a child from falling into the pit below. Families with several children sometimes had "three or four-holers."

Lee and Maude took advantage of the Works Progress Administration (WPA) in 1937 and had a new Chic Sales outhouse built. It was about the same size as the original but had a concrete base built above a deeper pit. It still was primitive, and the user still perused the catalog and, when duties were completed, carefully tore out a page or two for toilet tissue. There was no lighting, no plumbing.

Labor costs were assumed by the government as part of its program to provide jobs for the unemployed. Lee paid for the materials. The new edifice, which would last the remainder of his life, cost him $12.

Part III: The Children

Many Hands Make Light Work

*The children came too close together,
they had illnesses that left us tired and ill-tempered,
but they brought the happy sounds of laughter
to our home.*

ONE

*F*our children were born to Maude and Lee within six years and three months of their wedding. After Mildred Ilo (July 20, 1903) came son Mardo Allen (August 15, 1905), then Beatrice Eleanor, who made her entrance on January 7, 1907, and, finally, Bernice Pauline, born May 19, 1909.

The work multiplied with the growth of the family. With no indoor plumbing, efforts were made to ensure that drinking water be brought from the well and stored in buckets within the kitchen so a supply was always present. The bath water, which came from a pitcher pump installed outside above the cistern, had to be carried in and heated a panful at a time.

The kitchen became a fog-filled room on Saturdays, for Maude insisted that every child get a tub bath at least once a week. She and Lee might get away with sponge baths during the cold winter months but each child got dunked in the 10-gallon galvanized laundry tub--an activity that sometimes lasted from mid-morning until late afternoon, especially if one or another of the bathers was reluctant to get in the bath and decided to play hide-and-seek.

Diapers were homemade (cut from pieces of old blankets). After each use, they were soaked, rinsed out and washed again and again--by hand.

Home remedies were an integral part of healthy farm life in the early part of the century. The young couple had to learn when to use the knowledge available to themselves and their neighbors, and when to call their physician. For a time, Dr. J.D. Vassar of Ridgeway was available, then Dr. Harry Titsworth of Mt. Victory, and finally, from about 1909, Dr. C.L. Thompson of West Mansfield.

Maude and Lee relied on ointments, compresses and patented medicines for run-of-the-mill colds, bee stings, and sprains. Kerosene and lard, applied to a bandage around the chest, sometimes could break up a cold. Or Vick's Vaporub (launched in 1905) might be used, accompanied by inhalation of steam from a pan of hot water at the bedside.

The children had all the "popular" diseases--whooping cough, chicken pox, two kinds of measles, croup, and mumps. "We took them in stride--had no idea that they were as potentially dangerous as they later were found to be," Maude observed.

The family learned to cope. Luckily, there were no broken bones. "When the rare emergency came," Maude said, "we had the best doctors around."

The couple's first medical crisis came in September, 1905. Mardo, one month old, was asleep in the living room. Maude was busy in the kitchen making apple jelly, using fruit from the orchard adjoining the house. Mildred, a toddler of two, was playing on the kitchen floor with a homemade doll.

Maude heard the infant make a choking noise, she said, and went to make sure he was all right. He was. But ever-active Mildred chose that moment to grab the handle of the pan in which the jelly was simmering. It toppled toward the floor, spilling boiling liquid over the child's right arm. Luckily, the jelly solution was still thin and rolled right off the flesh.

But Mildred, who underwent emergency treatment in the office of Dr. Harry Titsworth in Mt. Victory, carried the elbow-to-wrist scars the rest of her life. There was no effective burn treatment in those days. Poultices were deemed sufficient and in cases of less serious burns, housewives often were advised to gently apply butter or baking soda, wrap the area loosely and try to prevent bumps that would tear the burned skin.

Maude's illness after the birth of her youngest child, Pauline, in May, 1909, was a potential disaster. Her internal organs were damaged and, before Lee convinced her to see a physician, had become infected. Dr. C.L. Thompson advised immediate surgery and scheduled a hysterectomy--comparatively rare in those days--to remove the damaged tissue. She entered Grant Hospital, Columbus in April 1910, underwent a five-hour operation which left the ovaries intact.

She wrote longing postcards to her family: To Mardo: "You must be a big boy if you can plow. Mama won't know you, will she? Do you take good care of Beatrice?"

To Mildred: "I am afraid you children will be so big I won't know you. You must be good. Take care of little Pauline."

And finally: "I will be home next week. You don't know how bad I want to see you all."

She returned to the farm 14 days after surgery. Her recovery was slow. Lee spent as much time with her as he could. Her mother, Nora Allen, came down from Toledo and remained until called home by the illness of her husband. Maude tried it alone but four active children--the youngest only two--were just too many to cope with in her weakened state.

Plans were made and the two eldest, Mildred, age seven, and Mardo, age five, were sent by train to Toledo to spend most of the summer with Grandma and Grandpa Allen. The entire family was at the Ridgeway depot to bid the youngsters a tearful good-bye. They were met at the Union Station in Toledo by the grandparents and their three sons, Waldo, Gene, and Harley (the children's uncles).

Mildred and Mardo got the royal treatment. They went to Toledo Beach, a resort-type playground where Mardo thought he would try out the giant slide. As he watched from the top, another youngster pushed off with an excited shout. About halfway down, his rump got ahead of his body, he overturned, and slid the rest of the way on his side. The Rush Creek farm boy reconsidered and backed down the stairway to laughter and jeers.

The summer was a long one for all involved. The children had little to do, and few playmates of their age. They sent yearning postcards to the family at home. Mardo's plea in August was: "Dear Mama, How are you? When are you coming up? Please tell us soon."

The parents missed them too, and wrote that Bea and little Pauline were getting tired of each other's company. But the summer's respite was a godsend to Maude. She started feeling better almost at once, gained weight and strength, and no longer had the dragged down feeling she'd grown to expect.

The next event could have been much more serious, even tragic. In 1910, three-year-old Bea developed what the parents considered a mild illness. It turned out to be polio. Both feet became severely twisted so that she could only walk on her toes and the sides of her feet.

Dr. C.L. Thompson of West Mansfield, the attending physician, recommended that remedial surgery be undertaken. The child, he explained, might be able to hobble about painfully on the tips of her toes as she grew older, but she might be so disabled as to be confined to a wheel chair. The alternative, he said, was a surgical procedure to weaken the controlling ligaments so that, with therapy, Bea could regain almost complete use of her feet. The doctor conceded that, even with surgery, her ankles would probably always be weak and that she might not be able to skate or run and play ball with the other children.

A few months later, the parents authorized the procedure. They had watched their daughter attempt to walk, with almost disastrous results. They had witnessed her pain at not being able to play the rough and tumble games with her sister Mildred and brother Mardo.

And Bea, Maude noticed, was growing so fearful of her capabilities that she disliked trying to entertain Pauline, the much-coddled youngster of the family. At age two, Pauline was walking everywhere and that may have been a factor in Bea's growing dissatisfaction with her disability.

Four-year-old Bea entered the hospital at Bellefontaine, Ohio, early in 1911. The unexpected happened during surgery when, under deep anesthesia, Bea's heart began to fail. By using all the known procedures of the time--"coupled with some luck," Maude said later--the little girl was revived.

The surgery was a limited success. Bea's ankles were double-jointed but she could don shoes; she could walk, hesitantly at first; she could even dance and one winter when she was eight years old, Santa brought her a pair of bobsled skates. That year, she skated on her four-runners and joined the other winter enthusiasts on the ice on Rush Creek. She skidded, was pushed and prodded, laughed and shouted as loudly as any.

Her mom and dad were proud of her, were afraid for her in the new, more active role she was assuming, and pampered her. But the other kids, Maude said, treated her as an equal and prevented her from becoming spoiled.

TWO

As the children grew older, "There's nothing to do," became a common complaint, especially on those rainy or snowy days, so Maude introduced games like charades, hide and seek and "andy over," in which one child would toss a ball over the house and another would toss it back.

Maude and Lee patiently played the simpler games with them-- dominoes and checkers. Then Lee introduced cards and taught them how each card, from the Ace (one) to the King (13) related to each other. By the time he or she learned to read, the child could play Euchre, Seven-Up and Sell-Out.

Lee had gained for himself a coterie of eager players who made up in enthusiasm for their lack of expertise. He won relentlessly, showed no mercy, and explained time after time where each of his opponents had erred. His partner, when they teamed up, two against two, received the same criticism (which Lee termed helpful hints on how to improve).

To Lee's undying regret, he was unable to teach either Maude or the children how to play Pinochle with any finesse. In that game, certain cards have different values than in most others. There also is an involved method of "melding" points before start of play and of counting the total at conclusion of each hand.

Lee liked Euchre with its 24 playing cards and right and left bowers (Jack of the trump suit paired with Jack of the sister suit--like Spades with Clubs, Hearts with Diamonds). Compared to Pinochle, it was a simple game, like kids playing pick-up, where one child scatters the entire deck on the floor and another has to pick up the cards, one by one.

When Maude was engaged in what she considered necessary evening duties, cards, dominoes, checkers, crossword puzzles, even popcorn, would fail to attract her interest. Lee couldn't entice her with promises or rewards as she patiently sorted through the clothing of two adults and four children, mending tears, sewing rips, patching holes.

She thought every sock had to be darned as soon as a small hole appeared in the heel. If Lee wanted popcorn, he had to get out the popper (an oblong metal pan mounted on a long handle, with a sliding lid that could be opened and closed with a pull cord), stir up the fire and do it himself. "I thought that when I got married, I would have someone to do those things for me," he'd joke.

While Lee was pushing the card skills, Maude was touting the necessity of reading well. She introduced each child to the land of make-believe through Grimm's Fairy Tales. The book was so well used that its pages were falling apart when Pauline, the youngest, started reading it for herself.

Book after book was obtained, even though money was so scarce that a coloring book and the necessary crayons might be available only at Christmas. Books were borrowed from the neighbors, obtained through school projects and once in awhile even purchased at second hand bookstores. People in rural areas respected the written word and had achieved an even greater degree of literacy than people in the cities.

All four read children's tales before progressing to stories of survival against the odds, adventure, and mystery. One of the most popular was *Girl of the Limberlost*, day-to-day life in primitive conditions in Appalachia. The children liked the Tarzan stories and Zane Gray's dramas of the Wild West. *Little Women* and other Alcott books were read and re-read. The longest and weightiest volume, *Les Miserables*, came as a high school assignment. All waded through it but were less than laudatory. Maude heard them discussing it later, shocked by the imprisonment and harsh treatment Jean Valjean had received--all for stealing a loaf of bread.

Mysteries became their number one choice, followed by adventure. Romance entranced the girls and they dreamed of being rescued from a raging torrent by an ideal man--preferably six feet tall and with dark hair and eyes. But all married schoolmates and only one (at five feet, 11 inches) approached the six-foot mark.

"Mom and Dad are psychologists" Mardo told Mildred once when they were growing up. "You mean how they get us to do the things we don't want to do?" she asked.

And they discussed how their parents contrived to get them interested in playing dominoes or checkers, reading books and magazines, or solving puzzles. It always started with an order "to quit pestering"--and to go play with their toys or a childhood game. It ended with "Mom and Dad getting out the dominoes or checkers or cards and showing so much interest in the game themselves that we demanded to be allowed to play."

The parents then gave up their seats to the youngsters, instructed them in the basics and returned to reading and conversing--until one or another child shattered the peace with a cry of "Unfair!" or a demand that mother and father keep a sibling from cheating.

Lee liked to sing baritone in duets and quartets. "Dad was our most popular performer," the children agreed. If they could talk him into singing one of his bawdy songs--*Actors Boarding House* was their favorite--all activities came to a halt. Mildred, Mardo, Bea and Pauline would stand entranced, just outside the range of his swinging arms. Even Maude, who was usually too busy, would stop and join the group, watching with a pleased smile on her face.

Lee was at his best in 1913, with his favorite fans surrounding him and no other entertainment for competition. The youngsters were four, six, eight, and ten that year. It was fun to see their dad in this comic role, seemingly without a care in the world. He sang--baritone and without musical accompaniment--in a freestyle manner.

He gestured and grimaced. He pranced, walked up steps, and enacted the various scenes that were described in this 14-verse song about a down-at-the heels actor living in competition with other actors in a rundown boarding house in New York City.

I'll sing you a song of an actor's boarding house that's run by a Dutchman, Herman Krouse.

It's No. 22 Great Jones, and the price per week is just six bones.
I'm up eleven flights of stairs, and in my room there are no chairs,
No sign of a gas or candlelight, in fact my room is out of sight.
We sleep 11 in one bed, and in the morning six are dead.
The first one up the best one dressed, today I lost my coat and vest;
Some other actor stole my shoes, and took them out to buy some booze.
They feed on hash three times a day, and the serio comics all chew hay.
The house is full of museum freaks, for a season of just forty weeks.
They are a dizzy looking troupe, and the turtle boy fell in the soup.
They all have English pugs to pet, and their picture's in the Police Gazette.
They played Delaware and Water Gap, and other towns not on the map,
*   Then comic songs all night they sing.*
When they hear the dinner bell, oh, how like Indians they do yell;
They surround the little tables in pairs and read the gaudy bill of fares.
We had some steak called Lafayette, ate some and I'm laffing yet.
Oh, the coffee it was awful weak, hadn't strength enough to speak.
It with the butter fought just two rounds, and had to settle on its grounds.
And when they passed the apple pie, oh me, oh me, oh me, oh my!
Upon my piece I found a hair, for things like that I do not care;
The boarder next to me named John ate his piece with the jo-jo's on!
When we're through we say our prayers and hope we climb the golden stairs.
We have a party every night, always busts up in a fight.
Pound parties are the fad you see, at the one last night they pounded me.
Then Christmas was the game they played, with their stockings on a line arrayed--
I had none but to get a chance, upon the line I hung my pants.
Some got presents, oh, so fine; some son-of-a-gun got into mine.

Into my room I made a retreat--And went to breakfast in a sheet.
AND the band played "Annie Laurie-e-e-e-e."

The children thought it was wonderful the way he brought the song to an end. He'd fling his hands out wide and make his voice deep and gruff, groaning out the final words, "Annie Laurie-e-e-e-e."

Winter evenings were customarily spent together in the living room, near the stove. "A popular picture in my memory," Maude said, as she contemplated her early life, "is of the kids playing on the floor, Lee and I are seated at the table, reading by lamplight. He has a paring knife in his hands and is carefully scraping an apple."

She explained this graphic memory: Lee had just received his ill-fitting dentures and had learned the hard way that the teeth just couldn't bite into his favorite fresh fruit. He solved the problem by halving an apple and scraping enough of the pulp to get the taste.

He told Maude, who was soon to get her teeth pulled because of pyorrhea, that the result was highly unsatisfactory; the dentures had caused him to lose his sense of taste. "Even apples don't taste good," he complained. He stopped singing shortly after he discovered that his voice was never the same with a mouthful of dentures. The tone was different, he explained, and it was embarrassing when he had to stop and relocate an ill-fitting upper or lower.

Lee and Maude grew more insistent that the children brush their teeth regularly. So each night after supper, wash basin and drinking water were placed on the kitchen table. The youngsters were lined up and, one by one, used their index finger and salt or baking soda to brush aside the day's food particles.

"We had no tooth brush and no tooth paste," Maude explained, "so we wrapped a clean white cloth around the finger and dampened it. The child dipped his or her finger in the cleaning agent (they had the choice--either salt or soda) and began rubbing the teeth--upper and lower, inner and outer surfaces.

"We emphasized the necessity of brushing teeth as frequently as possible, with the bare finger if no cloth was available, and always after the last meal of the day. We felt that sleeping with a clean mouth would help control tooth decay and that rubbing the gums would prevent the pyorrhea that caused us to lose our teeth so early in life."

Sometime during those informal winter evenings, the parents decided that their children had enough recreational gimmicks, hobbies, and chores to avert boredom; that now was the time to teach them some principles to guide them through life.

"A stitch in time saves nine," quoted Maude as she taught the girls to sew and darn. She bought them each a thimble to keep them from injuring their fingers, although she felt she couldn't afford a thimble for herself and never used one during all her years of hand-stitching. She made their little dresses entirely by hand until she acquired a Singer foot treadle sewing machine in 1910.

She taught neatness with the admonition that "cleanliness is next to Godliness." She was their mentor as the girls became experienced in cooking, baking, canning, and caring for the house.

Mildred, Bea and Pauline had their own sorority. They played together, wrapped corncobs in tattered clothing to form rag dolls, talked of their dreams, and shared secrets. They blew the fuzz from the mature dandelions, stripped the hollyhocks of their blooms to form heads on match sticks, and dressed up in their mother's clothing to play "make believe." When they weren't playing, they did their chores and learned new skills using thread and thimble, frying skillet and baking pan. Mardo didn't feel left out. He didn't want to learn their secrets, and he had no desire to become a housewife.

The three girls were proficient in every respect when they married, yet none could match their mother in flavor of the puddings, flakiness of the pie crusts, and wholesome heartiness of the meats. Gravies were made from the meat drippings and whole milk, and were never lumpy.

Lee, who was not given to needless praise, would wonder out loud how Maude could have made such a good cook of herself when she had so many other things to do. She did the laundry bending over a washboard-- and that included the dirty diapers for four babies until all were potty trained. The hand cranked washing machine came later.

Kotex was unheard of. So sanitary napkins, under some other name like "granny rags," were of folded cloth (light blanket material, if available) and had to be laundered by hand after each use. A bucket of cold water, to which a small amount of soap or vinegar was added, served as depository for soiled diapers and napkins until they could be washed.

The instruction of the son differed somewhat from the daughters and met with a little disquietude on Maude's part. Lee was careful to impart the message and procedure for using the crosscut saw, for example. But he was inclined to be boisterous and thought that his son, as he grew older, was old enough to hear "plain talk" and the facts of life, told in a somewhat ribald manner.

One time, shortly after the boy had been introduced to the rigors of sawing down hickory trees for firewood, Lee was trying to lift a heavy piece of wood and steer it into the fast turning buzz saw.

As Lee vainly tried to keep the six-foot piece of timber from striking the saw at an angle, and as Mardo watched with interest to see what was going to happen, Lee shouted: "Don't stand there like a turd on a tussock, give me a hand."

Work times were joke times when the worker became tired. Lee liked jokes that had a moral.

This little long-tailed dog, he told his son, liked to chase trains on a track at the rear of the farm where he lived. He never caught any but he kept trying. One day as he was gamely racing the locomotive, barking all the way, his tail drifted under a wheel and was cut off.

Angered at the pain, the dog snapped at the churning wheel and was crushed. The moral, Dad told the unworldly 13-year-old, is "Never lose your head over a piece of tail!"

THREE

Every child, from three or four years of age, had specific chores. They started--the boy as well as the girls--with the drying of dishes after each meal. Maude would heat the water in the dish pan on the wood-burning kitchen range, then move it to the kitchen table.

As mother washed, Mildred dried the dishes and stacked them carefully on the table. A year or two later, Mildred was trusted with the dishwashing and Mardo became the dryer (under mother's supervision, of course). Each child got the same instruction. Eventually, Maude was able to leave the entire after-dinner operation to the children--and she had time for other duties.'

By that time, additional chores were being assigned and the children (who considered dishwashing and drying the most menial) were arguing about whose turn it was for the table clearing and washing-drying. At least two youngsters were assigned--one to wash and one to dry--but after "company" had eaten dinner with the Williamses the entire family, including Maude (but exempting Lee), might be called into action.

Every child got the same basic training in chores that were added to the regimen by Maude and Lee. The woodbox had to be filled regularly so the baking, cooking and laundry could proceed unimpeded. The coal bucket had to be full and placed at the side of the heating stove that was kept burning throughout the winter months (in a smoldering stage at night so the flame could easily be restored by Lee when he arose in the darkness of early morning).

Lee tried to convince the youngsters it was part of their duties to clean his cuspidor periodically. He offered a bribe--ten cents at first and eventually a quarter--but usually would have to do it himself. The spittoon would become so cruddy, with stains so dried and the cuds of tobacco so hard that it would have to be filled with water, placed in the sun for a day and then roughly scrubbed with a broom. It would sparkle after the next application of soap and clean water, and a brisk hand brushing.

The cuspidor was of a glazed material and beautifully decorated in a light green floral pattern. The bottom was formed as a rounded bowl, pinched in, then flared out at the top to catch any dribbles that might stray.

Maude termed tobacco chewing a dirty habit and tried vainly to get her spouse to quit. He said it was safer than cigarette smoking, which would be hazardous when he was in the barn or field, or doing any of the harvesting operations. There was no concern then about tobacco's effect on the user's health.

The girls had to help their mother with the dusting and cleaning. All the children started picking vegetables in the garden when they were three or four. They learned to snap beans, hull peas, and peel apples from the 30-tree orchard at the west side of the house. They pared potatoes, and prepared tomatoes and other vegetables for Maude's incessant canning activities. They joined Mom and Dad in picking cherries from the trees near the house. These were the sour red cherries and were reserved for pies--either fresh or later from the canned surplus.

There were times to daydream too. The children liked to lie in the sun on the banks of Rush Creek while they watched the fleecy, variously shaped clouds floating overhead, and listened to the music of meadow larks, robins, red birds, and the "Bob White" or "Where Are You" call of the quail. When they grew tired of being lazy, there was always the creek at their feet beckoning them to wade, or swim, or overturn rocks to watch the elusive crawdad scoot away backwards.

FOUR

"Who's ready to pick me some cherries?" Maude asked one June day in 1914. When she received no answer from youngsters who suddenly got too busy, or became hard of hearing, she ruminated that she might have to substitute liver and onions for the pie she planned for Lee's birthday, June 17. The response was overwhelming. Even five-year-old Pauline volunteered.

The children made it a group effort. Bea and Pauline plucked from the lower limbs, using stool and stepladder; Mildred and Mardo climbed the tree, hooking baling wire over a branch to hold their small pails. When they had picked all they could reach, the four reported to their mother with enough fruit for two pies and dessert cherries for two meals.

They even aided Maude in the pitting process, removing the seeds and discarding those cherries which had been hosting a worm--as unsprayed fruit sometimes does.

All would help harvest other fruit as the season advanced--black raspberries in early August, blackberries from the woods that same month. Sugar pears would become pickled pears late that month and the Concord grapes from the arbor would be made into jelly and jam during the early part of autumn. Elderberries--too bland by themselves--would become jellies or pies after raisins, lemon juice or grapes were added.

Apples were a part of the Williams family menu from the time the first

Early Harvests were picked from the 30-tree orchard during late July. Those apples were quick to become rotten so were eaten from the tree or stewed at once to become sauce for the table. Red Asterkins ripened in early August. They were not keepers, but could be canned, baked or stewed. They were too sour to be sought as an eating apple. Rambos were harvested in early October and were relished for eating. Winesaps and Baldwins were delicious raw, were sought for pies and sauce, and would keep in a cool spot for most of the winter.

Over the years, one apple tree after another fell to the high winds, cold winters, the sleet, or heavy snows which snapped off limb after limb. The children were left with no place to climb, the birds with no place to nest or to sing the songs that had captivated listeners from windy March to bleak November. The orchard became a feed lot for the hogs, then a garden site. Finally, Lee planted a row of red raspberry bushes down the middle.

Gathering hickory nuts became a fall ritual for the children. The first killing frost loosened the nuts on their twigs, but it took some rain or a high wind to send them skittering to the ground. That was when the youngsters took their pails to tramp the fence rows and the woods to compete for the biggest, the best and the most.

If the nuts still clung tightly, one or two members of the party would climb the tree and shake the branches as violently as possible. They cheered whenever they found a leafless tree, its nuts spread in profusion around its trunk. They found one such tree--its leaves whipped away by the winds--along the fence row between Lee's and his dad's farms in 1915. The nuts, bright and shiny with the outside hulls already broken open, were lying on the open ground.

The children went wild. It was a bonanza. They gathered two pails full in less than 30 minutes. The pails held about two and one-half gallons each and would provide Maude with nutmeats for the winter--and the children with what they would care to pick from the hulls for their own use. Cracking the shells and gouging the kernels out of the intricate grooves were chores no one usually cared to assume unless there was some reward involved (like hickory nut cake).

The harvested nuts were spread on the floor in the granary, carefully screened from rats and marauding squirrels, and left to dry. Three weeks later, Maude instructed the older children to crack some of the choice nuts; she was about to prepare a mystery dish everyone would like. With visions of cakes, or pies, or candy, the youngsters raced to the granary.

They came back with long faces and told their mother that she could forget her surprise--no nuts were available. No, the squirrels hadn't confiscated them. The worms had. Every nut was riddled with holes. The floor held the dried shed skins of worms. One or two nuts looked untouched but when cracked open revealed plump worms eating away at remnants of the last nutmeats.

Maude consoled them. Lee told them to take along a rock or hammer on the next outing, crack a nut or two under every tree before picking them up. Then he offered his own brand of sympathy. He went with them that same fall to replenish the store the worms had taken.

The youngsters for a time relished gathering black walnuts. They had a strong, slightly rotten taste and were encased in a covering that was both difficult to remove and stained the hands. The children liked to stomp on each nut separately, remove the hull and carry the nuts to a dry place to cure. They displayed their deeply stained hands to friends with a sense of pride. Later, as the girls grew older and more concerned about their appearance, they begged off from the hulling or, under protest, wore gloves in reluctant assistance. The black walnuts were used in baking rarely. Lee maintained that one black walnut was enough for four men.

The son was impressed into service for all domestic activities, along with his sisters, until he was promoted by Lee to be his number two farming assistant. The hired hand remained the number one aide but Mardo learned to do the milking when Lee was busy in the fields. He assisted in more and more of the planting, cultivating and harvesting.

One of his early responsibilities, starting when he was eight, was to mount a spring seat attached to the tongue of Lee's corn plow and drive the team of horses for the crucial first cultivation of the tender plants.

He had to keep the horses a-straddle of each row of corn, holding them on course while they battled the flies with tossing heads and switching tails. If the horses staggered out of line, Lee would lose control of the gang of plows and a whole string of plants could be destroyed. The two worked from morning until evening, with a break at noon.

The son was not needed on the equipment as the corn gained stature. The plants usually were knee-high in early July and ready to be left uncultivated two or three weeks later. The larger stalks could control weeds and their widespread blades would catch practically every rain drop.

"Lee was able to utilize the children in a variety of ways as they grew up," Maude said. Both Mardo and Mildred drove the hay wagon, freeing Lee or the hired hand to do the loading. A seat was hung from the high front standards of the wagon, from which perch the child drove the team. "The child who drove the hay wagon automatically followed the load to the barn where he or she led the horse in the unloading operation."

Re-arranging the hay after it dropped in a heap from the track overhead was a chore for the strongest man. For teenage Mardo and his younger sister Bea it was an ordeal. Hot and dusty, they plunged the pitchfork time after time into the mass of hay and dragged the clumps to the farthest reaches of the mow. They had to work fast, before their dad sent in another 400-pound forkload to top the first.

They made a game of it to improve morale. Bea would shout about "the Elysian fragrance wafting from the hay," and Mardo would expound on the "cooling breezes" or the pleasures of wading knee deep in the perfumed substance, and the unalterable pleasure of their undertaking.

Exaggerations and combining of words of the same meanings, like "pulchritudinous beauty," became contests that kept them from dwelling on how tired they were, how difficult the work had become, how the sweat had soaked every scrap of clothing, and how the dry chaff was making every move an irritant.

When Bea and Mardo worked in the mow, Pauline, the youngest, drove the team down the windrow in the field, and Mildred helped her dad spread another layer of hay on the wagon bed as it fell from the mouth of the hay loader.

Maude recalled one instance when Pauline, then age 8, narrowly escaped serious injury. Everyone but Maude was helping store hay at the home place (where Lee's parents lived and where he was born). Lee had placed the hay fork into the forage for its transfer to the mow. Mildred was leading the horse that pulled the loaded hay fork to the track at the peak of the barn. Mardo and Bea were in the mow to help distribute the hay.

Pauline was tending to the heavy twine rope that was used to haul the grapple fork from the wagon to the mow with its 400 pounds of hay. Lee called to Pauline to tighten the rope, as he had been having problems tripping the mechanism. When he pulled the cord to release the catch, the fork separated from the track and crashed into the mow with its load.

Pauline had a tight grip on the rope and was yanked 10 feet off the floor. Her hand was pulled into a pulley (one of a series of the grooved wheels through which the rope passes to carry the fork from wagon to the track under the barn roof and along that track to the mow where hay is stored). Luckily, the fork came to rest on a pile of hay a foot before Pauline's hand would have been forced through the pulley, crushed and broken.

There was a lot of screaming and crying before Lee was able to reach her side and free her. She suffered only bruises. It was a narrow escape, the family concluded, and a valuable safety lesson, especially for Lee.

Maude had barely recovered from the scare with Pauline when she had another. She and the girls were busy sweeping and cleaning in the house when Mildred suggested that they had better light the kerosene lamps if they wanted to see what they were doing. The room had become dark, almost as black as night and it was only three o'clock.

Rushing outdoors, Maude saw turbulent black clouds sweeping in from the west. She remembered them as being the most threatening she had ever seen, before or since. A black streamer hung down in one spot and filled her with fear of a tornado.

She knew the girls were safe in the house. Her husband and son were in the field, crushing clods of earth to get the soil ready for the fall planting of wheat. They were apparently unaware of the fast-moving storm. She called to them but couldn't make herself heard. Almost panic-stricken, she ran to the dinner bell and sent its alarm sounding.

Lee, who had told her early in their marriage to use the bell to summon him in case of need, looked up from his work, sensed his wife's foreboding and rushed into action. He and his son unhooked the horses' traces from the heavily laden harrow, leaped astride the horses and drove them at a fast trot toward the buildings.

First gusts of wind, bearing stinging drops of rain, hit them as they rode into the barn. With a wave to his watching wife, Lee waited out the storm with Mardo at his side. Wind tore the galvanized roofing from the granary, leaving the adjacent house and barn unscathed. The tornado touched down a few miles away in open country, leveling trees but doing no other damage.

Nature staged an elemental show of another kind a few days later. Maude, who had just completed picking tomatoes from the vines in the front garden, stopped to watch the sun, an angry red ball, dip toward the western horizon. Ribbons of clouds streaked the lower heavens and the weakening rays were diffused through the pervading light haze.

She said she watched in wonder, then in awe, as the sun sank slowly out of sight. Rays of various shades lighted the flimsy cloud structures, from lavender and pink to orange and red. The effect was dramatized by the novel shape of the clouds which pulsated with color.

"I have never seen such a spectacular sunset," she declared. "A wide range of colors covered the western sky. As the sun sank below the horizon, its rays seemed to set the clouds on fire. The colors--from deep red to soft purples--shimmered for minutes after the sun sank from sight." She said she waited until only a faint glow marked the ending of a wondrous show, then made her way to the house in near darkness.

FIVE

Maude and Lee had little money, even for necessities during the first 15 years, so early Christmases were almost devoid of gifts. There were a lot of cheery greetings, a piece of coal sometimes in a child's stocking to warn him or her that Santa had been displeased, and always a tree on which strands of popcorn were hung.

The focal point of gift-giving for the first few years of the child's life was in the large stocking, hung on mantle or chair, and saved year after year. The parents placed small sacks of hard candy, a memento or two and perhaps a pair of stockings in each.

A small toy might be found by one child, with a written notice that it was to be shared. Each might get an orange or a banana, for they were a rarity in the Williams household and were treasured. When the children grew older, the gifts became wearables. The youngsters might protest silently that these were basic things they surely would have received anyway. But they were thankful that the sweaters and skirts and underwear and stockings and trousers were new, and not hand-me-downs from relatives.

By the time they started to school, Maude reminisced, each was searching the catalogs for the toys and clothing they would like to receive. They left lists around in the hopes that Santa would find them and bring at least some of the gifts on Christmas eve.

They made a game of reporting the picture of each Santa they found in a catalog or magazine. Other children at school had told them that Santa was a mythical figure but they held on to their faith. And they continued to put out their mother's cookies in the belief that Old Kris Kringle would sense their desperate need and leave some luxury item they never had.

When they found an asked-for gift under the tree, their joy was expressed loudly, and often. They were thrilled on succeeding Christmases, when their parents' fortunes had improved, by gaily painted sleds, wagons, huge wind-up tops, coloring books and card games. Twelve-year- old Mardo received the ice skates he had penned on his wish list for three years.

These skates were very basic--two blades on a little framework and with adjustable clamps that could be fitted to the skater's own shoe. They came in sizes too, so you could be sure the skate was long enough for the foot--and wide enough. A key turned the mechanism to lock the front clamps around the shoe sole and the back clamps to gouge into the leather heel. The cost was 89 cents a pair in 1917.

Mardo's first ice skating expedition took him five miles down Rush Creek. He had to skate-walk across the ripples and through snow-crusted areas. It took him two hours to reach the turning point and three hours to get back. He was carrying his skates the last mile. The clamps had torn a heel off one shoe and damaged the other. Lee was called upon to do a little cobbling before his son would resume his skating career.

Lee's makeshift cobbler's kit was pressed into service frequently, as he tried to keep his children's bare feet off the ground. He'd nailed an anchoring bracket to a 30-inch section of hickory, cut to the proper height when he buzz-sawed young trees for the winter's firewood. One of three different sizes of last (a block or form shaped like a human foot) could be fitted to the bracket, the damaged shoe placed on it, and the loose heel or sole fastened.

There was no reliable glue so Lee used brads (small nails) and hammered them through the outside leather so firmly that the head of the nail would bend against the iron last over which the shoe fit. Once, Mildred came hobbling home, complaining that a pebble had lodged in her shoe--and still was hurting her. Dad investigated. One nail had not clinched during his emergency repairs. The point had barely penetrated the sole of her foot, but necessitated a little iodine and some tender loving care.

Lee could also do some rough sewing on a torn leather upper, using an awl which came with the cobbling set, but ordinarily begged off--preferring to let the more experienced and better equipped professional shoe repair man do the work. Lee grinned when he spoke of an incident involving Lauren (Sonny) Ansley (who a few years later would become his son-in-law). The high school sophomore had torn the heel off his shoe during some rough scrimmage on the playground and took it to Old Man Bob McElheny.

Mac, a gruff man of 68 or 70 who had little sympathy for the younger set, unsmilingly took the shoe, nailed the heel back on and said: "That will be ten cents." Young Ansley told the repairman he had no money and, during the impasse, demanded that Mr. McElheny remove the heel and forget about payment. Each considered himself the winner and that evening the boy limped home where his dad re-attached the heel--without cost!

SIX

On a hot, muggy day in late summer of 1912 Lee made a surprise announcement. He said he might be gone for 10 days or two weeks in the spring. He feared to leave Maude and the children alone.

She understood Lee's apparent nervousness when he blurted out:

"Dad and I have purchased a freight carload of calves. They will be delivered in early fall. Next spring, when they've been fattened, I'll have to accompany them to Buffalo for the livestock auction. Can you get along, alone in the house, with four little children? What if you become ill or there's an emergency?"

She tried to assure him that she and the children would be safe. "If the need arises," she insisted, "I can send the two older children to the neighbors for help." Lee remained unconvinced. After all, Pauline was only three years old, Bea a little more than five; Mardo was not yet seven, and Mildred wouldn't be nine until July.

They agreed on the solution--a telephone to link the family to neighbors, to the doctor, to assistance. The phone company had recently established an exchange in Mt. Victory and was seeking new customers. Lee was assured that the line could be extended to reach him and service started within three months--ample time before he had to go away.

Crews were sent to install poles along the lane, string wires from road to house. A telephone was hung on the wall of the living room, near the kitchen door. Service began in February, 1913--and Lee had nearly two months to make sure it would fill the need, that Maude could summon help, if needed.

Today that telephone would be a collector's item. A cabinet about 24 inches high and 12 inches wide contained the transmission and receiving equipment, the wiring, and, on the top front, were the bells that announced incoming calls.

The receiver hung on the left side of the case and the "call out" crank was on the right. The crank had to be turned at least twice around for one long ring. This got the attention of the operator at Mt. Victory, who took over, plugged in the necessary wires to connect the caller to the desired party, or to the Ridgeway, Bellefontaine, or West Mansfield exchanges. Choices were meager. Not everyone had a phone.

Maude soon learned it wasn't necessary to go through the exchange if she wished to talk to a person on her own line. Each had a designated number of rings--three longs might get the Rob Richardsons, three shorts the Charles Marmons or two shorts and one long ring might belong to the Jeff Kellers. Maude's ring was two longs.

The operator was exceedingly helpful. She reported back if the party's line was busy. She discussed the weather, advised about doctors and dentists, if asked, and would pass along any news of fires, accidents, births, and deaths that came to her attention from reliable sources or perhaps from having "accidentally" overheard another customer talking to a friend.

Telephones of that era provided no privacy. If you wanted to discuss love, finances, or any confidential matter, you would ride horseback or hitch Old Dobbin to the buggy and go see the other party personally (unless you wanted to take a chance on the erratic postal service).

Maude said she might hear only one or two receivers lift up after she answered a call but she could be sure that every subscriber on that line was listening unless engaged in some more important activity.

"They're not nosy--just interested," she'd say. "I know that if they heard me call for a doctor, they would contact me to offer help before the doctor was even on the way." It was unusual to have an unhelpful neighbor, and all were honest. Most houses were never locked yet there were very few reports of theft or vandalism. "We were off the beaten path of vagrants and too far away from railroad tracks to attract hoboes," she observed.

She told Lee that the telephone made her feel safer and she would not feel so alone knowing that help was just a ring or two away if she needed it. So he left in early April with his carload of fattened beef, convinced he wouldn't need to worry during the two weeks he'd be gone.

He rode in the stock car with his cattle most of the long trip to Buffalo. He saw that they were fed and watered, quieted them when they became uneasy, and made sure the debris was cleaned out underfoot. He left them in professional hands when they reached the stockyards.

While awaiting the auction, Lee wrote postcards, took in a burlesque show, dined at the most economical restaurants, and, as a special treat to himself, made a day-long tour of the Niagara Falls area. He sent back a picture of himself seated in the cavern directly under the falls and said the roar of the water almost deafened him.

Maude and the children were surprised at how often he wrote. They were deluged with cards advising the youngsters to be good and help their mother, urging all to keep well, saying that he was having a wonderful time while intimating he was already homesick and couldn't wait to see them. They saved the cards and showed them to every visitor.

One of Lee's postcards to Mardo read: "Dear Boy, You can tell by looking at the picture on the other side [a buffalo] where I am. You want to be good." To make sure the card wouldn't get lost on its long journey to Ridgeway, Lee had added Hardin County to the address.

Part IV: Lessons

Hold on to your hats! We're going!

ONE

*I*n 1910, Mardo, age five, started his schooling, along with his sister Mildred, age 7. They walked in all but the worst weather to rural Spice Wood Glen school, a half mile distant. The teacher was Bessie Ziegler Hill, a close friend of Maude since her own earliest school days. Mrs. Hill remarked on the absence of childcare facilities in deciding to take two five-year-olds for instruction. Her own son, Bob, became five in September and Mardo was five in August.

"Two will be no worse than one," Bessie Hill told Maude. "I can be my own baby-sitter and you can have more time to yourself if you only have two to watch." The school board voiced no objection to the rule change in accepting a five-year-old if instruction proceeded among the eight grades and there were no childish disturbances.

School became a real adventure for Mildred and Mardo. Where they had been accustomed to playing with one or two neighbor children, now they had more than 20 of varying ages with whom to converse (or vie with in gaining the teacher's attention). The children came from three miles around and were at various levels of education. So the smaller ones sat on benches and listened to fellow students discuss the lessons that would become theirs in the future.

The school room was approximately 30 feet by 40 feet, with a four-foot-high blackboard ranging across most of the front wall. This permitted teaching from any point in the room, with no need to move classes. A different portion of the blackboard was used for each class. And, the teacher explained, confusion was minimized.

A pot-bellied coal-burning stove was anchored in the center of the room, sending heat in every direction during winter months. There were no desks, only long tables, in this early 1900s school. Pupils sat, facing the blackboard, on long hard benches with no backs. The children were arranged by age, classes and sometimes congeniality at the pleasure of the teacher. The first graders were stationed at the left of the room so a space could be left between them and those who were reciting their lessons. Everyone could listen to each other's class or they could spend the time preparing for the next day's assignment. If anyone had to go to the toilet, a hand was raised for permission, then he or she went to one of the two outhouses.

The teachers gave out picture postcards to the children as rewards, charming, colorful reproductions of animals, flowers, children at play. On the back, the card might read: "To Mardo Williams, For good behavior. From your teacher, Bessie Hill." Getting a postcard was unusual in those days. The children were so pleased with receiving recognition in this way, they were easier for the teachers to control. Several awards for good behavior were given to Mardo (a prankster like his dad), either as encouragement or as a bribe to continue on the virtuous path.

Picture postcards were exchanged for the holidays also, Christmas, Easter, Thanksgiving, Valentine's Day, and birthdays. Greeting cards, as we know them today, came later. Maude had saved many of the postcards, among them a surprising Valentine's Day greeting to Mardo from his teacher. The picture was of a little black boy with big eyes, that said "Yoo's ma honey chile." Above the boy's head was a border of heart-shaped watermelon wedges. On the back was written, "To Mardo, From your teacher, B.Z.H."

Maude and Lee saved their pennies to buy school supplies for their children--yellow tablets and pencils. Textbooks might be bought from the older children, secondhand. Ridgeway, where they later went to school, had a small library of about 100 donated books, but rarely had the one assigned by the English teacher for review. Maude and Lee both had a high school education and insisted that their children get their diploma too, just as parents today want their children to go through college.

Mildred and Mardo attended Spice Wood Glen for five years. Bea was there for two years. One day, after school, Bea and Mildred were so engrossed in discussing the inequities of life that they never noticed their mother hovering nearby. Seven-year-old Bea was incensed by the selfishness of one of her classmates and was venting that displeasure to her older sister. Mildred, four years older, should know all the answers, she reasoned. Pauline, a mere five was just an eavesdropper.

"I lost my stub of a pencil and asked Dorothy for one so I could do my lesson," Bea complained. "She picked out the shortest and most tooth-marked one." Mildred soothed her with the thought that at least she got to finish the teaching assignment.

"But she had three or four larger ones and a new one that had never been sharpened," Bea protested. Then Mother Maude intervened. "Never look a gift horse in the mouth," she said.

"What does that mean? We weren't talking about a horse," the little girls said. Maude told them it meant you should be thankful for any gift, not complain because it wasn't as great or as costly as you'd like.

"It started a long time ago," she explained, "when a farmer gave his son a horse so he could begin farming for himself. The young man immediately pried open the animal's mouth to gauge its age by the condition of its teeth--a sign that he felt misgivings about the gift and questioned the generosity of the giver."

"Since then," she said, "the saying, once restricted to horse traders, has been expanded to include any disappointing gift." The girls went out of their way during the next few days offering one another small gifts so they could urge each other "not to look a gift horse in the mouth."

Four teachers served at Spice Wood Glen during the five-year period that Mildred and Mardo attended the school--Miss Faye Lemley, Miss Mae Cook, and Mr. Harry Marmon, in addition to Mrs. Hill. Marmon later became Alice Williams' husband and Lee's brother-in-law. He also became the seventh-eighth grade teacher at Ridgeway in 1915 when the rural one-room school was abandoned and a horse-drawn school wagon began hauling the rural children to the newly centralized Ridgeway schools. He again became their teacher when the oldest Williams children entered the seventh grade in 1916.

Consolidation of the various rural schools for four miles in every direction from Ridgeway presented problems for both administrators and farmers. The school board had to obtain "buses" and drivers, establish routes and assure child safety. The farmers lost a portion of each child's services due to the time spent traveling to and from the central school. This was important, especially in key planting or harvest times when every potential worker was needed.

Everything was eventually worked out, if not to everyone's satisfaction. Enclosed horse-drawn wagons bused the children. The driver on each route was a private contractor who provided his own team.

Each bus had glass windows and a metal roof, was equipped with forward facing seats capable of carrying 30 to 40 boys and girls, and was heated, at least partially, by a coal-burning unit attached under the floor to the wagon frame. The only register was centered above the stove and provided enough heat only for moderate winter days. It was necessary therefore that everyone wear clothing on the bus that would be comfortable outdoors.

In 1915, during their first year at Ridgeway, sixth-graders Mildred and Mardo, third-grader Bea, and first-grader Pauline, found the three mile, 90-minute ride to and from school both exciting and boring. They were able to get choice seats because they were among the early boarders. They could choose to sit with each other--or alone if they wished to take a chance on who might want to sit with them.

Lynn Stevenson, the driver, was a poor conversationalist and had a team of plug-ugly horses almost ready for the glue factory. He spent most of his time exhorting the horses to go faster, the children told their parents, and when he got them going faster than a fast walk would shout excitedly, "Hold on to your hats. We're going!"

Regardless, it was a slow trip--especially to four energetic youngsters eager to see their new friends at school and just as eager to get home and relive all the interesting details with their parents.

One year later, they gained a new interest in the school bus ride when their young neighbor friend became the driver. John Marmon, brother of school teacher Harry Marmon, was 18. He became the confidant of every to child, the cheerful friend of all, the trusted adviser, second perhaps mother or teacher. His charges told him of their birthdays, what they got for Christmas, where they were going for Thanksgiving. They told him of their problems, of their fears and that "Janie" now was in love with someone else.

He listened to all, joked with some and commiserated with those who felt forlorn. In 1918, he died of tuberculosis. His parents, Charles and Lizzie Marmon, were stricken. The neighbors were saddened. And the children felt they had lost a lifelong friend.

A blizzard raged for three days after John's death. His body laid in state at the Marmon home as the snow blew and the temperature plunged to 20 below zero. Neighbors came in to stand vigil so their bereaved friends could get some rest. His burial was delayed for several days because of the frozen earth. When the storm passed and the grave could be dug, the burial ritual was held.

Bus riding would be humdrum after this. The Williams children, now aged 9, 11, 13, and 15 threw themselves into school activities. Each Ridgeway class was larger than the group that had attended all eight grades at Spice Wood Glen so each child had more opportunities to make new friends. But they missed eavesdropping on the older children as they recited their lessons, the impromptu ball games in which all participated at recess and the ringing of the bell on the crown of the roof, calling them back to class. Besides, they knew everyone at Spice Wood and there were scores of pupils in other grades at Ridgeway that they would never know.

They learned to play with classmates in special areas of the spacious grounds. Mardo took part in baseball and became adept at "One and Over," an athletic game that involved both skill and coordination.

There were certain rules. A base line was established and anyone who stepped over it in competition was immediately disqualified. A boy was selected by lottery to be the first "dummy." He had to stoop over and face away from the action, standing about three feet from the base line.

The leader of the first game, also selected by lottery, would run forward and, at the last moment, "leapfrog" the dummy. The spot where his feet first set down was the mark which each succeeding player had to meet or exceed to remain in the game. The dummy moved up to the new mark at each round. When the distance from base to the dummy became too far for anyone to reach with a single leap, the leader would take a broad jump, then leapfrog the boy. That gave the game its title of "One and Over."

As the distance became more and more difficult, contenders would start to fail, with the first loser being the dummy for the next game and the winner becoming the leader.

Harry Whetsel was the acknowledged expert for the three years he was in high school. He was a black youth who barely topped 5 feet, 8 inches, but who had both speed and coordination. He could leap farther than even the older boys nearing graduation. He was so good that he never had to serve as dummy unless he was unfortunate enough to be selected by lottery for the first game.

Recess was unsupervised--there was no coach or physical-education director--and the result was bedlam. The smaller boys were bullied by the larger ones. "Bumstarching" was the least popular sport, matching the bullies against the weaker. Two larger boys would grab the arms and legs of a smaller boy and bump his bum several times (and hard) against the metal railings in the schoolyard.

Shouts and screams from the playground made some neighbors so angry they moved away; others vented their displeasure by calling school officials to protest.

Classrooms were lighted electrically but there was no running water. If you wanted a drink, you went to the pump. If nature called, you went to a glorified outhouse where planks were stretched across an open pit and--as you performed--read the revised passages from Shakespeare and other graffiti on the walls.

"Here I sit in silent bliss," began one ditty. "Listening to the falling piss." Those with a clever bent for words continued to try to outdo the existing literature by fashioning new slogans. The walls were covered by the end of the term.

All graffiti had to be re-composed at the start of the next school year. Workmen had repainted during the summer and carefully blotted out the priceless words. This presented a challenge for budding authors.

Maude said the children did well in school, made friends and presented the parents with no growing-up problems. Mardo received high grades in English--above 90 on each paper until the grading system was changed and he got "A's," his mother recalled. His sisters didn't like that subject as well.

He found ways to express his thoughts, to describe panoramic views, and to extol the virtues of forays in the fields. During his sophomore year at Ridgeway High School, he wrote an essay in which he forecast what his classmates would be doing in 1970, 50 years in the future. (Later, it was determined, none of the predictions came true.) At age 16, he penned a description of mythical Keel Island which drew praise from his teacher, Mrs. Hattie Surface, and the school superintendent, Frank C. Ransdell.

Mrs. Surface would give him the highest grades in the class, except for behavior--which she always listed on his report card as "unsatisfactory." Once she returned to her class after a visit to the restroom to find two of her pupils missing. Mardo and classmate Robert Hill, lured by spring weather in March, had clambered through the second story window onto the roof. Soft-hearted Hattie, Maude said, listened to their abject apologies and decided not to send them to the principal for punishment.

When he was graduated at age 16, Mardo had a four-year average of 92.4 points--the highest score in the eight-member class (despite all the little episodes which added up to multiple "unsatisfactory" deportment ratings). He gave the valedictory address at the Commencement exercises and expounded learnedly about the way to succeed--a subject about which he knew nothing!

There was no drug use at that time and the consumption of alcohol was limited. In fact, most families had no intoxicants in their home so, in the event the child wanted to vent his or her rebellion, it had to be done without drugs or alcohol.

Few black families lived in the Ridgeway School District--the Mayles, Whetsels, McGinnises, Scotts, and Baileys. Each of the Williamses had at least one black child in his or her grade. All got along well--without bickering or violence. There was no indication that one race resented the other.

LaMotte Mayle was a dark, handsome Spanish-appearing youth who played center on the Ridgeway High School basketball team for three years (Mardo and Forrest LeValley were too short, Olen White too ungainly to make the varsity squad so they formed their own team). LaMotte Mayle and Marie Whetsel were black classmates of Mildred and Mardo. They were friends but after graduation never fraternized again. The same relationships applied to black classmates of Bea and Pauline--due as much to the retiring attitudes of all blacks at the time as the failure of the white children to make that special effort at becoming friends. The parents and grandparents had not been slaves but sensed the widespread prejudice prevalent at the time and trained their youngsters to ignore personal feelings, keep silent even when they disagreed with their Caucasian playmates.

In school, Mardo was more mischievous and inclined to skate on the brink of breaking regulations. Maude recalled that she and Lee had to lecture him at one time. He was introduced to the "F" word by a neighbor boy. Thrilled at the addition of a new word to his vocabulary, he immediately tried it out on a girl who lived only a mile away from the Williamses.

"Want to----?" he wrote on a slip of paper and passed it to her during a class. His intentions were innocent, Mardo explained. He wouldn't have known what to do if she had accepted the invitation but he could not tell her that. It would be too embarrassing. She refused to return the note. Instead, she passed it along to his sister, Mildred.

Mildred knew what to do with the incriminating evidence. She tried to blackmail her brother, saying she would return the paper if he agreed to do all her chores at home for two weeks. That was too much. He envisioned having to wash the dishes and perform Mildred's duties while the others played outdoors during the failing daylight, completed their assignments for the next day, read a book, or played games like dominoes and checkers. He told her "NO!"

"When Mildred gave us the note, we were astounded," Maude said. "Both Lee and I lectured him. I told him that such an act was wrong, that it was morally indefensible, and that I wouldn't be surprised if the girl never talked with him again." Lee gave him a lesson in legalese. "If you want to make an off-color remark, say it orally and with no witness around.

Never put it in writing," he advised.

Both Mildred and the neighbor girl went about their studies with a sly smile for weeks. Mardo never knew with how many friends they shared the note. It was a valuable lesson.

At about the same time, Lee entertained Maude with a story of the recent trip he and Mardo had taken to a neighbor's house two miles away. The tale: The youngest cow in their small herd was "in heat." So he and his son put a rope halter on her head. The heifer was very nervous and had to be dragged across the bridge, which had a wooden floor and made reverberating sounds when trod upon. Forty-five minutes later, the three arrived at the Billy Bird place, tired and sweaty.

When the bull was brought out of the barn, the boy was more alarmed than the cow. The bull was a massive animal, weighing close to a ton, with red-looking eyes. Fearful that the bull might forget the service he was committed to perform, Mardo hid behind his father.

Lee told him: "There's no reason to be frightened so long as the heifer is here," which proved to be true. The road back was uneventful. The cow walked docilely home, with a slight hump in its back.

TWO

When Lee had "leisure" time from field work, he could be found in the barn. There were endless chores and the sprawling, two-level structure could accommodate them all. Tasks could be accomplished in comparative comfort. A bank of earth insulated the lower level from wintry blasts. Wide swinging doors permitted north-south cross ventilation of the ground-level floor in summer.

Routine operations, like milking the cows, feeding and caring for cattle, horses and hogs, and normal housekeeping chores gave way to machinery repair in the off season--those times after hay had been stored, grains had been binned and corn had been husked.

A major project each winter was the maintenance of the massive equipment used to thresh wheat and oats. Moving parts were cleaned and adjusted, bearings that had started to wear were replaced and all nuts were tightened. The cutting arms at the front of the machine, where sheaves started their shattering journey to the straw stack, got careful attention. Knives were sharpened. Bushings, in which all moving parts were anchored, had to be tested. When the shaft's housing was cracked or worn, Lee prepared a molten mixture of metals to replace the babbiting, thereby producing a new bearing.

Corn shredder, clover huller, and smaller pieces of farm equipment like the corn planter, hay rake, hay loader, corn binder, wheat binder, and mowing machine got similar attention. End wrenches in all sizes and lengths, plus a giant pipe wrench or two, assured the removal of every nut from the rustiest and most recalcitrant bolt.

The monotony of machinery repair in the cavernous barn sometimes was broken by the fluttering of scores of sparrows in the upper areas near the roof. The commotion increased when a pigeon or two left their nests (between the rafters in the lower level) to invade Lee's domain. And more than once he had to stop work to rescue one or the other of his children-- usually the youngest, Pauline, who thought she was as big as anyone and would occasionally get herself stranded on a high, narrow beam, unable to go up or down, forward or backwards. Lee would enter the haymow, and climb up on the crossbeam to reach her and steer her to safety. For some reason, he said he always felt rested when he resumed work.

If feed for the stock became depleted, Lee would haul loads of corn stalks to the ground floor location and use the husking peg to strip corn from fodder. The peg was a hook attached to a leather strap wrapped around his hand. Lee used the peg sparingly in those early days of autumn, and only until the mechanized corn shredder could be placed in service. The barn offered comparative comfort to the worker on all but the coldest days. Hay in both the east and west mows provided a measure of insulation so the work of husking corn or repairing machinery could proceed in all kinds of weather.

Lower levels of the barn were dim at all times, making a lamp of some kind necessary by twilight. Lee had no powerful flashlight or incandescent lamp, so a metal lantern, with the fuel tank filled, hung on a nail at the barn entrance. It held enough kerosene to provide light for six hours.

The lantern dimly illuminated an eight-foot-square area, letting the work proceed in a sort of twilight haze. The lamp was very similar to ones that switchmen swung to signal "stop" and "go" to the locomotive engineers. With the glass chimney clamped in place, its flame was covered. It was wind resistant and waterproof. It was considered the safest light for barn usage at the time. If held upright, it would be almost impossible to start an accidental fire in hay or chaff.

Lee hated to do the routine chores by dim lantern light, but his worst job in the barn came in early spring when the new crop of pigs became eight or nine weeks old. Sows would farrow (give birth) in February so he would have time to watch over the new arrivals. Late March or early April became the time for neutering the males.

If permitted to become boars, when there is no need for breeding stock, the animals become too large and their meat is coarser-grained. They do not fatten properly, are in less demand at the livestock auctions and therefore sell at a lower price. Including even one unneutered male in the sales lot of several prime animals could bring down the prices for all.

This distasteful duty involved, first, the separation of males and females. One group of excited, squealing animals was enough to contend with. Next he needed an assistant (a helper was mandatory if the operation were to succeed). The aide would catch and hold the elusive pigs, one at a time.

Lee, who had equipped himself with a very sharp knife, a jar of Vaseline and possibly a pair of pliable rubber gloves, called for the number one victim. With the pig positioned in the arms of his surgical assistant, Lee slashed, pulled and treated each emasculated animal with salve. Approximately one-half of the entire birth group were males and were subject to the surgery.

His biggest patient count for a single year was 28, the male progeny of eight sows. Normally only five sows were bred, he said, and each could be counted on to raise eight pigs.

Another little relished chore each spring also required physical exertion and skillful action. Lee and his hired man herded the 10- or 12-week-old swine from the barn into a small barricaded portion of the hog pen, one animal at a time. While one attempted to hold the struggling pig immobile, the other inserted the open jaws of the "loaded" pincer-like device astraddle the nasal cartilage. A forceful squeeze closed the brass half-ring through the flesh.

The appliance was a sort of plier with a curved head in which the open metal rings were placed. The jaws holding the ring were placed on that portion of the nose to be pierced and then squeezed shut. If the pig's head moved even a fraction, the ring might be only partially anchored, or attached in the wrong place. In that event, the ring would be removed at considerable pain and opposition of the animal--and re-embedded.

Properly done, two rings in the snout effectively curbed for months tendencies of the pigs to "root" big holes in the ground and around fences. Without the nose rings, pigs rooted quite deeply, searching for acorns and minerals in the soil, making the ground dangerously uneven. If they rooted under a fence row and destroyed the neighbors' corn, the pigs' owners were to blame and might be sued for the loss.

The lower level of the bank barn was home not only for pigs but also for the horses and cows. Calves and pigs were born there. Horses were stabled in one section. They required special care when with foal so only a few colts were born on the farm during the 54 years Lee called it home.

Cows usually dropped their calves without complications, but Maude remembered a rain-chilled April evening in 1912 when a young milk cow failed to return to the barn. Calfing time was so near that concern mounted as darkness neared.

It was dark when Lee completed the milking chores and the cow was still missing. There was no response to repeated calling. The next move was a search of the woods by lantern light. Wet from the cold rain and left bedraggled by his conflict with the bushes and bog, he returned to the house before midnight to await first light of a new day.

At dawn, Lee awakened his seven-year-old son to continue the search. They found her at last, near death. The calf was hung up crosswise in the birth canal. It took the efforts of both father and son to pull the dead calf free.

The mother cow had struggled so violently that her head had carved a trench in the earth six feet long. She was weak but still breathing. A veterinarian was rushed to the scene to administer a stimulant and medication. She died the next day. Lee mourned the valuable cow and the fully developed calf, a loss he could not afford.

The couple recounted other losses and varied setbacks. Maude remembered the death of a work horse during those first years. Lee had forgotten to place a block of salt in the pasture. The animal, in its desire for salt, grazed along the fence line where rusted wire had created a substitute. The horse swallowed a number of staples and pieces of wire, dying of an internal hemorrhage while the veterinarian worked to save it.

Another animal tragedy occurred two years later. A three-year-old that Lee was training as a buggy horse became ill and started kicking its stall to pieces. The violence could not be controlled, even after the veterinarian injected it with a massive dose of tranquilizer.

As demolition of the stall continued, the vet decided the horse had encephalitis and gave the colt a lethal injection. In its final throes, it broke a hind leg.

Lee blamed the malady on a mosquito bite. Uncertain as to how the affliction might be spread, he dragged the carcass to the woods, piled branches over and around it and started a fire. For three days, the fuel was replenished to keep the blaze going until only ashes were left.

After this, other problems with the horses were merely irritants. Lee spoke of vainly trying to fit one of the big draft animals with a collar.

"The collar was too narrow, or too wide, or not supple enough--or the horse's neck was not shaped right. No matter how I remedied it, Bell (the horse's name) ended up with an open sore on the shoulder at the base of the neck."

It was very difficult to heal. After treatment with salves and the purchase of a new collar fitted to the horse's neck dimensions, the ultimate solution was found to be a four-day rest.

Importance of a well-fitting collar cannot be over-emphasized. It fits around the neck, not too tightly, and rests on the shoulder above the front legs. The harness fits over it so that the pull is distributed over the front of the body. There should be no stress on back or joints--only to the muscles, Lee said. He learned this lesson by costly experience--four days loss of the services of the animal at a crucial time--during planting season.

THREE

Maude never harnessed a horse, although she learned to drive the run-about, the single-seated buggy hitched to Topsy. She knew how to guide the animal. "Gee" meant right, and "haw" meant left. A "whoa" might stop the horse in her tracks or a pull on the reins might steer her toward the ditch, but nothing Maude did or said could prevent the inevitable from happening after Topsy lifted her tail. It wasn't a pretty sight, when viewed over the dashboard, just three feet away.

Maude, of course, knew to toss a blanket over the overheated animal after returning her to the barn, and to use the curry comb to brush her matted hair. She would loosen the yoke at the horse's neck before calling for someone to lift off the bulky harness and arrange it on the pegs at the side of the stall.

She used the rig to travel to neighbors' houses and to Spice Wood Glen school functions, but tried to limit her solo excursions. All in all, she said, gadding about the neighborhood that way wasn't a whole lot of fun for her.

FOUR

The porch was Maude's favorite summer work-and-play place, as it was for all the family. She and Lee had made it more comfortable by stretching meshed wire between pillars one and two and pillars three and four, then planting morning glory and honeysuckle vines, which provided nectar for the bees and an aroma of delight for the humans. The vines were porous enough to allow the passage of gentle breezes, on which were wafted the delicate fragrance of the flowers. By early summer, the vines formed a solid mass across two-thirds of the outer porch and made it a bower, shaded from the hot sun, yet light enough to be cheery, and protected from wind gusts or rain.

The porch was left open in the middle and on the end leading to woodshed and grape arbor.

"We made it the family room," Maude said. "That was where I sat in my favorite chair to snap beans, hull peas, do the churning and much of the necessary sewing and mending." All the canning preparations as well as other housekeeping duties that could be performed in the open air were transacted on the spacious, cheery porch. It was the selected spot for placing the hand-operated washing machine in 1916 when Maude at last was able to retire the laundry stand, galvanized tub, and washboard (which she'd used while all four children grew through "potty training"). "We kept the wood flooring painted," Maude observed, "making it easy to clean up after the sloppiest job or the messiest youngster."

The children scattered toys about Maude's chair as she sewed or processed vegetables. In playing marbles, the children drew an imaginary circle on the porch floor and placed the smaller ones, called commies, inside the line. Then they placed a larger glass-like marble (called agate) between index finger and thumb, and flipped it into the circle. The game was to knock the commies out of the circle with the agate.

"I heard them warning one another not to 'hunch.' I took it to mean not to add impetus to the agate by arm or shoulder movement." The one who collected the most commies was the winner.

Jacks was a game the children tried but never finished, Maude recalled. The players started with 10 of the small five-pronged metal pieces (specially designed to land on three legs when thrown). The first round required the player to bounce a rubber ball, pick up one jack and catch the ball on its first bounce, in the same hand--continuing until all ten jacks had been retrieved one at a time. The same rules applied to picking up two at a time, threes, fours, and so on. "It seemed to be a game of skill, coordination, and patience--and the children didn't have much of any of the three," Maude said.

"Mumblety Peg" was played in the grass in front of the porch. It was made much more interesting to her progeny, she thought, by the permission Lee gave them to use his treasured Barlow knife. The blades at one end were opened so that the long one extended straight, the smaller one bent at a right angle.

With the short blade embedded lightly in the soil, the player would slip an index finger under the lower end of the knife and carefully cause it to flip end-over-end. If it landed on the long blade, a certain number of points would be scored; on the shorter blade, a lesser number. If a blade failed to stick in the ground, the player received no score and he gave up the play to the next contender.

"When they got tired of opening and closing the knife, they put it back on the shelf and sought other diversions," she said.

Summer evenings were quality time for the family. When work permitted, they sat on the porch until the mosquitoes drove them inside. The children, quiet after a busy day, propelled the porch swing back and forth as they renewed their strength and awaited the inspiration for some new game. Maude and Lee also were quiet, each in a reed rocking chair-- Maude with a bit of darning or needlework in her lap and Lee reading a book or farm journal.

The tranquility always was interrupted. One child or the other would seek a new place in the swing, demand that Dad or Mom devise another game, play horsy-back, oversee a contest--they had to be busy every moment. If one was bored, the cry went up, "There's nothing to do."

Maude remembered the many times that peace was restored by the hundreds of fireflies that soared two or three feet off the ground, intermittently flashing their little tail-lights. It was a challenge no child could resist. Soon the growing dusk was filled with happy shouts and running feet. Each child competed with the others to see how many "lightning bugs" could be captured and placed in her or his own glass jar. Perhaps there might be enough to light the way to bed?

The children were always disappointed. Once in the jar, the fireflies clung together so as to hide each other's light. Yet the lighting extravaganza in the Williams's front yard was so dramatic that each of the viewers kept hoping that sometime the little flames would all go on at once and illuminate the entire area. It never happened.

One night Lee tried to dispel the children's apparent boredom by taking all four on a mystery expedition. He carried the farm lantern to lead the way to the creek bank in a more remote spot in the front pasture, overgrown with willows and shrubs. To the four youngsters (the oldest was 10), it looked like a wilderness.

He cautioned them to be quiet as the very seclusive "shike poke," for which they were to watch, was a shy bird. The best time to see it was when daylight was gone and the moon was approaching its brightest, which was now.

Lee described the bird as being unusual in appearance, with a dark beak, white tuft on top of the head, black body, red wings and yellow tail. "It is about the size of one of our farm hens," he explained. "It doesn't like to fly so it usually runs along the ground in a sort of crippled hop. I have seen it only once," he admitted.

With that, he blew out the light with a final instruction to the youngsters, huddled together under the bushes on the creek bank. "Don't talk. If you have to move, do it quietly. And if you haven't sighted the shike-poke by ten o'clock, you either have missed it or it decided to stay home for the night."

Now for a few minutes of quiet, thought Lee, as he dropped into his chair on the porch. But Maude, who had seen Lee enjoy his game, had different ideas. She told him how cruel it was to let those four youngsters cringe in fear in the dark as the bullfrogs opened their symphony, the hoot owls contributed their plaintive "Who, Who-o-o" and some unknown animal slithered through the brush.

Maude was in full voice as Lee vainly tried to assure her that their children were in no danger, that no one would want to kidnap four such demanding children and that the bright moonlight would erase any fears they might have of the boogeyman.

His arguments fell on deaf ears. "I'll go get them if you won't," she cried, then fell silent at the sound of childish voices approaching in the darkness. Each parent claimed responsibility for the intelligence shown by the four in deciding that it was only a game and there was no "shike-poke."

There was one lasting effect. The youngsters decided it was such a swell game that it would be a crime to let it die. They played it with their city cousins and any others they could convince that an hour or two "in solitary" along the creek bank would be educational.

The porch also was the launching spot for contests to see the first star, catch the flare from a falling meteor, identify the mysterious soundings of the night. The crickets made music by rubbing their hind legs together. The night birds sang. Some noises were never identified but the call of the owl brought forth quotations of the unheeded message their mother made repeatedly:

"The wise old owl sat in an oak,
     The more he saw, the less he spoke;
     The less he spoke, the more he heard.
        Wasn't that a wise old bird?"

Maude was the one who took that counsel to heart, became known as the best listener around--and often helped others to solve problems without opening her mouth.

Mardo recalled one such incident. The youngster listened as a recently married young woman poured out a tale of woe to his mother who was only a few years older than the complainant. Mrs. Rose or Mrs. Brown--Mardo wasn't sure of the name--had awakened to find her house a picture of demoralization, with men's clothing scattered everywhere, the furniture pushed out of place, and newly soiled dishes from a late evening snack on the kitchen table.

Mrs. Rose (we'll conclude that was her name) told Maude that she prepared her husband's breakfast and, as soon as he left for the fields, she gathered up his discarded clothing and pushed the furniture back where it belonged. "When I got to those soiled dishes, encrusted with dried foodstuff, my mind snapped," she said, "and I just had to talk to someone."

She was boiling mad when she drove down the Williamses lane, one and one-half miles from her house. She started talking to Maude before she got the horse tied to a fencepost in front of the house. Maude hurriedly seated her visitor in a chair by her side on the porch. She handed her a pan, with the request that she help her snap some beans for canning--without interrupting Mrs. Rose's flow of words.

For a half hour Mrs. Rose talked of her husband's carelessness, his failure to pick up for himself, his demands for special foods "like his mother used to make," his habit of leaving his clothes lie on the floor wherever he stepped out of them. "I thought about nailing them to the floor like a friend of mine did," she confessed.

Maude listened, interjected a sympathetic word or two, asked the young woman to take into consideration the good things about him, and was about to advise the angry young woman to "sleep on it" before taking any action, when she blurted out: "I love him, but I thought he would be more helpful when he learned I was carrying his baby."

Mrs. Rose left just as abruptly as she arrived, after crying a little, and thanking Maude profusely for "having solved a problem for me." The couple was still together and apparently in a very good relationship--when the baby girl was born six months later.

Mrs. Rose may have felt embarrassed by her outpouring to a comparative stranger. At least, she never reported back, and failed to say good-bye when they moved, shortly after the baby's birth, to a farm ten miles away. The Williamses were left wondering if Mr. Rose was able to change the careless habits of a lifetime and hoping that the little one had lessened the tensions, if any still existed.

During the summer, chores multiplied but there was time for wondering about the why and wherefore of simple things. One of the early mysteries was why the hens suddenly squatted every time anyone passed through the poultry yard. It remained for Lee to explain that the horny flock was missing the male leader. He had neglected to buy a replacement when the old rooster was sold or killed.

Ducks once waddled around the barnyard, but they were messy. They left gooey gobs everywhere. No one in the family liked the meat, Maude said. Several were lost to the turtles which would come up under a duck in the creek, grab it by the leg and gnaw the foot off before it could escape.

Hen eggs were in popular demand. Maude would take the surplus to town where she could trade for coffee, sugar and other groceries. Sometimes the hens quit laying and a mysterious shortage of the "hen-fruit" developed, especially in late March or early April.

"The missing eggs showed up on Easter Sunday," Maude said. "The children competed to see who could bring in the most eggs. We always had a big ham and egg breakfast then--but sometimes the eggs may not have been the freshest."

The children picked up all the eggs available--finding those stashed in out of the way places in the barn, from nests the hens had hidden away--with no concern about the length of time the hens may have been sitting on the nest. Some eggs were "over-ripe," others near the hatching stage when Maude cracked them open.

FIVE

The Williams youngsters were no exception--they wanted a pony! Bell and Daisy, the gentle work horses, would have been appalled, had they known. They were big, with backs too broad for a child to straddle. And it was no fun, Pauline, the littlest, noted, riding a sweaty animal, clutching mane or harness to keep from tumbling five feet to the ground.

Convinced that no pony was forthcoming, the children sought alternatives. Mildred, the tomboy, mounted a cow as it drank at the watering tank. She stayed on without benefit of bridle or saddle for half the distance across the barnyard, then was sloughed off as the unhappy cow wriggled to free itself of its unwanted burden. Bea was dared into climbing aboard the back of a dozing sow, who resented the intrusion. Bea's ride was even shorter.

No one was hurt, but as the four were debating what adventure was next, and whether Mardo or Pauline would be first, Lee burst onto the scene. He had been alerted by the confusion in the barnyard, where all should have been quiet in the middle of a hot August afternoon. He warned against any further disruption, apparently more concerned about the welfare of the animals than the safety of his little darlings.

SIX

As winter approached, the collecting of firewood became a prime consideration. Lee and his hired hand were in the woods day after day during November and early December, seeking fallen trees, which were denuded of limbs before being dragged to the area back of the woodhouse. They also felled hickory trees, stripped them of branches, wrapped the heavy log chain around their base, and used the team of horses to drag them, one or two at a time, to the same site.

Cutting the standing timber--always in a clump or an area that benefited from clearing--was a back-breaking task. The cut was made as close to the ground as possible (usually 10 inches or less above the surface) so every movement of the crosscut saw was made from a stooped position. It took two men to operate the saw--one pulled while the other rested. Neither could push or the six-foot-long saw would buckle and the men's pull-rest rhythm would be lost.

If the saw teeth had been set (sharpened), two men who were in synchrony could cut through a 12-inch tree trunk in less than ten minutes. First, a shallow cut was made on one side of the trunk, an axe was swung to make a notch above the cut, then the sawers began their rhythmic back and forth action with the saw. The tree fell outward from the notched cut. Lee became an expert--could drop the tree within inches of his target without twisting or tearing out strips of bark at the tree's base.

The saw had peg-like handles on each end. One edge was smooth. Teeth extended down the other. The teeth could be "set" to cut a coarse groove (for green wood) or a thinner fissure (for seasoned wood). The crosscut could be used horizontally, to fell standing trees, or perpendicularly, to saw through trunks or posts lying on the ground. Lee attempted to instruct his son in the art, found himself shouting, "Don't ride the saw." It took a while for Mardo to learn not to push or put weight on the saw in its back-and-forth motion.

The son became proficient enough to help his dad prepare the mounting pile of slender logs at the side of the woodhouse for the steam-engine-powered buzz saw. The pieces had to be short enough for two men to lift them safely to the table and steer them at cross angles into the whirring blade as it lopped off a section of firewood every 22 to 24 inches (the maximum lengths to fit in cooking range or heating stove)--as measured by the built-in ruler at the side of the saw.

The pieces were stored in the woodhouse. The thicker blocks were propped on end and split with a blow from the axe. The largest might require use of a steel wedge and a sledge hammer to drive the wedge into the grain of the wood.

Lee had little love for the firewood chore, switched to coal whenever funds permitted. He said that when he came home, all bent over from cutting down trees, it reminded him of the story Beryl Wallace told him. A neighbor was complaining about how stupid his father was. "You think that's stooped?" Beryl asked facetiously. "You ought to see my dad--he walks like this" (assuming a very bent over position).

Lee said he was overjoyed when the woodpile was replenished--

although the next step was to winterize the steam engine (which had been pressed into service to power the buzz saw). He would have to drain the water from each line prior to the first freeze--due at any time--before he could store it in a lean-to at the home of his parents. The buzz saw would be put away too, until the next season!

With luck--and normal winter weather--the woodpile would last until the following spring. If it didn't, coal would be bought in Mt. Victory or Ridgeway.

SEVEN

It was a little party in recognition of Bea's birthday. A dozen children were too many for the parlor of the Williams home. Maude became a little apprehensive as sounds of revelry mounted behind the closed doors, but she had promised not to interfere unless a child barged into the heating stove or someone fell and was injured.

She was beginning to regret having invited so many--Stewart, Ruth, Boyd and Daisy of the Rob Richardson family, Charles, Jr. and Isabel Marmon (next door neighbors), Velda and Willie, the two youngest of the Will Engle clan. The parents came too but, like Maude, were relegated to the living room. Occasionally, one or the other would cautiously crack open the double doors between living room and parlor, sneak a look at the boisterous group, and quietly close it.

Maude had promised her daughter a party for years, but kept putting it off because of unpredictable January weather. Other years were too cold or too snowy for the guests to make the trip by horse and buggy. Bea should have been born in spring or summer, like the other children, Maude thought, instead of making her appearance on a January 7th.

When the noise from the front room changed tempo--almost total silence, followed by shouts, the pounding of feet and the scraping of chairs on bare floor--the parents feared total chaos. They rushed to see for themselves what was going on. Some looked through a crack in the double doors, others watched through a partially opened door which led from Lee's and Maude's bedroom to the parlor.

The youngsters had cleared the floor of furniture and moved chairs to form two parallel lines on opposite sides of the room. There were seats for only eleven--the twelfth was the leader, who mumbled a little speech before unexpectedly shouting "breadbasket." All 11 had to cross the room to find their new places. As they shouted, pushed, and bumped into each other, the "leader" slipped into one of the vacant seats, leaving the one without a chair to make his own little speech and set the turbulence in motion again.

Maude said she could stand only so much of the action. "I called a halt to what they had named 'upsetting the bread basket,' and served refreshments of apples, cider, and popcorn to children and parents." Later, she proposed one celebration for all four birthdays and said it would take place in the summer months when guests of the celebrants could congregate on the porch. There would be no need to worry about broken chairs or overturned stoves.

Maude and Lee admitted they found the winter months less enjoyable. That season presented its own annoyances--hauling water, traipsing to the outhouse, going to town for supplies. The best thing that could be done about it was to sit inside and look at falling snow. It painted the fields a dazzling white. It made of every tree a Christmas tree.

"The children loved it," Maude remembered, "made angels in it, took goblets of the freshly fallen stuff and made their own ice cream by adding a little sugar and a drop of vanilla extract."

When the chill winds of January and early February swept the snow into huge drifts, the 500-foot lane leading from the house to the traveled roadway was buried three feet deep.

The children floundered in it, slipped and slid about, laughing. Maude refused to venture out. And Lee, before he made the trip to town for groceries or coal for the heating stoves, first had to hitch the team to the heavy drag (used in the spring to break up clods of earth in the fields before planting) and scrape away at the drifts until the snow was cleared or packed down for the buggy's path. When the weather warmed, and a light rain fell--as it usually did after a heavy snowfall--the lane became a glare of ice, too uneven for anything but a sled.

Unless someone telephoned them, Lee and Maude wouldn't know the school wagon couldn't get through the roads until it didn't show up. So the children stood out in the yard, in coats and boots, watching the east. They could see it coming for 3/8 of a mile. If it appeared, they staggered through the drifts to the end of the lane. If it didn't come, they'd know school was out for the day.

The house stood alone on a knoll overlooking Rush Creek and was fair game for every wintry gust. Wind-driven snow seeped through every crack in the windows, stacked in little drifts behind all the outside doors. Maude recalled one cold day when the dishrag froze solid while hanging on one end of the heated stove!

On the most frigid days, the family wore their boots in the house, as well as long pants, long underwear, and layers of sweaters. The back parlor, where Mardo's bedroom was, was closed off in winter to conserve fuel. When he left the heated living room, the walk was short but cold. He jumped into bed with his socks and long johns on, sleeping under such a pile of blankets, he'd be tired out the next morning.

Maude told a story that tended to the more disagreeable part of the snowy cold. Bessie Hill, the teacher at the rural one-room school the Williams children attended, passed it on to her.

After a very troublesome day, school was over and the kids were rushing to don coats and boots before venturing into the four-inch snow and near-zero temperatures. Bessie, already with a headache, was getting the smallest ones on their way. At last, only one little girl was left. She had her coat on and a pair of four-buckle overshoes in her hands.

"Come here, young lady, and I'll help you," Bessie said. Then she struggled and struggled and finally got the four-buckles over the child's shoes. She was congratulating herself when the girl casually volunteered, "They're not my overshoes."

The child awaited a response or a question, and the teacher barely held her temper as she pulled and tugged to remove the too small overshoes from the girl's feet. After the boots were off again, the little girl said, "They're my brother's. Mine were wet inside and mother made me wear his today." Bessie worked for another 10 minutes to get the boots back on.

Bessie never said so, and Maude never asked, but Maude concluded in her own mind that the child was Mildred. It sounded just like her. "She can be just that exasperating."

The rush of springtime was a welcome relief. There would be sudden showers, mud tracked across the floors, children with snotty noses--but there would also be greening grass, budding trees, and the outpouring of song by early arriving robins, meadowlarks, cardinals and mockingbirds. Each season brought its own rewards to Rush Creek.

EIGHT

The *Saturday Evening Post*, late in 1897, told seventh-grader Maude and other present or potential housewives that proper care of their coal oil lamps was essential for both safety and economy. It listed common sense precautions in selection and use: "Choose a lamp with a shallow reservoir to assure a steady flame as the fuel level dips; a lamp that has been set aside for any length of time must not be relighted until all kerosene left in the reservoir has been emptied, a new wick installed, all parts thoroughly cleaned, and fresh oil supplied."

Maude said she also learned to turn the wick low, so the chimney didn't become overheated at first lighting--then raise it carefully to obtain the required light. To extinguish the flame at the end of the evening, she was advised, "lower the wick a half turn of the winder, then blow a sharp puff across the top of the glass chimney."

She found she was breaking many lamp chimneys by the way she was cleaning them. She washed them in warm, soapy water, but failed to dry them completely. The combination of heat and moisture caused them to crack. The solution: Use a soft, dry cloth and a lamp brush.

Maude kept three or four coal oil lamps ready for immediate use. Each lamp had the same basic features--a leg or wider base supporting a bowl-like oil reservoir from which a wick would siphon the fuel to the base of the chimney.

The family sat around the living room in the evening with two lamps burning and eyes straining in the dim yellow light. They welcomed the new Aladdin lamp. It also used kerosene but had a gas mantel instead of a wick. The light was white instead of yellow and the difference was like night and day.

The Aladdin was no more trouble for Maude, she said, than any of the other lamps. It burned even cleaner, with fewer smoked chimneys. It used a mantel of delicate filament to diffuse the light. After she learned not to push her finger through the filament, it was no problem. Propane and natural gas lights would use the same principle to spread an even more intense light. The family swore by the Aladdin and thought there could be nothing better--until the house was wired for electricity in 1947.

NINE

One of the least popular yearly summer projects, in which everyone took part, was the removal of ground-in grime from the carpets. A broom, and later a push hand-sweeper, could not pick up the dirt tracked in by six or more pairs of feet for 365 days of the year. So Maude became the supervisor, and the rugs (two of them, 9 by 12 and 12 by 15 feet in size) were manhandled across the clothes line at the west side of the house. The line was fashioned of heavy wire stretched between the pine tree and the black walnut tree at a height of six feet and was propped up in the middle to prevent the fabric from dragging on the ground.

Only one rug could be "cleaned" at a time. The day, ideally, should be sunny with a light southerly breeze that would carry the dust away from house and driveway. When preparations were complete, Lee and Maude would arm themselves with broomsticks and, from either side of the line, batter the rug with enough force to send out clouds of dust.

They were amazed at the amount of dirt embedded in the fabric that first time they did the spring cleaning. But the dirt had been tracked inside by residents and visitors for an entire year (or more)--through dust from the lane, grime from the barnyard, mud from the fields and through thawing snow. Dust had been blown under the ill-fitting doors during every gusty wind in the summer and snow filtered in with each winter blizzard.

When the children were big enough, rug beating became one of their least favored spring "pastimes." They competed with each other to see who could send out the largest clouds of dust or beat out the best muffled tunes with their makeshift clubs. There were arguments, of course, as one child or the other fought to gain his or her place in the breeze and stay out of the choking and ill-smelling dust. Mardo and Mildred, as the eldest, set the pace, and if one slipped or fell, he or she might blame the other for the mishap, calling on "Mom" to come and solve the dispute.

When they were tired out from flailing the fabric with various length cudgels (salvaged from brooms that had been worn to a nub by repeated daily attempts to keep surfaces clean during the previous year), they reported the job completed. But if Maude inspected, and she always did, the rest period could be ended suddenly. The rugs might pass visual inspection but if a light tap of the club raised a minor cloud of dust, the children were sent back into the fray.

The carpet was adjusted on the line to make higher points reachable and the youngsters renewed their onslaught. Complaints of tiredness went unheeded but the child who showed a blister on the hands was given time out for loving and a medical treatment before being sent back into action.

Everyone breathed a sigh of relief when the rug-bashing was over. And when the next cleaning season approached, the children carefully did not mention rug cleaning in the hope that it would be forgotten until another year. It never was.

TEN

Maude was a meticulous housekeeper and prided herself on keeping surfaces clean, clutter to a minimum and daily tasks--like care of the lamps, cooking, canning in season, laundry, sweeping and dusting-- completely on schedule. She reluctantly made concessions during childbearing times and various emergencies. Neighbors who helped at those times were not expected to do other than routine duties.

Maude reserved Tuesdays for breadmaking--Mondays for laundering and Fridays for sweeping and dusting. Other days of the week could be used for canning, sewing or any number of impromptu activities but Lee could be sure that Maude would be bent over the washboard each Monday, wielding broom, mop, bucket, and dust cloth every Friday, and mixing bread dough on Tuesday--her gingham apron covered with flour.

Breadmaking was a weekly chore in that period before commercial bakeries spawned an endless variety of enriched white breads, supplemented by sister loaves of oat and whole wheat--all carefully sliced and wrapped in cellophane to ensure freshness.

During the first year of Maude's marriage, Lee's mother, Sarah Williams, had demonstrated how "simple" it was. "You just combine flour, lard, water and yeast in the proper proportions," she told her daughter-in-law, "knead the dough vigorously, let it start to rise in an oblong pan, then put it in the oven."

Maude learned through experience that the quality of the bread was governed by the housewife's control over the yeast process--if the dough went into the oven too soon, the loaf was flat, the bread sodden; if too late, the loaf spread above the sides of the pan and the texture was coarse, with large holes throughout.

On this breadmaking occasion, Maude felt like an expert. The children, aged one to seven, were playing on the linoleum floor, within her sight. Pauline was attempting to drop a clothespin into an empty milk bottle. Mardo was notching the ends of a small spool so as to make a noise-maker when rotated across a window pane. Bea and Mildred were playing with a doll they'd made, using a corncob and an old sock.

Maude's routine was always the same. She cleared the table and wiped the oil cloth with a clean cloth. Then she placed a container under the spout of the large wooden flour bin (it held 25 pounds) in the kitchen cabinet. She sifted the required amount--two cups for each loaf--and dumped the flour in the center of the oil cloth. This flour was natural, with no additives, and made from wheat only.

She added a handful of lard, a little water, some salt, and began working them into the dry flour with her hands. More lard, more water, and a half hour later the dough was ready for the yeast. Maude--and most farm wives--used a culture made from cakes of dry or moist yeast. It could be maintained from week to week and supplemented by the addition of water and sugar after a portion was used.

Kneading now became important, to distribute the yeast so the bread would rise evenly. The dough was put into three loaf pans, covered with clean dish towels, and allowed to rise. When the mixture swelled to near the rim of the pan, it was ready for baking--any delay could result in a coarsened texture of the finished product.

As the first batch baked, three more loaves were readied and put into pans. If all six had been prepared at the same time, three would have risen above their pans before reaching the oven, and half the week's consignment of bread would have been of inferior quality and taste.

One December day, Maude took the time to answer the children's pleas for doughnuts. She formed round globules of dough from her bread-making supply and dropped them carefully into a pan of boiling lard. A sort of forceps was used to lift the light brown morsels from the sizzling fat and place them on the plates of four hungry youngsters.

Two factors combined to end her breadmaking activities. One was the developing concern among the girls about their weight--and their reduction in the intake of bread and butter (with sugar sprinkled on it). The other was the arrival of the couple's first car in 1920--which made the store only 15 minutes away. Bread, wrapped in waxed paper, could be purchased for 12 cents a loaf, and replenished whenever Lee had a spare coin or Maude had butter and eggs to trade.

During the decade of the 1920s, the commercial bakers made another bid for the bread trade by slicing the loaves and wrapping them in waterproof-airproof cellophane. Fleischmann's, the nationally operated supplier of packaged yeasts, began an advertising program advising housewives to buy their bread--not bake it!

The yeast maker was signaling the decreasing home market for yeast, and the increasing number of commercial bakeries (who purchased larger amounts of yeast). Commercially made bread was never as good as the home-baked loaves. Maude said it was light and airy, lacking in solid texture. Bread eventually would be made from grains, from which natural nutrients were removed or altered before being "enriched" with vitamins.

Maude said there was another "never mentioned" reason that she abandoned the culinary art at which she'd become expert. "Mice invaded our house each autumn, multiplied, and left their droppings everywhere," she explained.

Lee set traps on every shelf and in every runway. But no matter how many were trapped, the mouse population was always replenished. The little animals would come through cracks--or a child would leave a door ajar. The use of poison was considered, but discarded as a potential danger to curious youngsters seeking the candies their parents were known to hide on pantry shelves. The use of a cat, which could have been brought in from the barn, was unthinkable. Grandmother Allen had indoctrinated daughter Maude against having cats in the house.

The trap used by the Williamses was designed to kill one animal at a time. It was a loop of steel wire and spring, mounted on a flat piece of wood. The spring tightened when the loop was fastened to the bait in the open position. A particle of cheese on the tripping device became the bait. Even the lightest nibble caused the steel wire to snap shut, usually with fatal results.

It wasn't unusual for three or more mice to be trapped in one night. "We were sitting around the dining room one night--all six of us busy (reading, studying, mending)--when we heard a trap shut," Maude recalled. "Lee investigated, removed the animal and re-set the trap. Before he got back to his chair, the trap was sprung again and we had another victim."

There were so many rodents hiding in the kitchen and pantry, where the food was, that Lee bought a wire mesh trap. Little one-way doors permitted the mice to enter. When the cage had several occupants, it was submerged in a barrel of water. Lee said he couldn't stand the sight of the mice drowning before his eyes. He said the spring traps were more humane and junked the cage.

Maude, who'd begun to feel sympathy for the unwelcome visitors, said the crowning blow in the battle came one Tuesday when she prepared for her weekly bread-baking. She noticed little black pellets in the mound of white flour she'd sifted onto the table. It can't be, she thought. It was-- mice had gnawed through the wooden canister and contaminated her last 20 pounds of flour.

The entire supply was thrown out. Storage hereafter would be in metal containers, resistant to sharp teeth and to pests, like the ants she'd noticed infrequently on the kitchen floor. A 5-gallon lard can was pressed into service, and would be used as long as Maude had need of flour.

ELEVEN

Pauline, the youngest child, was four when Maude and Lee began making the weekly trips to town a regular part of the family agenda--and thought she was as big as anyone. There was a lot of shouting and arguing if the adults decided that the weather was too bad (rain, high winds or a sudden drop in temperature) to risk the one-hour trip each way in the open carriage. No one questioned Topsy, the means of locomotion, as to her desires, but she may have been content to stay in the barn and munch hay!

One Saturday evening in 1915, when Pauline was 6, a minor disagreement between the youngest of the family and her father almost became a crisis, in the minds of the other children. Lee, who was a kind and loving father, nevertheless had established a strict code of behavior. At the top of the list was the admonition that no child was to "sass" the parents. Another prime rule, strictly enforced, set forth that everyone of the household had to eat all of the food he or she ladled onto the plate.

Pauline had broken both commandments that evening. Dad ordered his daughter to eat the remainder of the food on her plate. She talked back and said she wasn't hungry any more and that she wasn't going to eat it. During the clash of wills, Lee said if she didn't do so, the entire family would miss their anticipated visit to the amusement capital of their world-- Mt. Victory, a rural town with a population of 800, a grocery, hardware store, bank, dry goods establishment, and restaurant along Main Street.

The older children watched anxiously as the clock ticked ominously toward the time when it would be too late to start out. Both stubborn Pauline and indomitable Lee refused to budge. Then, Mildred, 12, Mardo, 10, and Bea, 8, took action.

They surreptitiously ate the food for Pauline, told her that if she didn't tell her father she was sorry for her actions she would suffer at their hands during the coming week, and convinced Lee he shouldn't punish everyone for Pauline's shortcomings. Finally, Maude noted, "We all got going."

The Saturday night excursions were enjoyed by the whole family for chance meetings with old-time friends like the Chet McMahons, the Hank Rosebrooks, the Joe Earlys, the Rob Richardsons and others, and the opportunity to shop, watch the passersby and ignore for a time the continual responsibilities.

Those uneventful rides in the family carriage behind the slowly trotting horse were pleasurable too. The three-mile trip took about an hour. Maude and Lee had the opportunity to talk without interruption while the four youngsters played their games and watched for the rising moon or the appearance of that first star. The games were, in effect, contests and were conceived as a way of heading off those endless questions, "Are we almost there?" and "When will we get there?"

There were no sign boards, no radio music and no brightly shining lights along the way to distract attention from the game at hand. Popular was the contest to see and identify the most hogs, or sheep, or cattle or horses within a certain time or distance frame.

This activity was accompanied by the "stamping" of every white cow, horse or mule in sight. Stamping was effected by placing an index finger to the lips, pressing it to the palm of the other hand and then striking the palm with a closed fist.

When the magic total of 100 stampings was reached--counting one for each cow and horse and ten for the less prevalent white horse or mule--the child, according to the rules of the game as interpreted by the parents, would glance down as he or she walked about the town and find in his or her path a coin. This was usually a penny, but it could be a nickel, dime or even a quarter.

"We never attempted to change fate," Maude insisted. "The children would lose count, but when the magic 100 arrived, there was no doubt in our minds that a penny or more would certainly appear on the ground in their path. That's why when the children were in town, they were always looking down."

Word games were introduced early. This competition embraced the spelling and meaning of words and was expanded to identifying plants and objects along the road. The youngsters enjoyed riddles, and a favorite might be sprung on friends, relatives or playmates a hundred times before patience wore out.

And when daylight faded to dusk, the search began to find that first, dimly twinkling star. Soon, a childish voice could be heard reciting the only poem known: "Star light, star bright-- first star I see tonight; I wish I may, I wish I might have the wish I wish tonight."

The wish, more frequently than not, might relate to the survival of the heroine in the melodramatic movie serial they were about to see. Last week, in "The Perils of Pauline," the attractive young woman had been left tied to the railroad tracks in the path of a speeding train. This week, she might be catapulted over a raging waterfall, stranded on the sawmill platform edging toward the whirling buzz saw blades, or aboard a raft traveling along Borneo's crocodile-infested rivers.

The movie, climax to an evening of window and store shopping, of eyeing farm folk from miles around in their freshly laundered work clothes, bonnets and straw hats, and of sitting on curb-side benches as the people paraded past, was the drawing card.

It was free, a promotion by the merchants--the magnet that attracted hundreds from six miles away to the little town each show night. The movie was projected on the outside wall of the two-story feed store, high enough so the audience of 300 to 400, who stood to watch, could easily see the flickering images.

Maude said the movies were of the same basic plot, each episode ending with a "cliffhanger" to hold the interest of the audience from week to week throughout the summer. Silent serial stars were usually women, invincible heroines who survived snakes, explosions, kidnappings, collapsing buildings, and bizarre native rituals.

The best known was Pearl White, whose serials included (besides "The Perils of Pauline") "The Exploits of Elaine," "The Fatal Ring," and "Plunder." The movies were cheaply made. The pictures were blurry, made more so by the rough texture of the painted brick store wall. When the film broke, the operator of the projector took forever, it seemed, to make repairs.

The only sounds from the audience were the occasional cough, the shout of warning to the endangered hero or heroine, and the cries of exasperation when a movie reel had to be exchanged or the dialogue written on the screen (like the subtitles of today's foreign films) or the picture became so indistinct that viewers couldn't determine what was happening. Was the villain fast approaching? Would the hero arrive in time? When the picture faded from the white store front just off the village square, viewers quietly gathered their families and stole away. There was no roar from untamed mufflers, no screeching of suddenly applied brakes, no burning of rubber--only the clip-clop of hooves on the hard street surface. Then, only quiet.

The Williamses were too tired to resume their games on the ride home. After a few grumbles and a battle or two for a choice seat, the children settled down and when Maude glanced back, all four were huddled in the back seat, sleeping. Taking advantage of the quiet, she and Lee resumed their conversation where they had left off on the trip to town.

The couple shared their desire to better plan their future and to take some time each day to enjoy the youngsters. "We always agreed we should live our lives more freely, savor the sunrises and sunsets, the caroling of birds, the flow of fleecy white clouds in the blue skies, the sudden storms, and every facet of nature," Maude recalled.

"We vowed to discount the fussiness of the youngsters and take in stride the trials and tribulations that would be forthcoming." But that, she admitted, was a lot to expect of mere mortals.

As Lee and Maude talked, they held hands. They were still talking when Lee suddenly realized that they were stopped in the roadway. Topsy had brought them safely home and was waiting patiently in front of the farm gate.

"Get up, sleepyhead!" Lee shouted to his son. "Open the gate so we can make it up the lane and to bed."

That was the way it was during those summers when the Williams family found Saturday movies in Mt. Victory an irresistible lure.

TWELVE

It wasn't a nurse-doctor experiment as she first suspected, Maude told Lee on that day in July. She explained. "I needed one of the children to run an errand for me and couldn't get an answer to my calls. After doing the chore myself, I saw our four trooping out of the barn. Along with them were Stewart and Ruth Richardson (Rob and Mattie's oldest), and Isabel and Charlie Marmon (youngest children of Charles, Sr. and Lizzie).

"I couldn't imagine what was interesting enough to keep eight children quiet for that length of time. So after the neighbor children left, I called nine-year-old Mildred to my side and gave her the third degree."

Under pressure, Mildred told the following story, naming 13-year-old Isabel Marmon as the instigator:

The girls approached the boys with the proposition of a mutual private showing in the empty oats bin. Boys were to do the showing first. So as the girls waited in the privacy of the enclosed bin, Isabel announced the first "victim" as Stewart Richardson, 10. He was followed by Charles Marmon, eight, then by Mardo Williams, seven.

Appropriate fanfare preceded each boy's entry into the inner sanctum. Alone and helpless in the spotlight, each hurried through the humiliation, looking forward to the upcoming show when the girls would be onstage.

"What did you do when it came your turn?" Maude questioned.

"We cheated," Mildred said. "The boys insisted we had promised, but suddenly Isabel remembered that she had to go home and finish some work she'd started."

The episode was over, except in the minds of three boys who throughout their lives would ponder on the deviousness of the gentler sex.

There were so many minor emergencies, comedic incidents and educational happenings that Maude had to grapple for them in her memory as she grew older.

When Pauline was seven years old, she got her hand caught while exploring high in the huge bank barn. She was seeking the nest of a sparrow and plunged her fingers into a hole that had been cut in the upright timber. Almost her entire weight was born by one arm as she balanced, one-footed, on a narrow cross piece.

As the diminutive Pauline screamed (she wasn't quite four feet tall) and the other children shouted for help, Lee anchored an extension ladder at the scene. He mounted, rung by rung, until he was two feet above her. Then he reached down, took the frightened 55-pound child in his arms and gently lifted her until the hand was pulled clear. She suffered bruises, a loss of confidence, and a severe case of lice infestation. The sparrow was long gone but had left ample evidence of its past presence.

Mildred, who had the reputation of being the ring leader in many of the childish adventures, escaped injury (and even the blame) most of the time. Maude thought fate helped her oldest child as recompense for the burns she had experienced in September 1905 when she pulled the pan of boiling jelly off the kitchen range.

Both Mildred and Pauline loved to whistle, but Pauline could whistle a tune. Maude would quote, with a smile, "Whistling girls and singing hens always come to some bad end," meaning that singing hens didn't lay eggs and always ended up in the stew pot.

Bea, the most tractable of the children, nevertheless had a will of her own. Maude found her one day threatening her five-year-old cousin, Edith Williams, with dire punishment. It seems that seven-year-old Bea had consented to take Edith to the outhouse, where the smaller cousin had refused to sit and do her stuff as commanded. Whether the outhouse visit was Bea's idea was never determined. Relations were strained for a while between the two but all was forgotten when they met the next day.

Most of the time Bea was cheerful, disliked arguments and was amenable to the wishes of others.

Maude remembered an occasion that aptly portrayed Bea's laudatory traits. At age 13, she had become dissatisfied with her long tresses. She wanted them cut and beveled up the back. There was no money for a barber and the quest seemed hopeless UNTIL...Mardo offered...and Bea consented...to some experimental barbering. All of it to be done under Bea's careful supervision, of course.

Armed with a pair of household shears, he began cutting away at those light brown strands of hair. As he hacked, she watched through her mirror and advised: "Even it up! Take a little more off there."

The barber envisioned a new career. He complied enthusiastically, if not expertly. Each succeeding cut left the hair more uneven. An attempt to bevel the hair on the back of her head left the remaining hair in ragged clumps, separated by a few almost bald spots.

Bea wore a tam o'shanter to classes for a month, too ashamed to let the teachers see the results of her tonsorial experimentation. Despite her mother's threat to punish her brother for such blatant butchery, she insisted: "We did it together."

And Maude said that both were punished without anyone taking action. "Bea suffered through a month of teasing by classmates. And Mardo felt guilty for having taken part in her humiliation."

His barbering days were over. Those who had seen his sister's haircut said they could have done better blindfolded. Mildred and Pauline wouldn't even let him trim their bangs. If they saw him with scissors in hand, they ran in mock terror and pretended to seek help from their parents.

Mildred led the way in changing the dress code. When she started to notice that boys could be exciting, she became more interested in her appearance. It was apparent that she was combing her hair more carefully, washing her face more thoroughly, and seeking ways to improve both dress and bearing.

"The first evidence of her dissatisfaction hit us one winter day when she stepped off the school bus with her legs bare from shoe top to knee," Maude noted. "She had rolled up the legs of her long johns." It was a protest to unsightly underwear and unattractive leg coverings that would be continued day after day, until spring arrived with its warmer weather and light underthings.

Maude did all she could to speed the change from the purely utilitarian to the more comely styles. The high button shoes already were gone. They had been difficult to button, especially for younger children--requiring a hand-held tool with a hook at the end of a steel wire. The hook was latched around each button and pulled through each eyelet on the opposite flap. Buttons were lost when the thread broke as the hook tried to force them through the holes in the leather. Laced shoes were much easier to don and more comfortable to wear.

Mercerized stockings--a lighter weight cotton product, made more attractive by its closer weave--became the vogue for the active youngster. Bloomers and cotton underthings were becoming popular. Heavy four-buckle boots, fastened with metal clamps, had replaced the felt boots that elderly men depended on during winter's coldest blasts and their recurrent bouts with arthritis.

Women, who had witnessed the passing of the ankle-length dresses of the previous century, were eager to follow the trend of styles even if it meant baring the knees.

The Williams girls enthusiastically endorsed change and said they would be glad to shiver in winter gusts if they could but wear attractive things.

They shared feelings with the school friends they visited frequently. Favorite friends of Mildred for overnight conferences were Hazel Predmore and Geneva Ansley. Mildred confided to her mother that Geneva (who later became Mardo's wife) used the dishpan in shampooing her hair. The implied criticism: The dish pan should be used only for the washing of tableware, pots and pans.

Bea was never critical of her school friends but then she never stayed overnight with any of them. She was more of an introvert and a homebody and preferred her own home and her own bed.

Pauline's favored schoolmates remained her best friends for life. If phone conversations could have been more private, Helen Seedle, Erma Rostorfer, Martha Perry and Pauline Williams would have continued their private discussions every night and each week-end. Like the Williamses, Pauline's friends were on party lines which were open at all times to the six or eight other families sharing the same circuit.

Mardo stayed overnight from time to time with his cousin, William Newell, who lived on the south side of Ridgeway, Maude said. One of Mardo's visits with Cousin Bill became memorable when the Newells received a consignment of Georgia peanuts from his dad's sister. The small in-shell goobers, when roasted, took on a delicate flavor. That feature made up for the difficulty in opening them.

Mardo told his parents he was a little afraid of his Uncle Forrest Newell, a gruff-looking man of six feet, three inches and 190 pounds. He concealed an underlying neighborliness with solemn visage. He thought children's activities should be watched carefully and closely supervised--and he kept his son Bill under strict control.

"We would be playing and if a whistle sounded, Bill would take off at a fast run," Mardo reported. Bill said: A shrill whistle meant "stop everything wherever you are and come home immediately." It was a sure way of keeping the son out of devilment--and out of the neighbors' homes.

Mardo decided he didn't want to live in town if he had to be as closely watched as Cousin Bill. He preferred the way his dad and mom supervised. Even additional chores were welcome when compared to being shouted at or whistled to like a dog, Maude was told. Mardo found excuses not to stay overnight.

Mardo and Mildred agreed that they began to realize how fortunate they were when they started to high school. "Our parents were always there and they listened. They treated us like adults."

Pauline's complaint about a gift from an uncle brought the admonition: "Be thankful for small favors." Everything was to be enjoyed. There was to be no rancor, no jealousy, no envy of anyone else.

"Our youngsters learned to share and take pleasure in another's good fortune," Maude said. "They never gave us cause to worry."

The couple remembered when Bea accidentally dropped her glass of milk on the kitchen floor and had her tears dried with the admonition, "Don't cry over spilled milk."

Pauline received comparable advice a few weeks later when she tripped (four or five eggs were broken) while returning from the poultry house with the "hen fruit" she had just gathered. She was sobbing, both from embarrassment and from pain of the scratched leg she had suffered, when she heard her mother telling her the injury was trivial and her mishap could have meant a foodless breakfast for someone.

"Don't put all your eggs in one basket," she advised the little girl, then took time to explain that the adage, passed down through generations of farm folks, could apply to many developments throughout life. It simply meant that you shouldn't go overboard, that you shouldn't bet all your money on one horse or one project, she said.

THIRTEEN

Taffy pulls were popular in the early 1900s. Maude invited two or three other couples, usually at holiday times, and both women and men vied for the honor of fashioning the clearest ropes of candy. The hostess did the cooking--and woe befall her if she cooked the sugar and water mixture either too little or too much. In the one case, the candy remained sticky; in the other, it hardened into a chalk-like substance.

But cooked just right, a person could snatch up a huge ball and, by expert pulling and wrapping the strings of candy around thumb and elbow, form it into perfect loops. After it cooled, the candy was broken in pieces by a blow from a knife handle. It wasn't so much a contest as a way of helping a neighbor acquire sweets for a special occasion.

Most of the taffy pullers were adept at the art before they appeared in Maude's kitchen. Her younger brother Harley (12 years younger than Maude) often stayed at the farm. He wasn't skilled at taffy pulling, but he insisted he was a quick learner. So a small heap of the sweet mass was ladled on a plate for his use. At first, it was too hot to handle; then he permitted it to become too cool.

At last, he got the hang of it. He pulled the ropes of pliable candy back and forth in his hands, finally made circles around thumb and elbow as he saw his sister Maude do. Wearing the candy loops, he moved around the room, flexing his muscles, and claiming to be the best of the group at the night's session. As Maude prepared to warn him that "pride goeth before a fall," he stumbled, threw up his hands, and lost control of the candy. It fell into the coal bucket--and Harley was relegated to the living room where he could do no more damage.

There were quilting parties too. Each woman brought her own patches cut from old clothing and used her decorative ability to sew the various colors into intricate patterns. These events became educational challenges, opportunities for gossip, and the basis of sewing, knitting, cooking and baking competitions.

The husking bees outside Lee's barn were just as entertaining in a different way. No one passed up the opportunity to attend. The men competed. The women socialized, knitted, crocheted, made comforters. Everyone enjoyed pumpkin pie, cookies and cider. Children always had the range of the lantern-lighted farmyard--until hungry mosquitoes drove them into the house.

Sometimes, the competition was staged in the afternoon. If the weather was bad, fodder was moved to the barn floor--and the men followed. But everyone preferred the outdoor farmyard setting, either in the sunshine or under the stars. There was loud talking, joking, and the issuing of challenges as contestants settled into the routine of grabbing a stalk with its one or more ears of corn, slashing the husking peg through the husk and tearing it away in one movement.

Some used a peg attached to the fingers by a leather band, but most used a leather glove without fingers (with the peg attached in the middle of the palm). Each type took a different movement but both required coordination, strength, and the stamina to propel the hand and lower arm back and forth hundreds of times during a contest session.

Lee sometimes competed, with mixed results. Ross Engle, his nephew and hired hand for three years, was the champion or runner-up at many husking bees in the area for several years. Mardo never gave it a try. He was too young, too small and too inexperienced--so was given the chore of gathering up the ears of corn that were flung far and wide by the contestants.

The aim was to get the husked ear off the stalk--not to toss it accurately into a pile. A bystander--even another competitor--sometimes was struck by the flying corn. Points were lost if any husk was left attached to the ear-- none was deducted for conking another during the heads-down melee.

One feature that added some piquancy to the meet was the special "prize" for those who husked a blue or red ear from his pile. He was made to seek out his wife, or girl friend, and in the presence of jeers and catcalls give her both a bear hug and a resounding kiss.

FOURTEEN

The annual butchering was a dreaded--and necessary--event in Maude's and Lee's life. The killing, scalding, cutting, rendering, and packaging took only one dawn-to-dusk day. But the gathering of the necessary tools before and the later clean-up of grease and hair, blood and entrails stretched the ordeal into a week.

The huge iron kettle, in which cubes of fat were boiled, had to be leveled carefully on slabs of stone, with chunks of wood and coal distributed beneath it. An empty barrel had to be anchored at an angle against the woodshed. At least two structures, on which hogs would be hung for scraping of the skin and disemboweling, must be in place.

The kettle and the barrel were used each year and stored, either at the Williams' place or at the neighbor's, who shared the ownership. The lard press and sausage grinder also must be located and cleaned. Knives had to be sharpened, scrapers prepared and the wooden paddles readied for stirring the fatty pieces as they boiled.

The rendering kettle was smooth on the inside and a textured black on the outside. No one knew if it was of a weathered black enamel or if the color was the result of being subjected to coal and wood smoke over the years. Its first usage this year would come as the butchering got under way. It would heat the water in which each carcass would be scalded.

The barrel, from which the top had been removed, was crucial in early stages of the operation. In it, each carcass would be dipped back and forth in near boiling water to loosen the hair. Scraping was accomplished by a hand-held tool--basically a six-inch circle of steel that was slightly dished and sharp on the edges. It was mounted at right angles to the wooden peg which served as a handle to facilitate the scraping.

With the major accessories in place, Lee awaited the first November (or early December) day with frost on the ground. Temperatures, he said, should hover around the freezing mark. A light snow would be acceptable, but muddy conditions made the work much more difficult.

Six of his best young hogs had been placed in a pen to one side and fed a ration of grains and milk for two weeks, to promote the meat's tenderness and flavor. Everything was ready and today was the day!

Two helpers, Lee's hired hand, Enoch Spain, and a neighbor, Charles Marmon, herded the first animal to the chute at the side of the pen. As the hog scrambled up the incline, Lee used a 22-caliber rifle to shoot it at the base of the skull. In almost the same move, he dropped the rifle, grabbed a knife and plunged the long, slender blade into its neck, severing the jugular vein.

The procedure was never assigned to a novice. It had to be completed before the hog started its reflexive struggles. There must be no repetitive searches for the jugular, and the sharp point must be retracted before it penetrated the shoulder muscle.

In the event of a miscue, a blood clot would form deep within the shoulder. This meant that the meat could not be preserved for long. It could not be stored safely. Even with the most meticulous curing process known at the time, spoilage would start at the site of the pooled blood and spread throughout, Lee said.

With its life blood gushing out, the hog was dragged from the slaughter site by handled hooks inserted through its Achilles tendons, and strung upside down to facilitate the draining and assure that blood would not pool in the joints. It hung on hooks, the hind legs attached to two of the three poles assembled in a tripod arrangement. Each post was extended to help brace the structure and, when erected, it looked like the framework of a tepee.

Carried by three men, the carcass next was plunged head first, then tail end, into the barrel of near-boiling water. It hung on the "tripod" again for the scraping, eviscerating and separating into two halves. Each half went to a work bench in the covered shed near the kitchen, and became a ham, a shoulder, and a side (bacon). The backbone became porkchops. The leftover lean trimmings would go into sausage, the fat into the big black kettle after it had served its purpose of heating the water for scalding.

The same procedure was followed for each of the six hogs. As the parcels of meat and trimmings multiplied so did the duties. Someone had to man the rendering kettle. Another must cut and trim the hams, shoulders, and sides.

Someone must carefully clean the small intestines and place them in a salt solution. They later would be threaded on the spout of the sausage grinder and become casings for the link sausage.

The livers and hearts were always saved but most farm folk didn't like the other abdominal parts or the brains. Kidneys were welcome if one had cats. And the cuts around the jowls were favored for mincemeat. Most farmers liked mincemeat pies, a combination of the head meat, apples and raisins within two savory crusts.

By noon, Lee and his two helpers had called in the reserves. The women would help. So would another neighbor man or two. And Fred Bondley was always available, for the promise of a good meal, a pouch of chewing tobacco and one of the livers.

Fred, a personable Dutchman, liked to be called Fritz. He was a widower who lived in the village of Mt. Victory, and was 62 years old when Lee called on him to help with the 1913 butchering. He was a colorful character first and an avid hunter second. With a small glass of whiskey in hand or a cud of tobacco in mouth, he was willing to talk at length about that terrible winter day when he tracked a deer over parts of three counties and lost it in a blizzard-like snowstorm when he was 12 miles from home.

Fritz would describe each move, each tracking device he used to follow the snow-obliterated trail--never missing a stroke of his assigned task. When the call came for dinner, he took the wad of chewing tobacco out of his mouth, wrapped it in a piece of paper and carefully placed it on a post. He would reclaim it later.

A prankster (Maude's youngest brother Harley) thought he would add a little flavor and just as carefully implanted a small hen turd in the cud. Fritz never got to resume his chew. Lee, who had noticed the prank, offered him a fresh one from his newly opened Red Man.

"I thought it would be the height of ill manners to let him chew the polluted tobacco when he helped me out on such short notice," Lee said.

The day had turned leaden with a light wind-driven snow sizzling in the fire under the vat when Lee shot the sixth (and last) hog. Maude and her cohorts had long since started grinding and stuffing sausage, and the first of the lard had been rendered. It would be stored in five-gallon covered metal containers for use as needed.

For some reason, sausage-making had become the sole responsibility of the housewives. The men carefully trimmed away the fatty surplus as they shaped hams, shoulders, and bacon sides, and prepared the backbone for either chops or tenderloin (the rolls of choice meat at either side of the spinal column). Fat went to the rendering kettle; strips of lean meat went to the sausage-making brigade in the kitchen.

Maude always organized her women helpers into an assembly line team. One trimmed even more fat from the strips (you could never get the sausage too lean, she said); another fed the sausage grinder; a third took the ground meat and ran it through the hand-cranked press; and a fourth, if Maude had that many assistants, threaded the casings on the outlet tube of the sausage press and tied off the filled sections into "links."

The grinder was clamped to the top of the kitchen table, near the press.

Both were manually operated. Through the cutting knives and perforated plates of the grinder oozed the ground meat; through a tube at the bottom of the press, sausage flowed in a stream into the casings, or into a pan to be formed into patties.

The press required a little more strength than the grinder. As the crank turned, it revolved a set of cogs that forced a circular steel plate downward into the cage that held the raw sausage. The product's only outlet was the spout at the bottom.

Maude took the sausage link or patty, fried it to the desired doneness, and placed section after section, or patty after patty, in two-gallon earthenware jars. Each would be filled nearly to the brim with the hot, liquefied lard, effectively preserving the product for weeks--even months --until Maude claimed the meat for some future breakfast. The lard, somewhat tainted by the sausage smell, could be used for all frying but would be unsuitable for cakes, pies or puddings.

Lee personally supervised the lard rendering, leaving his other tasks to make sure the fatty mixture was being stirred periodically with the wooden paddle at the site. The paddle also was used to press chunks against the side of the vat to gauge how done they were or how much longer they would have to cook.

When the experts concurred the mixture was done and there was no danger of the lard developing a slightly rancid taste in the storage can, the liquid was removed. The chunks of cooked fat were placed in the lard press. The crushed material was called "cracklings" by the farmers, who found it too greasy to eat--except in moderation. Commercial enterprises later were formed, removed more of the fat, enhanced the taste and made a profit selling it to the public.

Lard, once the exclusive fat for baked goods and frying, lost ground in the 1920s with the advent of a product called oleomargarine. Originally, it too was made largely of animal fats (later, with vegetable oils). But it came with a little pouch of food coloring that, when properly mixed, made the product look like butter. Many housewives started using oleo, but Maude remained faithful to lard.

All six hogs had been processed by day's end, Fritz had been returned to his hunting dreams, the neighbors had gone home, and Lee, with greasy hands, was milking Old Bossy. There would be several days more of work for Maude--and perhaps Lee--as she preserved the rest of the sausage and cleaned up the mess.

During the first few years, Lee had preserved the hams and shoulders by treating them with hickory smoke. A small room at one end of the woodshed had been set aside for that purpose, complete with galvanized barrel to hold the wood, and flues to carry away the smoke.

When he increased the number of hogs butchered (from two in the early years of marriage to the six now required by the growing family), smoking became too slow a treatment, he said.

Now he rolled each section of meat in a mixture of brown sugar and smoked salt, poked a hole all the way to the bone's joint and lined it with the smoked salt so the meat wouldn't spoil from the inside out.

Hams and shoulders were wrapped separately in muslin cloth, placed in 25-pound flour sacks, and hung on nails in an unheated upstairs room of the house. The meat was cured in four to six weeks. The salt preserved them so they remained edible for about 10 months, until late the next summer.

The distasteful clean-up was left until the last. Who could enjoy scrubbing away at the hog grease on the lard press and sausage grinder, rendering vat and work bench (where each animal was laid to be dismembered) and on the knives and utensils? The smell and feel of raw and rendered fat had become almost sickening.

Lee dismantled the chute and tepee-like tripod, cleaned up the scalding barrel and returned any borrowed equipment.

The gory trauma was ended for another year--the killing, bleeding, scraping, gutting (with all the entrails toppled into a wash tub), amputating and processing. The next one was only twelve months away for every family member but Lee, who would be executioner, lard renderer, and master of all trades, as his neighbors enacted their own butchering dramas (with his assistance)!

Part V: Events and Entertainments

The Devil finds things for idle hands to do.

ONE

*C*ounty fairs were attractions for every family member. "We tried to get to either the Logan County Fair at Bellefontaine or the Hardin County Fair at Kenton once a year," Maude recalled. "We started at daybreak, equipped for an all-day stay. The 12-mile trip by horse and buggy took about four hours each way, so shortly after we arrived at noon, we spread a blanket on the ground and ate a picnic of fried chicken, potato salad, cookies, and lemonade.

"The children sought the rides and side shows if they had the money. Lee and I inspected the livestock, culinary and domestic arts exhibits. We met back at the carriage in the early evening, made the long trip home and Lee finished the milking at ten o'clock."

It was worth the extra effort and lost sleep once a year, the couple agreed. To go more often would be too much. Maude remembered son Mardo working in the hot sun for 10 cents per hour to clear fence rows for his grandfather. "He saved ten dimes to take to the fair, then stopped at the first booth and spent it all trying to burst a balloon with a dull dart. 'What's the matter with these spendthrifty kids,' his father wondered. 'Don't they know the value of money?'"

About once a summer, Lee and his brother-in-law, Will Engle, celebrated for no apparent reason, and without the approval of either Maude or Neola (Lee's sister). The parties were held in the horse stable area at the Engle farm. A case of Crystal Rock beer was iced and when the beer was gone, "we hitched up Old Topsy and she knew the way home," Maude said. The time of departure was governed largely by how many neighbors heard of the party in time to join in.

The celebrations continued until 1914 when Will became ill with what he described as an upset stomach. After he vomited what looked like coffee grounds, his diagnosis changed. He became seriously ill and died a few months later of cancer.

Each summer the family traveled to the Ansley-Johnson-Rosebrook reunion which attracted more than 500 persons. Foot races, horseshoe pitching and watermelon eating contests were featured.

And once a year, Lee, his five sisters, his brother and their families got together at the farm home of parents Rawson W. and Sarah Witcraft Williams for a potluck dinner. It was held in mid-to-late October to commemorate Ross's and Sarah's wedding anniversary (October 26), both of their birthdays and various other October anniversaries of the family.

The annual gathering attracted 60 or more Williamses each year. They would congregate in small groups by ages and special interests. Some of the men were expert horseshoe players, could score a ringer from 80 feet away every second or third toss despite the inferior equipment. The pegs at each end of the court would be of wood if no iron rods could be found. The horseshoes were always of different sizes and weights--warped or scarred in spots from rugged use on the feet of work animals Ceilum and Daisy, Bell and Minerva, Topsy and Warrior.

The shouting and laughter were a magnet that attracted the wives to the scene, sometimes for a not-so-friendly challenge to the "superior" men. Each game ended when the first contender reached 21 points, scored on the basis of five points for a ringer (encirclement of the peg by a horseshoe), three points for a leaner (reposing against the peg), and one point for the horseshoe nearest the peg in the event there were no ringers or leaners.

Competition could be between individuals, pairs and teams of five. If one of the early "pitchers" got a ringer or leaner, the opposition would try to knock it away. Teammates would build up horseshoes in front of the vulnerable horseshoe to protect it. After each player had taken his or her turn, the points were counted, the horseshoes gathered up and the next frame started. One game ended and another was started only when the 21st point was counted.

Younger members deemed the baseball game an integral part of every reunion. Plans had been set in motion for the current contest with selection of Ralph Engle and Fred Smith (grandsons of Ross and Sarah) as captains of the opposing ball teams. A bat was tossed and caught by one of them. The two older boys went hand over hand until there was no room on the bat. The one with the last hand-hold got to pick his first player.

The captains continued choosing sides until everyone who wanted to play had been assigned to one team or the other. Each determined which players would be pitcher, catcher, first baseman, and so on. Small children were discouraged, primarily because they would prove a handicap when it came their turn to bat in the five-inning game.

A playing area was stepped off in the livestock pasture with a home plate, first, second, and third bases, and an outfield that ranged to the encircling fences.

No quarter was asked, none given. One team would be ahead, then the other. In this memorable game, the Reds were leading by one run in the last half of the fifth when the Blues sent up their power batsmen. With two out, men on second and third, and a key hitter at the plate, excitement mounted.

All at once, a shout went up from the spectators. Lee Williams had boldly dashed down the base line attempting to steal second base. The Red defensive team trapped him and eventually got him out. Meantime, the tying run had scored, a runner had advanced to third, and the batter was awaiting the pitch.

Making himself heard over the frenzied laughter and applause, Captain Engle of the Reds demanded that the scoring runner be sent back to third base, that the Reds one-run lead be restored, and that Lee Williams, the runner who had been put out trying to steal second, be barred from even watching the game. Captain Engle was evidently one of the few who'd seen Lee, a spectator only moments earlier, dart from the sidelines toward second base, determined that the Blue team should be given a fighting chance to win.

Umpire Roy Ansley ruled that non-player Lee Williams was illegally on the playing field and suspended him from any further participation for the season. The scoring problem, he said, would require some study. The confusion on the field was not the fault of the Blues. But, he said, the Red team should have caught Lee's trick at once.

Finally, Roy resolved that the two teams agree on a tie and adjourn to the dining table where the meal was waiting.

Baseball, called Roundhouse by the participants to differentiate it from an earlier two-base version of the game played with a club and a string ball, attracted more players at the Williams reunions than spectators. Children always watched, some attracted by the antics of Uncles Lee and Roy, some because they hoped for a belated invitation to join one team or the other. The girls wanted to join the fun but most couldn't hit or throw as well as the boys. And the women were just not interested in watching their husbands or sons play catch, strike at a ball with a club, or run around a circle of bases between heaps of cow dung.

Wives said their mates had to be rolled, protesting, out of bed the next day. They had swung the bat or tossed the baseball or hurled the horseshoe so many times that their arms and sides were a mass of aches.

Lee had a lifetime love of baseball. He attended every home game of the Ridgeway Reds between 1915 and 1924. Games were played Sunday afternoons in the Newell's pasture field at the side of Forrest's and Margaret's home in Ridgeway. Maude wasn't a fan so visited with her sister-in-law while Lee and the kids sat on the grass or stood at the sidelines with the other 80 to 100 spectators, cheering and jeering. For years, Ridgeway fielded the best team in the small inter-village league, or, at least, the team that had to be defeated to win the title.

The only player who was assured pay for appearing was the veteran pitcher, Glenn Jeffers. When he pitched and Fay "Red" Craig caught, Ridgeway won. The squad was assembled from the surrounding community. If the receipts exceeded the costs of renting the field plus Jeffers' retainer, all team members participated in the surplus. No one got rich, and there was no strike. Like school boys, they played for the love of the game.

TWO

Maude Allen Williams was a descendant of strong-willed people who took a passionate stand when they were displeased by religious intolerance or any kind of prejudice in the community where they lived. Her colonial ancestors were politicians, industrialists, educators, doctors --and farmers! Many served their churches as deacons or ministers and Maude said she always hoped son Mardo would become a clergyman.

Maude's great-great-grandfather Joseph was a deacon in the church of the Reverend Jonathan Edwards, who by his forceful preaching and powerful logic in support of Calvinist doctrine had gained a wide following. Joseph Allen was one of 19 friends who remained true to the last when the Reverend Edwards was dismissed from his Northampton, Massachusetts church in 1750 because of his stern demands for strict orthodoxy and his refusal to compromise in a membership controversy.

Joseph's sons Moses, Solomon, and Thomas (Maude's great-grand uncles) were as devout as their father. The Reverend Moses Allen became a chaplain in the Army of Independence in Georgia. "His warm exhortations from the pulpit" angered the British and they arrested him. He jumped off a British prison ship and swam three miles to land. He turned back to help a comrade and was drowned at age 30.

Solomon Allen, at the age of 40, was chosen deacon of the church of Northampton and at 50, went into Western New York, where for 20 years he preached the Gospel to the poor and destitute. His only compensation was bread and board. He came back to New York City to "set his house in order" and died there at the age of 70.

As a result of a bequest, Joseph's son Thomas was educated at Harvard and graduated in 1762, ranking among the best scholars of his day, and was ordained at Pittsfield, Massachusetts, becoming its first minister. Thomas's son William not only was a minister but became the author of the *American Biographical Dictionary*.

Maude's great-grandfather Adam was the only one of Joseph's eight sons who headed West, enlisted in the Army of Washington in Pennsylvania, and later emigrated to Ohio. Maude concluded that he didn't have the religious calling of brothers Thomas, Solomon, and Moses.

Adventurer and Revolutionary War hero, General Ethan Allen, and third cousin to Maude's great-grandfather Adam, was as much of a renegade in religious matters as he was in everything else. He wrote the first essay on Deism, proclaiming that the teachings of the Church of England and the Puritans of America were built on fraud. He maintained that the soul of man, after death, would transmigrate into beasts, birds and other living creatures and often said he should live after death as a white horse.

Maude was almost as proud of Lee's ancestors as she was of her own. They too had assumed roles of leadership in the colonial communities. They had maintained their inherited principles. They had spoken out against slavery for years before it became a popular cause in the North. Many fled North Carolina as the Civil War neared, rather than be forced to serve in an army supporting a way of life they condemned.

As members of the "Religious Society of Friends" (Quakers), they had been persecuted in England where the Church of England conducted the only approved services. After settling in Rhode Island (founded by Roger Williams), in Pennsylvania (under William Penn), and in Maryland and North Carolina, they asked only to be free to worship in their own way.

George Williams arrived at Philadelphia with a wagon train of fellow Friends (or Quakers) in 1690, and proceeded to Prince Georges County, Maryland, which later became a part of Frederick County, Virginia. His son, Richard Williams, Lee's great-great-great-grandfather, moved with his wife, Prudence Beals Williams, and two children into the wilderness area of North Carolina in 1749 (later to become the town of New Garden).

Richard's brother-in-law Thomas Beals, a minister in the Society of Friends, and his wife accompanied them. They probably came by the Great Pennsylvania Wagon Road through the Shenandoah Valley into North Carolina, sleeping nights in their covered wagon, and after they arrived at their chosen spot, lived in the wagon until a home could be built. They were the first white settlers in that community.

Few early settlers in America traveled about more than the Quakers. One writer said "that they were always looking for a better place and usually found it."

They carried certificates testifying to their membership in the Society of Friends, and were expected to have written permission from their monthly meeting to migrate. Scouts usually checked out the territory in advance for safety and suitability.

Richard and his family attended Quaker meetings 30 miles away in Cane Creek, until their community grew and they were allowed to set up a meeting in New Garden. From the 874 acres Richard Williams was granted by agents of Lord Granville, he deeded in 1757--for a token sum of five shillings (about $1.25)--53 acres of land and donated the timbers for the New Garden Meeting House and Burial Ground in Guilford County. It became the "mother" for many other meeting places erected across the state of North Carolina. The denomination's Guilford College now is located at the New Garden site (near Greensboro, North Carolina).

During those early pioneering days, wild game was almost the only source of meat. Shooting contests were held by the Friends at New Garden and many became expert shots, able to "shoot out both eyes of a wild turkey with a single shot at a distance of 100 feet," according to Addison Coffin (of the Levi Coffin branch of the Williamses).

Coffin, in his "Pioneer Days in Guilford County, North Carolina," related that at one such meet, a beautiful, buckskin-clad damsel emerged from the woods to compete in all the events. She won at will, to the chagrin of the younger men, and when she left--just as mysteriously as she had arrived--she was known only as "Ann, the huntress."

The Friends services consisted of silent waiting upon the Lord. There was no singing or Bible reading. If anyone felt led by the Spirit to give a message, they stood and did so. Some were more gifted than others. Everyone was a potential "minister"--men and women. Friends believed everyone was created equal and gave women equal duties and respect in their religious services.

Friends helped the poor and unfortunate, they testified against all flattery, and bowing and scraping, they treated American Indians with respect, and they were leaders in the attack upon Negro slavery.

Quakers had to marry within the faith or they would be disowned and in those early days, settlements were small and appropriate mates hard to come by. They couldn't marry any closer than second cousin.

Richard Williams opened his house for the care and treatment of

British soldiers after the Battle of Guilford Courthouse, one of the final battles of the Revolutionary War. He caught smallpox from one of them and died on May 6, 1781. He was buried under the old oak tree (named for him and also called the "Revolutionary Oak") in the New Garden Burial Ground.

When Mardo and daughter Kay stopped by the site of the Old Meeting House and Burial Ground at Guilford College in 1995, the "Revolutionary Oak" was gone, a stone monument in its place. The tree had been dynamited in 1955 while Eleanor Roosevelt was speaking to a racially mixed group at the college.

Even though as a Quaker he refused to bear arms, Richard Williams has been recognized as a Revolutionary Patriot by the Daughters of the American Revolution and the Sons of the American Revolution for his service in helping establish American Independence.

During the Revolutionary War, the Quakers paid double, sometimes triple, taxes because they refused to carry arms. They raised crops to feed the army. They fed and clothed the poor and provided free schools for them. They endured cruelty and persecution and never failed to do their duty as they saw it.

Richard's and Prudence's daughter, Prudence Williams, married Levi Coffin, Sr. in 1786. Their son, Levi, Jr., born in 1798, became an anti-slavery crusader and was widely known in the 1860s as "the president of the Underground Railroad." He helped establish a line of "safe houses" from the Mason-Dixon line to Canada, channeling more than 3,000 escaped slaves to freedom.

Harriet Beecher Stowe based many of the incidents in *Uncle Tom's Cabin* on escapees traveling the route established by distant cousin Levi Coffin, Jr., Lee said. It was Levi who harbored the slave girl, Eliza Harris, after her flight across the Ohio River on floating cakes of ice, he maintained.

Levi never arranged the escapes, but helped slaves on their way after they had taken the step. Many people did not approve of Coffin's efforts. The Reverend Dr. Rust, secretary of the Freedman's Aid Society, wrote that Levi Coffin "walked through the streets, hooted at and threatened by mobs."

Lee said the Quaker religion and its precepts governed every action of his ancestors. Many were "readers," if not ministers in the faith. Great-great-grandfather Silas Williams was active in business meetings of the New Garden Meeting House. In 1770, he married Mary Hunt, whose uncle, William Hunt, was a famous minister--praised by author Richard Jordan as "the greatest man North Carolina ever held!" When Silas asked Eleazar Hunt for permission to marry his daughter Mary, then 16, her father said she was too young. "But," answered Silas, "she will get older every day." Which she did until she was 100 years old and had about 300 descendants.

In 1793, Silas, wife Mary, and children William, Richard, Silas, Jr. and Asa (Lee's great-grandfather) were granted certificate from New Garden to Westfield Monthly Meeting in Surrey County, North Carolina. They moved from there to the Mt. Pleasant Monthly Meeting in Grayson County, Virginia.

Between 1805 and 1835, the migration of the Williamses from the Southern states to Ohio and Indiana (then called the Far West) intensified, as they became more vocal in their opposition to slavery. In 1813, Silas and his family were granted certificate to Darby Creek Monthly Meeting, Ohio, and moved to that state. With courage, they then began the work of restoring their lost lands and homes, thankful their children could grow up without coming into contact with slavery. Silas Williams died in Champaign County, Ohio in 1840 at age 93.

In the Rush Creek neighborhood, as elsewhere, the first concern became the establishment of a meeting place. Lee's grandparents, Jesse and Elizabeth Hammond Williams, took an active role at the Quaker Meeting House that stood on a little knoll at the side of the Mt. Victory-West Mansfield Pike, three miles south of Mt. Victory. After Jesse's death in 1874, his son, Rawson, and his wife, Sarah Witcraft Williams, made it their responsibility to help with the its upkeep.

Ross and Sarah donated $20 each month (about the cost of a hired hand) to help maintain the building and to help purchase coal when the firewood supply was depleted. They regularly attended meetings. The meeting house was replaced about 1890. Now it is gone. But the graveyard next to it remains. Lee's grandparents, Jesse and

Elizabeth, are buried there.

Lee and Maude seldom attended the Quaker services, although throughout her life, Maude always referred to herself as a Friend. Their children remembered going to the Meeting House only once or twice. There was no paid minister during that period (1910-1925). Parishioners sat quietly on benches after the lay reader said a few opening words. Silence was broken only by those who felt "urged by the spirit" to proclaim their faith in the Supreme Being, or who had feelings of guilt or inadequacy. Some spent the entire evening in contemplation, speaking only to greet acquaintances at the start or close of the session.

No one dressed up; all wore work clothes. Women had to wear a head covering. The interior of the hall, as unassuming as the parishioners, consisted of four bare walls in drab colors and was lighted by four coal oil lamps in brackets along two walls.

When a special program was advertised by handbill and word of mouth, the one-room building--barely 40 feet by 50 feet--would be crowded with more than 200 persons from six or seven miles around, each hoping to hear the featured leader make a passionate plea that would sway that tricky neighbor (who had just cheated you in a horse trade) to change his ways or face an eternity in hell.

Lee and Maude took the children to a special program one evening when Mardo was 13. The hall was crowded. The silence was interrupted repeatedly by shouts of "Amen" and "Lord, Save Us!" And the closing was delayed by the scores of men and women who had to give testimony "while the spirit was with them." It was impossible to keep the four children quiet. All left early, Maude said, and never tried it with the children again.

During these same years (1910-1924), Chautauquas were popular in the Ridgeway-Mt. Victory community. Scheduling was made a year or more in advance and subscriptions solicited by the Parent-Teacher groups. Prominent inspirational speakers were booked for afternoon and evening sessions of the two or three day program.

Strangers who passed the site might inquire if a circus was in town. For this Chautauqua, an offshoot of the nationally known forum on social, political and religious issues based in Chautauqua, New York, operated out of a tent. The advance crew hoisted the big top early on the day of the first performance, tore it down after the last performance and had it in place on time at the next stop.

The programs were always monitored by church and lay leaders, seeking talented speakers for their own group meetings. Ralph Parlette, who was featured at one of the Ridgeway High School commencements, impressed his audience during one of the early Chautauquas and found his services in demand throughout the district. On one or another of the programs were retired ministers, and those just starting out; business leaders, educators, inspirational speakers who made their living telling others how to attain success, and those politicians with a message.

Explorers, authors, even musicians were sometimes featured but the emphasis was placed on inspirational and religious topics. After all, it was sponsored initially by the First Methodist Episcopal Church during a camp meeting in Chautauqua, New York, in 1873, and later expanded to include a series of eight-week summer programs nationally.

Chautauquas attempted to become a powerful force in the religious and inspirational field. They were organized commercially in 1912, when they acquired a reputation of being somewhere between a revival meeting and a county fair.

The local Chautauquas had to play to an audience of 200 or more at each performance just to break even. So it became profitable to stagger the production among Ridgeway, Mt. Victory, West Mansfield, and LaRue-- appealing to the intelligentsia of the other three communities when it was staged in one. The lecture circuit was abandoned when interest lagged, when radio and other channels of entertainment developed.

THREE

The Williams children thought their Uncle Harley was pretty special. He was 12 years younger than his sister Maude and seemed almost like an older brother to the children. Whenever he stayed at the farm and went to Mt. Victory with Lee, he brought home candy--hard mixed candy to be sure--but he wasn't stingy with it. He always shared. The first hint that the children's idol might have feet of clay came when he was 18. The youngsters found a cache of chocolate candy in the pantry! He and their parents had saved the chocolate for themselves, doling out the cheaper sugar candy to the children "who wouldn't know the difference."

The children were told this was the first time any favoritism had been shown, and it was purely unpremeditated--since the chocolates were an unexpected windfall. Uncle Harley had started buying chances on a punch board at Rose's Restaurant in Mt. Victory. He was surprised at how much candy remained to be claimed and how few punches were left on the board.

He counted the remaining prizes: a three-pound box of caramels, three one-pound containers of varied chocolates and a few half pounders plus the five-pound one that went with the last play. He convinced Lee that for about $2.50 they could go home with nearly 15 pounds of fine chocolates. "Maude would like it," he argued. Lee contributed to the gambling fund and all were happy--until the youngsters demanded a share of the loot.

Ten-year-old Mildred, who stumbled upon the chocolate hoard in the pantry while seeking hard candy to satisfy her sweet tooth, didn't keep her secret long. She lugged the five-pound box of choice nougats, caramels and creams into the kitchen and notified her mother of her astounding find. With all four children now grouped around, Maude opened the box, passed the candy around, and shamefacedly congratulated her daughter upon making such a sensational discovery right under all their noses.

Harley considered Lee and Maude his second set of parents and took advantage of every opportunity to go to the farm after his parents, Arthur and Nora Allen, moved from nearby Kenton to Toledo, 80 miles away. Harley's older brothers, Waldo and Gene, could find jobs but in 1910 Harley was only 15. He had lost both his school friends and his proximity to Lee and Maude.

Harley was likable, a little ungainly and inclined to soldier on the job (stay back and hope someone else would do it). Maude enjoyed having him--he was a link to the Allen family and would be of aid in looking after the children. Lee tried to train him in farm ways. He taught him to harness the horses and get the rig ready for Maude if she wanted to go to town. All too frequently Harley wanted to go along, forgetting that the only time his sister could go was when he would be there to care for the youngsters.

Harley made friends easily. John Picon, grandson of Hank Rosebrook, a neighboring farmer, Harold Williams, a distant cousin, and Ralph Engle, eldest son of Lee's sister, Neola (Mrs. Will) Engle, were at the house so often Maude thought she should be charging rent.

Harry Marmon became a close friend. Harley and he competed, dared each other to accomplish impossible feats, and sometimes skated on the fringe of serious trouble. They were at loose end on one summer day in 1913. Harley had just turned 18 (August 5), Harry was 21, and they were in no mood for a siesta.

The sun was burning down. They didn't want to go swimming but they wanted to do something exciting--that didn't entail too much effort. Conveniently, they were prepared to ignore their parents' oft-expressed warning: "The devil finds things for idle hands to do."

Herbert Williams chose that moment to stride into view. Herb was headed for a refreshing, if not cooling, plunge in Rush Creek. Herb was a distant relative, his father Obadiah being a first cousin of Lee's father, Ross. He was 16, a skinny six-footer with a scraggly beard, a solemn demeanor and a total lack of humor.

Harry and Harley, bent on devilment, might have chosen another target if they had known of Herb's apparent instability. A sophomore at Ridgeway High School, he was known as an oddball, a loner and a "brain." He had a swarthy complexion, penetrating black eyes and already was sprouting whiskers, which he was inclined to let grow.

Teachers said he was brilliant in those subjects he consented to study. He spoke so precisely that he overawed most of his classmates. An older sister Helen had many of the same traits, but since she had a smile and a friendlier attitude, she finished school without being termed anything worse than eccentric. Both were much like their father Obadiah in appearance and temperament. Herb read the Bible every day and once lectured Mardo, who was eight years younger, about the evils of masturbation.

Harley and Harry waited until Herb was splashing contentedly in the water. They sneaked through the willow grove that screened one bank, grabbed his clothing and secreted it under some brush nearby. They couldn't let his predicament go unnoted, and to make certain that didn't happen, they stayed to watch.

The swimmer was having so much fun and seemed so cool in the almost stifling heat that the two jokesters considered giving up and joining him. But they restrained that mad impulse, using massive willpower. The clothing stayed hidden. And Herb was about to find that he had only his birthday suit to wear through the field on his one and one-half mile walk home.

Harley and Harry were laughing so hard as Herb vainly hunted for shirt and trousers that they feared he would hear them. Unable to see anyone or to understand what had caused his clothing to disappear, the bare-skinned youth started off at a half run. The first obstacle was the seldom-traveled road and the two fences at its side. If he could clear that without being seen, he wouldn't have to worry until he reached the road in front of his home.

Unable to keep their secret, the two men laughingly told friends about Herb tearing off a willow spray to conceal a part of himself and bragged that they still had his clothes--except for the shoes they had thoughtfully left for him to wear across the stubbled fields.

The next message came from neighbors of the Obadiah Williams family. Elder son Herb was going around wearing only a loin cloth. He had taken the experience as a divine sign. He was going to emulate the Lord Jesus.

Harry said it was Harley's idea in the first place so he should be the one to return the clothes, explain that it was a tasteless prank and apologize. They finally deposited the apparel in the mailbox and made no attempt to convince Herb to abandon his righteous calling.

He eventually began wearing all his clothes but the experience may have made a lasting impression. As an adult, Herb became a hermit, living in a corn crib after the house on his home farm burned down. Neighbors were afraid of him, possibly because of his oddities. He carried a gun or club with him when he rode his bicycle to town. He killed one dog that attacked him and was sued by the owner, wounded a neighbor boy, and escaped prison by accepting counseling at a mental institution.

Herb was too shy to seek the female companionship for which he yearned. Women generally were not attracted to him. And by the late 1930s, his stringy gray hair and bushy beard gave him a disreputable appearance. Also, he had cultivated a sullen attitude to discourage any friendly overtures by strangers.

He finally admitted to himself--although he would deny it to others--that he would welcome the presence of a woman in his life. The house was still standing on the home farm--it was destroyed by fire later--so Herb composed an advertisement for a lonely hearts magazine in Columbus, Ohio.

"Lonely 38-year-old farmer," he wrote, "seeks the company of attractive young woman who is seriously considering matrimony." He listed his address as Rural Route 1, Ridgeway, Ohio, and asked for letters. The response wasn't overwhelming--Ridgeway was just too far away from Columbus or members of the gentle sex were afraid to venture into the unknown.

He eventually got an answer that sounded promising. The 27-year-old woman sent the picture of a buxom, cheerful looking person and asked for a photo in return. Herb was afraid to take that chance but wrote her that he owned a 92-acre farm with a fine three-bedroom house, and had money in the bank. He offered to pay her way if she would just come up to see and talk with him.

Plans were made, and on the agreed-on evening, the romantic swain arrived at the train site in Ridgeway. The horse had been curried and the carriage cleaned. He was in his best suit, or at least a clean white shirt and pressed trousers.

The locomotive steamed into the station, halted to discharge passengers--and two women alighted. The young woman had brought her mother along as chaperone. Herb never showed his disappointment. He loaded them into the buggy and drove through the countryside in the gathering dusk. No one ever heard what the three talked about on the way or what the women thought as the horse turned down the lane to a dark, one-story house--screened from road and neighbors by trees and shrubs.

The only "after the happening" news came from the Toledo & Ohio Central station master at Ridgeway where Herb deposited the women the next day to catch the 9:00 A.M. train to Columbus. He left hurriedly with barely a goodbye. Disillusioned by the results of their search for a "sugar daddy," the women revealed they had been frightened by the physical appearance of their host, by the drabness of the home, and by the almost complete silence that surrounded them.

Station Master Knepper said that from what he overheard, the mother and daughter scarcely touched the dinner Herb had prepared for them. They had slept poorly on a lumpy mattress, had refused breakfast, and demanded immediate transportation back to civilization.

The incident cured Herb of lovesickness. He paid the double fare demanded, ignored future appeals from the lovelorn magazine, and chalked up the cost and stress to experience.

The incident provoked sly comments from Ira, Herb's brother. Not only was Ira, popularly known as Ike, more personable and outgoing than Herbert or his sister Helen, he was light-complected while they both were dark with flashing black eyes, like their father, Obadiah. The differences were so great that a wild rumor circulated that Ike was an adopted child.

Under the nickname Ike, he acquired a reputation as a jokester. Once he distributed a deck of playing cards through a Bible his father, Obadiah, carried to the Friends Church meeting. Obadiah was a devout Quaker, Maude said, and was violently opposed to card playing.

So he experienced the ultimate humiliation when he arose in front of his fellow worshipers to give his testimonial, opened his Bible to read a passage and the playing cards fluttered across the floor. He sank to his knees in prayer--or maybe he was asking for help in controlling Ike, his wayward son.

Ike was a constant companion, during those teenager summers, of both Mardo Williams and Wallace Early, who lived just two houses down the road. Lee told about one incident that clerks at Mt. Victory's leading soda fountain were discussing. Ike and Wallace apparently had decided on their purchases when the young soda jerk asked for their orders.

Wallace took a fudge sundae and Ike, trying to look innocent while watching the young woman clerk for signs of embarrassment, said: "I think I'll have a douche. Mother says they are so refreshing." Management asked the boys to get their douche elsewhere.

That summer of 1913, after their joke on Herb Williams backfired,

Maude's brother Harley and Harry Marmon kept out of trouble, Maude said, until the days turned cooler and education, temporary jobs and the near advent of war occupied their talents. Harry was preparing for a teaching career.

He was married to Lee's sister, Alice Williams, the youngest member of the Rawson and Sarah Williams family, on April 11, 1914. Alice was 24 and--until then--had been jokingly called "the old maid." Harry was 22. While the couple was visiting the Lee Williams home, the "bellers" arrived. During the shouting and pan-banging, Harley decided he would attempt to separate Harry and Alice for the night. Newlywed Harry resisted and, in the scuffle, fell against a table and broke a front tooth.

That was the most excitement on their wedding day. When the belling group left, the new Mr. and Mrs. Marmon returned to the "honeymoon suite" at the home of the bride's parents, Ross and Sarah, where they lived for almost three years. Harry taught school at Spice Wood Glen. Seven months after the marriage of Alice and Harry, their son Byron was born.

FOUR

"Keep outta corn" were the first words two-year-old Byron Marmon mouthed when he came running back to his mother from the corn crib. They were impressed upon the tot by his grandfather Ross, who found the toddler climbing a mound of ear corn in the farm granary. There was no explanation of the brusque order, but Byron's mother Alice thought her father was concerned that the corn might shift and trap the little explorer under its weight.

Years later, when asked, Byron would recall the words yelled by his stern grandfather who made no attempt to quiet the then-crying youngster. He steered clear of his grandfather after that--never went to the granary without adult supervision and, until early manhood, trembled whenever Ross spoke to anyone in a loud voice.

The granary was a forbidden spot for all the children, so attracted interest and was the object of secret incursions--when Granddad Ross was not around. The building held the corn crib along the west wall, a wide driveway in which some farm implement was always standing, and another narrower driveway where Ross kept his prized Buick touring car.

When Lee found out that Granddad Ross's auto was the principal attraction in the granary, he admonished his children to be very careful with the steering wheel, gear shift and the levers adjusting gasoline use and spark control, and to clean up any debris they might drag inside the car with them.

Ross's car was a 1914 model with engineering improvements from earlier models. For example, the opening to the front seat had been partially closed to alter the open carriage look. Entry to the rear seat was by way of a hinged door. It had a collapsible top and side openings that could be closed off with heavy canvas-like cloth, in which isinglass had been sewn for windows. The strips were held in place by twist buttons inserted through holes in the cloth.

In winter months, the car was mounted on cement blocks (placed under the frame) to keep the tires off the ground and thus conserve them.

Ross treasured that car--and the Elgin and DeSoto autos that replaced it. He was known throughout the district as the farmer with his own automobile--eight to ten years before others thought of owning one. When it stalled, as it frequently did, he was advised by rude spectators to "get a horse."

During later years, as his hearing faded, neighbors knew every time he took his car out of the shed. He could be heard coming down the roadway, the gas lever wide open, the gears grinding whenever he stopped and started. He sold his last car, the DeSoto, when he was in his late 70s, relying on Lee to run errands for him.

About the time of son Byron's corn crib episode, Alice and Harry learned that he had curvature of the spine. The specialist said the condition might have been aggravated by Byron's inclination to push himself across the floor one-handedly, using muscles only on one side of his body. The doctor prescribed a brace which was discarded a few months later. Alice and Harry felt it was doing no good and the boy complained bitterly about the chafing.

The child, born on November 13, 1914, was doomed to stunted growth (five feet, three inches, as compared to his father's six feet, one inch) and to lifelong adaptation to the hump on his back. He became the most even-tempered, the most uncomplaining, and the most cheerful person in the neighborhood. His father had tagged him with the word "fella" while the boy learned his way through childhood--and soon everyone was calling, "fella, do it this way" or "fella, look at this." It was "fella," "fella," "fella."

In 1924, when Byron was 10, his father Harry was stricken by tuberculosis. At that time, the couple and their three children--Byron, Doris, and Fern--had moved from Granddad Ross's and were living on the farm just east of the Lee Williamses--with Rush Creek at their back door.

"With Alice's untiring help, Harry battled his disease to a standstill," Maude asserted. "He wouldn't walk again for ten years. He would lie in the summer sun, become as brown as a nut and, buoyed on by Lee's sister, recover from every setback."

Doris Barnhart remembered as a child how her father reclined nude on a cot near the creek's edge, shielded by bushes from intrusion by a chance passerby. "He had a sheet at his side but used it only if a visitor appeared," she said.

Her mother was under more stress than her dad, Doris said. "She changed all the dressings, took care of him, cheered him on--and she had to prepare food for three hungry children, do the laundry and housekeeping, keep us all busy and reasonably happy."

Their spirit was almost broken when in 1929 the tuberculosis spread to his right knee. The flesh became a running sore. Salves, lotions and poultices were useless. Lymph and pus polluted every cover and soaked every cot or bed on which he rested.

His physician, as a last resort obtained a consignment of maggots and introduced them to the unhealable sore. The little white worms went to work, thrived and multiplied, and eventually cleaned the bone surfaces of all pollutants. Dead tissues and poisons were eliminated and the healing process started.

His spirits went up and down during the last three years of healing. He started writing current affairs letters to the editor of the *Ohio State Journal* in Columbus, Ohio, corresponded with Lowell Thomas, famed newsman of the 1920s, and found enjoyment in penning poems about his wife, his doctor, the day's activities, the cheering rays of the sun, and the welcome caroling of birds.

Harry progressed to a wheelchair and during the autumn of 1932, Lee loaded him into a two-wheel trailer that formerly had hauled hogs to market and, with Alice guarding her mate, took him to the Williams reunion. It was a triumph of faith that seemed more like a miracle to those who watched. Harry lived for 25 more years, with only a stiff knee slowing him down.

Part VI: The World Beyond the Farm

Isolation was a fact of life. The train passing through was a reminder of the world beyond the horizon.

ONE

*H*enry Ford tested a gas-powered buggy in 1893, the same year that Sears Roebuck advertised its horse-drawn run-about--with optional folding top, for $24.95.

In 1903 (the year Maude and Lee were married) the United States entered a pact with Panama to build a canal that would link two oceans for worldwide shipping.

That same year, Ohio's Orville and Wilbur Wright got a makeshift airplane off the ground at Kitty Hawk, North Carolina, giving impetus to man's dream of flying through the air like a bird.

Railroads became the favored means of transportation. Since that first American-built locomotive, the Tom Thumb, had lost the race with a horse-drawn train over a nine-mile track in the 1870s, the picture had changed. By 1890, freight and passenger service was being maintained over 200,000 miles of track.

Trains speeded the gold-rushers to the West Coast for the stampede to Alaska in 1897, as word spread of the stupendous Klondike discovery. Steam engines had been made more powerful. Freight and passenger cars had been improved--the train streamlined to some extent. The warning whistle--a mournful, drawn-out wail--was heard at every crossing, in every town along the transcontinental route.

TWO

Rail travel was an exciting experience for all the Williamses. The family, as a unit, traveled by train south to Peoria, for visits with the Ansleys, Roy and Dawn (Lee's close friend and favorite sister). Roy was stationed in the little Union County town as a branch troubleshooter for the railway. He was transferred later to the car shops at Kenton, where the Ansleys and Williamses continued to socialize and play cards.

On the train, the kids made a game of keeping out of sight of the disapproving conductor. They had to use the toilet, of course, and were surprised, Maude said, at how fast the earth was traveling under the train, as viewed through the toilet seat.

Lee said that the children's enthusiasm for the railroad privy reminded him of the time he was taking the Toledo & Ohio Central to Toledo. A farmer from south of Ridgeway revealed he'd been saving for a year and finally had the $35 needed to buy a fine dairy cow. He already had made arrangements for the purchase.

He talked with everyone in the coach about the sacrifices he'd made in order to save the necessary cash and how much the animal would contribute to his family's welfare. As he neared his destination, he asked about bathroom facilities and was directed to the small booth in one corner of the next car to the rear, Lee told Maude. He unbuttoned his trousers (this was before zippers) and was standing at the bowl relieving himself when he began re-counting his money--most of which was in $1 bills.

Casually, he opened the restroom door and started down the aisle, still counting his money--and with his John Henry out.

At the same time, the conductor entered the coach from the opposite end, saw a potential embarrassing development, and shouted: "Hey, you! Put that away."

"Sir, let me tell you," was the response, "I'll have that in a cow before night."

That was farm humor of the times. And it prompted another "true story" from Lee, told in his inimitable style, the tale of the farmer's wife who substituted for her husband when a neighbor brought his cow for a visit with their bull. All had proceeded well when the man leered at her and commented, "I'd sure like to do that!"

Her reply, which sent him and his bovine companion on their way: "I'm sure I have no objection if the cow doesn't!"

Maude recalled an over-the-holidays train excursion to Toledo in 1916 as the first extended "vacation" in which the parents and their four children participated. And it cost them very little. Her three brothers and their parents had sent the railroad tickets for all, as well as some clothing to the children as advance Christmas gifts.

"We boarded the train in Ridgeway on December 23rd so we could take part in the Christmas Eve festivities the following day," she said. "We had been to Peoria a time or two but this was to be 83 miles to the Toledo terminal--or some four hours in a confined space with four boisterous youngsters. We feared the worst, took lunch with us, and, optimistically, carried pillows in hopes that we could get them to rest their little heads on them when they grew tired."

But they never tired, Maude said. They asked endless questions. They had to traipse up and down the aisles, presumably to go to the toilet. The conductor could barely conceal his irritation and was heard to tell a passenger: "Thank God, mine are grown. These four are enough to try the patience of a saint."

In Toledo, Maude's brothers took charge of the children and tried to get them tired enough to sleep when they at last arrived home. The family was shown Toledo at night--the crowded streets, the Christmas decorations, the curbside stalls loaded with fruits and nuts, and the stores where choice wares were being offered to the chime of bells and the caroling of youthful voices.

"We had heard of Tiedtke's Department Store and each of us was entranced by it," Maude said. The children remembered the first floor selection of fruits and vegetables and meats. They were almost hypnotized by the sight that met their gaze when they reached the last display, she recalled. "The meat counter extended for 80 to 100 feet and spotlighted in the center, lying on mounds of chipped ice, was a grouping of the largest fish any of us had ever seen. They must have been six feet long--and their glass-like eyes were looking right at us."

In Rush Creek, the youngsters had seen minnows, crawfish, and pan fish that were less than 10 inches long, so their amazement at the size of these "denizens of the deep" was understandable. They had little interest in the displays of dolls, sleds, or coloring books in Toledo's showplace department store of the early 1900s. But they convinced their Uncle Harley, Uncle Gene or Uncle Waldo to take them back downtown to see the meat market at Tiedtke's over and over again. They marveled at the size of those fish, wondered a score of times what kind of bait and how strong a line was used in their capture. They boarded their return train on December 28 and slept all the way back.

All remembered that Christmas for the rest of their lives. No family vacation ever approached it for variety and adventure. The next most enjoyable vacation--at least, for the men--may have been the week spent on Indian Lake at Russells Point, Ohio, when the Roy Ansley and Lee Williams families shared a cottage, went fishing each day and played cards each evening.

Maude and Dawn got less enjoyment from the outing than the others for they had to do the meal planning, the cooking and the housekeeping. The two women had a lot of togetherness during the long week, the children ran out of places to explore and the men got sunburns but little else on their fishing forays.

The vacation was memorable to Lucille, Ronald and James Ansley, Mildred, Mardo, Beatrice and Pauline Williams for one reason. Mardo, 13 at the time, said they all got to row a boat and decided, "When you've rowed one boat you've rowed them all." Each refused to man the oars for their fishing dads. "It's just a lot of work and you're getting no place," explained Mildred.

THREE

Left far behind the trains in the transportation race were the automobile-makers who in 1900 boasted of only one established factory. Olds Company opened that year in Detroit and had produced only 4,000 units by 1903 when a government report revealed that gasoline-powered vehicles were in the minority. Forty of every 100 vehicles in operation were steam-powered, the report noted; 38 were electric and only 22 operated on gasoline. The V-8 engine wasn't perfected until 1912. In 1914, workers were paid the unheard of sum of $5 a day to work on Ford's assembly line production. Ford lowered prices until a Model T cost under $500, or less than a team of horses. Until then, the idea that a farmer could own a car was beyond conception. Autos were for rich people.

FOUR

At 10:00 A.M. on October 14, 1916, Lester Bird, a Mt. Victory auto buff, established a new speed record between his home and the Hardin County courthouse at Kenton.

As friends and neighbors watched, Lester loaded the back seat and trunk of his new Chevrolet touring car with concrete blocks. The added weight was needed, he explained, to keep the car from going out of control when it hit ruts, potholes and stones in the unpaved roadway. He banned other persons from the car because of the risk of injury.

Bird had fine-tuned the four cylinders, checked the leaf springs to make sure there were no weak or broken blades, and inflated the 30" x 3" tires to the recommended pressure of 35 pounds per square inch. In those early days of motoring, tires with a 30-inch diameter were necessary because the body of the car had to rise above the rutted roadway or obstacles thereon.

There were no balloon tires or shock absorbers. The springs were strips of spring steel, clamped together. When a car went down the road at 35 or 40 miles per hour, it rode little smoother than the old storm buggy.

Lester Bird donned a padded vest to protect his ribs from the steering wheel. There were no safety belts!

Stop watches were set. Lester, with the gas lever locked at wide open, took off in a blast of engine noise and the squeal of tires. He plunged and bounced, steered around some obstructions and into others, spent a good share of his time in the air and made the ten-mile trip in 14 minutes to set a 42.8 miles per hour speed record that never fell until the roadway had been paved and auto engines refined. Lee said Mr. Bird's feat, accomplished without a broken spring or blown-out tire, sold him on the Chevrolet. He bought one for the family four years later.

FIVE

Drafted in 1917 for service in World War I, Maude's youngest brother Harley convinced the Army that his farm training with Lee made him an expert in handling horses. He was placed in the Artillery and assigned to look after the animals that pulled the caissons into place for the big bombardments. He made sure that his steeds were fed, pampered as much as possible, and ready to haul the big guns any place at any time.

He served satisfactorily, if not with distinction, helped the Allies to save the world for democracy, and returned unwounded to resume his job as a fireman on the Elkhart Division of the New York Central's Toledo-Chicago link, shoveling coal into the fireboxes of those ever-larger locomotives pulling those ever-longer freight trains. He had outgrown the farm.

SIX

Shortly after war end, Maude's favorite brother Gene died of influenza, one of the estimated 50 million victims worldwide of the 1917-1919 epidemic. Eugene E. Allen was eight years younger than Maude and they almost shared a common birthdate. She was born October 23, 1883; he was born on October 25, 1891. He was only 27 years of age when he died in December, 1918.

Gene was a quiet, unassuming man, generous to a fault and loved by his sister and her four children. Mardo remembered him as being about five foot, ten inches tall, and weighing 155 pounds. He had the grayish blue eyes of the Allens, talked nasally and with a slight lisp, as did his father and both of his brothers, Harley and Waldo.

His speech impediment was due to a vestige of a cleft palate, attributed to cousins marrying cousins over the years. Maude wasn't afflicted--she apparently inherited genes of her mother and the Wilson branch of the family.

Gene had been recently married and was living away from his parents' home for the first time in his life. Arthur and Lenore told their daughter Maude they had received only meager information from their daughter-in-law as Gene battled for his life. They only knew that he'd been stricken with influenza but continued to work at his electrician's job.

Gene's wife, an attractive Polish girl whom he'd met at work, discouraged his parents from calling on them. Even when he developed double pneumonia as aftermath to the flu, she said their presence would only complicate things. They heard he was critically ill, with his chest packed in ice to control the fever.

They were allowed to see him only after he died. His widow--whom they met only once and whose given name they soon forgot--called them to say she had no money for the funeral. Arthur and Lenore Allen, with son Waldo's help, paid for Eugene's funeral. His widow attended the services, followed the body to Toledo's Forest Cemetery, and left.

"We never heard from her again," Lenore Allen told Maude when she herself was in her last illness. "We don't know how she is doing, where she is living, or if Gene left us a grandchild. Maybe that's the way she wanted it."

SEVEN

Home from overseas service, Harley related firsthand accounts of the bitter hand-to-hand fighting, the pounding his heavy artillery brigade gave the German entrenched positions, and the important role the "air force's" few propeller planes had assumed in both reconnoitering and bombing.

Solitary planes flew high over Central Ohio during the following summer. Airplanes were still a novelty so each sighting resulted in long conversations--were they just a fad or the start of a vast new trend? Could they be adapted for peaceful use? No one knew and no one could predict that passenger air travel would exceed travel by trains and buses, and challenge rail and truck enterprises for valuable freight cargo. It was just the beginning!

More prosaic developments held the interest of the Williamses. Bea found a robin with a broken wing, tied a piece of shingle around the break, watched over it for two days, then cried brokenheartedly when it died.

Pauline let her sympathy embrace a lamb, the runt from a neighbor's flock, orphaned at birth. She hugged it, taught it to drink its milk out of a bottle, fashioned a bed in the kitchen where it could be kept warm, and wept her tears when the orphan ignored her after being returned to the flock.

Tender-hearted Mildred generated her own trouble. An entire litter of kittens apparently had been dropped along the roadside or had escaped a planned drowning in the creek. Four of them made their way to the Williams' doorstep, begging for milk.

Mildred picked up the smallest--the one which was the scrawniest, meowed the most pitifully, looked almost ill enough to die. And she found some sort of parasite had buried itself in an open sore on its head. The problem needed immediate attention, she told her mother. So she got a pair of staple-pulling pliers from her dad's tool box, hooked onto the worm, and left a giant pus-filled hole. She cried--and cried again the next day when she buried the pitiful thing in a hole at the side of the garden.

Other events of the summer were less dramatic--but still memorable, Maude said. Year after year, the family attended Memorial Day and Fourth of July attractions at Mt. Victory. She recalled the patriotic parades from Mt. Victory to nearby Hale Cemetery (where both she and Lee are now buried) on each May 30th.

"Families like ours surrounded a cleared circle near the cemetery entrance--and with the graves of loved ones all around--listened as eloquent speakers extolled the sacrifices of those who served in the armed forces, some of whom had made the ultimate sacrifice and were resting nearby. Then we sought out the monuments to our own loved ones--sometimes depositing wild flowers we'd gathered from the woods behind the farm," she remembered.

"We celebrated the Fourth of July sanely," Maude recalled. "There were no rockets, only a few firecrackers but a good number of sparklers. The little ones ran around the lawn with lighted sparklers in hand, making believe they were fireflies. And no one got hurt."

Although summers were anticipated and enjoyed, the flies were persistent pests. They multiplied in the grass, in the brush, and in the barnyard manure. They proceeded by the hundreds and thousands to the farm house where they congregated on every screen. Each door when it opened became an invitation to enter.

So Lee's responsibility, Maude thought--since the flies originated in his barnyard domain--should be their eradication from the screens. He tried valiantly. He sprayed each screen two or three times daily with a kerosene emulsion, leaving scores dead on the porch floor and scores more flying drunkenly away after each barrage.

Maude said she swept thousands away each week. If the weather was a little cool, they were drawn in even greater numbers to the warmth emanating through the screens. Those that got inside were met with fly swatters and strips of odorous tape, to which they would stick.

On the worst days, Lee had to delay the milking until after dark when the flies became dormant. During daylight hours, the cows were so busy lashing out and trying to get away from the painful bites that the milker ran the danger of being stepped on, and of losing both stool and milk pail.

The flies were pests in house and barn. They were despised. Another form of life at the Rush Creek farm--the swallow--was admired for its voracious appetite for flies and its grace on wing. Each late summer and early fall evening, after the sun went down and darkness grew, scores of the fast moving birds would sweep like shadows from field to barn, safe in its confines until another day.

Part VII: The Grapevine Twist

"First gent take his lady by the wrist,
And through that couple with a grapevine twist."

ONE

*W*hen Mildred turned 12, Maude and Lee decided that the children were getting old enough to be trusted at social functions in other people's homes. They accepted an invitation in November to a square dance at the home of long-time friends, Lizzie and Charles Marmon, who lived just down the road.

Maude made sure the girls would have clean dresses, Mardo his knee-length pants, and Lee a pair of trousers, or a clean pair of overalls if he decided to dress as most of the other farmers would. She would wear the blue checked gingham dress she had remodeled to the season's fashionable length.

The household was in a turmoil of activity on the night of the event. The milking was done early, supper rushed, and all were seeking articles of clothing that had been mysteriously displaced or stolen by goblins. The dancing was to start at what now would be an ungodly early hour--7:30 o'clock. And all wanted to be there for the opening chord.

The two males were finished early and threatened to leave without the female contingent. Mother and daughters were being delayed--not by the application of eye liner, lipstick and face powder (they had none)--but by the long wait to comb their hair.

Only one comb could be found with its teeth intact and that was strong enough to tear the tangles from those long tresses. Maude, who was practically ready when she got up from the supper table, helped all the others and was the last to don her coat for the walk down the lane, across the bridge and to the Marmon house for a night of revelry.

The Williams children termed their first dance an exhilarating occasion. They arrived to find their neighbor's side yard and barn lot filled with standing horses, hitched to buggies. Lanterns hung from the trees to dimly show the way to the house.

There were no intoxicating beverages, no cleavage showing and no overt acts of passion. A two-piece combo (banjo and guitar) provided the music. A local farmer shouted the calls while four couples shuffled and paraded, swung their partners and "dosey-doed" on the corner. The first tune, the children remembered, was "Pop Goes the Weasel," followed by "Old Dan Tucker Missed His Supper," "The Cat and the Fiddle," "Three Blind Mice," "Oh, Suzanna, Don't You Cry for Me," and "Skip to My Lou, My Darling." Mildred triggered a discussion when she questioned if "Lou" was a girl's name or the slang expression for an outhouse.

The children kept time with the music, ran almost unsupervised through the house, noted that their dad was the best swinger of both his own partner and of someone else's when the call demanded, and reluctantly went to sleep in the Marmon's spare bedroom when Maude and Lee decided it was their bedtime (but not before gorging themselves on cookies and lemonade). Awakened after the party was over, the children found the walk home interminable.

The square dances continued from home to home, with the children interested spectators if included in the invitation.

The music was simple harmony--chords and improvisations to the popular tunes of the day, like "Red River Valley," "Comin' Round the Mountain," "Turkey in the Straw," "Darlin' Nellie Gray." One of the area's more versatile, self-taught musicians might change the tempo, compose chords from popular classical, religious and folk songs or romantic arias. He would fit words to them for the caller to use--like "swing your partner," "swing the lady across the hall," "dosey-do on the corner," "promenade all" or substitute more intricate phrases from the most prevalent country and western tunes to make new dance calls. Some calls were chanted, some were sung.

The "composer," ignoring all copyrights, then would improvise special arrangements for piano, banjo and guitar. No music was written down; it was all done by ear. There was no drummer and, rarely, a violinist. Wind instruments (trombone, saxophone, flute, and cornet) made infrequent appearances--and only because these musicians wanted to demonstrate their ability to blow a tune. They were never paid a formal wage.

The caller, pianist, banjo and guitar players, however, frequently received a small reward for their efforts from the collection taken from the dancers. The talent split the receipts at the end of the evening. Sometimes the musicians at the better attended public dances received more in a week of three or four jobs than farm laborers earned all month.

Most square dances had four parts: an introduction, consisting of a simple move in which all dancers were active at the same time; a main figure performed four times by all four couples simultaneously or by an individual or couples in turn; a break after each main figure was completed; and a terminating simple figure performed by the four couples.

If the caller could compose the words for a sequence that met with approval, he would launch a new square dance. When the effort failed, as it did more often than not because the moves were too intricate, the fans went back to the old time favorites.

One was called "The Grapevine Twist," but the wording and dance steps were so involved it might be called only once during the evening. It involved all the dancers, six or eight sets of four couples who weaved in and out among one another and reversed themselves to make similar moves in the opposite direction. "First gent take his lady by the wrist," the call went, "and through that couple with a grapevine twist."

There might be more than a dozen different calls each evening, with the most popular sequences repeated upon request. Lee and Maude grew to know them all. They remembered dancing to "Birdie in the Cage," "Chase the Rabbit," and "Take a Little Peek." Also "Butterfly Whirl," "Duck for the Oyster, Dig for the Clam," "The Suzy Q," "Roll the Barrel," and "Sally Good'in." There were others. After you learned the basics, Lee explained, you could do them all by listening to the caller.

Each call contained many of the moves of all the others, interspersed with the variations that made every one different. Four couples made up the set. In the event one had little knowledge of the calls and the movements that accompanied each, that man and woman became the last to go through the routine. They learned by watching the three couples ahead of them form circles, swing on the corner, promenade and hook arms, and follow the commands that were shouted in time to the beat of the music.

Sometimes a coach would stand behind the novices, instruct them as to what the caller was saying, and guide them through the sequences.

Every dancer used a different style. Some were graceful. Others were almost violent in their movements. It was splendid exercise, Maude and Lee agreed. The dancers strutted. They clogged (or tap-danced, if adept at that). They promenaded and circled, pivoted and swung both their partners and the other persons' partners. They never stopped moving until a rest period was announced.

When the Grand Parade was called, it was hailed as the evening's "Auld Lang Syne" and everyone took part. Eighty or more couples, at some of the better attended dances, would line up to follow a leader in a parade around the hall. The formation would change, couples would become singles, go hand-over-hand for a designated number of paces and claim another partner. As the closing overture began, the group always filed off the floor in orderly pattern to storm the cloakroom and prepare for the ride home through the wintry night.

Sometimes two or more callers performed during the same evening; one might be more popular than the other because he handled the calls with more finesse, calling out loudly and plainly so the commands could be understood. Some callers would only hum, relying on the dancers to know the moves. The best callers made the command calls more interesting by adding "patter" to help fill the silence between calls--"Go halfway round, the other way back, Make your feet go clickety-clack," or "Partner left and corner right, Keep on going if it takes all night."

Lee liked the sets that had a lot of intricate action--swinging, hopping, and foot-shuffling; Maude preferred those that called for dignified promenades and routine mixing of the partners.

Dancers changed partners or partners were replaced by new dancers after each set. While the commercial events in towns might last until midnight, dancing at the farm homes ended at 11:00 P.M. Farmers started the new day at five o'clock, so they gathered their families after a farewell cup of coffee, climbed into buggies, and clip-clopped homeward.

When it came their turn to host the festivities, Lee and Maude moved the furniture from the seldom-used parlor and lined the walls with folding chairs rented from the Mt. Victory undertaker. They arranged for the same musicians and caller that others had used.

All were relieved when they could eliminate dancing in private homes and pay a nominal fee to dance in the Ridgeway public hall and opera house. The admission initially was $1.00 a couple; it later was increased to $1.25--with an enterprising merchant sometimes providing refreshments (which the women served during breaks in the dancing).

A group of citizens contracted to rent the hall, starting in the fall of 1918, when it was not in use for other events. A three-piece combo (piano, banjo and guitar) agreed to provide square dance music. And Claude Collins, the most able caller in three counties, was hired to direct the evening's program.

Guest callers fought for attention with new sequences or variations of old favorites. The sponsors even arranged for round dances, with volunteer musicians, during two 20-minute "rest" periods.

Collins might require a little watching, the committee was told. He liked alcoholic beverages and, when he was in his cups, was inclined to make suggestive remarks to the women. Some resented his behavior (Maude was one of them) but all conceded he was superb in his field and would be an asset for that reason.

He appeared to be about 50 years old at the time, stood at around five feet, 10 inches tall, and had been crippled a few years earlier when his left arm was crushed in a farming accident. He had a pleasing baritone voice, strong enough to be heard throughout the hall without a megaphone, and boasted a wide variety of calls.

The hall was ideal for the purpose too. The front half was cleared of seats and chairs to offer an area roughly 60 feet by 80 feet for dancing. Opera seats remained in the back half for convenience of viewers and between-set dancers.

Most came to square dance but a few were doing the two-step, waltz and foxtrot. Tango, rhumba, bunnyhop, the Charleston and all the acrobatic dances came later. Children fashioned their own steps at the edge of the floor to the popular tunes of the day and the rhythmic cadence of country-western music. Some joined parents to learn the simpler square dance calls--and became avid fans in their own right.

The gallery of onlookers kept public demonstration of affection to a minimum. After all, this was a community of solid values and this was a time of moral commitment. Even the appearance of lewdness was wrong. So dancers refrained from getting too close, going cheek to cheek, or holding hands after the music stopped.

Later, Maude and the children joined Lee in regional square dances at Marysville, 20 miles distant. There, they were met by Lee's sister Dawn, her husband Roy Ansley and their children, Lucille, Ronald and James. Free hot dog sandwiches were served. "I ate seven once," Mardo recalled. He didn't get sick, but has never liked wieners so well since!

The Ridgeway Opera House was remembered by the Williamses for other reasons than the dances. Each of the children appeared there on the stage in school plays, accepted their high school diplomas there, participated in variety programs and, for a time, played basketball in the area devoted to dancing.

Maude and Lee recalled one program in which their son and three members of his class --LaMotte Mayle, Robert Hill and Olen White--sang at intermission of the class play. Jeanette Eaton, a talented member of the student body, had coached them.

In fine voice, they sang "Margie" and "Sonny Boy," then waited for the applause that would bring them back on stage for an encore. The hand-clapping was so meager that the boys got the message. None went on to become the first Bing Crosby. Although Beryl Wallace, a neighbor, commented that Mardo on stage looked and sounded just like his dad Lee had during his years at Mt. Victory High School.

Some of the school-sponsored programs were long remembered by the impressionable children. Ralph Parlette, a speaker on the Chautauqua circuit, left an indelible and inspiring message.

He used a pleasant speaking voice, clear diction and the stage aid of a jar of different size beans to stress each point. He displayed the container, with small beans on top and bottom, medium-sized beans throughout and the large beans just as widely dispersed.

His stage presence, the continuous shaking of the jar of beans, and his resonant voice held the audience in rapt attention as he delivered in various forms the message that perseverance is the key to success.

Those who try and try again become the leaders--the executives--he declared. One must have the desire and a goal. After that, all things are possible if one perseveres--and to prove his contention, Mr. Parlette brought forth his jar of beans. All the smaller ones had been replaced at the top by the largest during the course of his speech. The biggest, when shaken enough during life, always rose to the top, he declared.

Students may have been conditioned for Parlette's inspirational address by a similar one at the school assembly a few weeks earlier.

J.G. Evans, a Ridgeway businessman and civic leader, had told of an incident in which one gave up and another kept on trying.

These two mice, he explained, climbed to the top of an earthenware crock which was about two-thirds full of milk, and fell in. They tried vainly to climb the slick sides.

Around and around they paddled. The swim strokes became weaker until one concluded it was hopeless, stopped swimming and drowned. The other one, tired and with no hope of ever getting out, nevertheless kept paddling.

He paddled and paddled, floated a while, then paddled and paddled and paddled. At last the cream that had formed on the milk was churned into butter. Mr. Mouse, the persevering one who kept on paddling when there was no hope, climbed on the blob of butter and scrambled to safety.

The message, Mr. Evans told his listeners, is clear. Don't listen to those who say the game is lost, that there is no use to try any longer. "Just keep on paddling."

TWO

Charades became popular with Lee and Maude, were barely tolerated by the youngsters. There just was not enough action. "We couldn't appreciate the skill of the gestures and the variety of facial expressions," Mildred said once. Maude was good at solving the presentations; Lee enjoyed his role in the spotlight when he enacted the movements to portray farm activities, scenic attractions--even the pictures on a wall or the objects in a room.

He used his Welsh temperament to full advantage--grimaced, threw his weight around, waved his arms, beckoned, made pictures in the air. He portrayed Niagara Falls, enacted a thunder storm, and stumped his viewers with "The Last Supper." He had a lot of fun, as did the other adults.

No words were used by the performer after introduction of the subject of the skit. Viewers could ask questions and make comments. The "mime" would answer with gestures to continue that line of questioning, or to indicate that the questioner was totally off the track.

Maude recalled only one charade when their children (and the youngsters brought by neighbors for the evening's competition) displayed any interest. The two leaders--Harry Marmon on the one side and Lee on the other--had selected those who wanted to participate. They had decided the topic would be about farming or rural living, and Harry's team had been selected to perform first.

The presentation was started, with grandiose gestures and barely concealed chuckles. When Harry reached a certain point in his silent communication, he was interrupted by one youngster after another. First came a "moooo," then an "oink," followed by a whinny, the cackling of a hen, and the quack-quack of a duck. As Harry continued to mime, the sounds were repeated.

The children on both sides of the room laughed. Their elders shouted "barnyard madness," "farmyard extravaganza," "animal overture," and "hayseed musicale" before someone ended the hilarity with the correct answer--"The Gobble Family" (later known as "Old McDonald Had A Farm"). The "E-I-E-I-O" that some child shouted gave it away.

Wiener roasts were a favorite with both intimate family groups and neighborhood parties. In the family setting, the parents and children took turns roasting wieners and marshmallows. The larger parties might attract 20 or more families, each bringing their own food and utensils and socializing until late night in the flickering firelight.

Maude recalled one of those parties which almost got out of hand. Lee and his farm hand had spent two days clearing fallen trees from the creek pasture in front of the house. The brush, interlaced with trunks and larger limbs of trees, was piled high in an area far from buildings.

The word went out that the Williamses were going to have a huge bonfire on a certain night and that all friends and neighbors were welcome to help celebrate the near advent of winter. Aided by placement of kerosene at strategic points, the brush blazed high. Sparks soared into the heavens. Heat and smoke drove the revelers back, to shouts and bickering.

The heat abated at last, and family heads marshaled their hungry children into line for the toasting and roasting. There was one untoward development--some of the men had decided that the occasion merited some liquid libation and had brought beer. Before the evening was over, the male contingent was in the doghouse, two of their number had staggered away from the light and fallen into the creek, and the wives were making dire threats as to what was going to happen to erring mates.

After the children started classes in Ridgeway, box suppers were popular. Maude attended in her calicoes and ginghams. Most were school affairs and attracted 200 or more adults and children.

Every participant (usually female) fixed a box lunch for two, filled with delicacies (pie, cake, out-of-season fruit) designed to attract a member of the opposite sex. It didn't hurt for the more beautiful of the single ladies to spread the rumor that a certain gaily decorated box was hers. The object was to create as much bidding as possible for each box, with proceeds going to a popular school project.

Some boxes were auctioned for the almost unheard of price of $3.00 or more, depending upon comeliness of the lady, attractiveness of the box, and desire of the swain to impress. The competition extended to the children, too, but it was highly unusual if not downright risky for a man to provide an entry. On those rare occasions, there were no bidders or another male purchased his supper for one cent to a nickel! Girls hesitated to bid, even if the boy was the most popular classmate in school, because of the shouts of derision that resulted.

Mildred, Bea, and Pauline each tried her hand at catching the boy of her choice--John Perry, Buck Deerwester and Sonny Ansley, respectively--via the box meal auction. All usually succeeded--even though none of the bidders was supposed to know in advance who had offered a box. The name was revealed only to the purchaser when he tore away the ribbons and was ready to dine.

One time, 17-year-old Mildred tried to send word quietly to John Perry which box was hers, how it was decorated, and, in the event he needed an extra incentive to part with his hard-earned money, the delicacies that were enclosed.

John received Mildred's message, as did an eavesdropper who told a group of young men that a certain box would be in great demand. It was filled with such goodies as fried chicken, apple turnovers, coconut pie and banana cake--and, as a bonus, the purchaser would have an attractive young woman to share the meal.

The five young men pooled their resources, selected one of their number by lottery to bid on the desired supper, and gave him all their cash. John, who had come from his part-time job at the Ellza Limes garage with little more than $2 in his pocket, knew something was fishy when on every bid the price surged upward by 10 or 15 cents. The auctioneer had started the bidding at 50 cents, as with every other box supper. When the bid reached $1.75, only two young men remained in competition--Pat Lane (representing the group of five young men) and John.

As Mildred watched nervously, the price rose to $2, $2.25, $2.50, $2.75, and she was preparing herself to eat supper with someone other than her boy friend. Then Pat bid $2.80 and stopped. He had reached the limit of his resources. John topped it by a nickel, and searched through every pocket before coming up with two one dollar bills and eighty-four cents in change. Bob Hill, a classmate of Mildred's, slipped his friend a penny to keep the record straight.

Young John Perry, who was learning the mechanic's trade at the Limes' garage and Ford dealership, went without lunch until he got his next pay envelope two days later.

Lunch didn't cost much in 1921--he could buy a sandwich and a glass of milk for 25 cents at the Ridgeway restaurant. But he had spent too much for the pleasure of eating with his best girl. He suggested to Mildred that box supper messages be made more discreetly in the future--he wasn't made of money!

John remembered an occasion two years earlier when Palmer Romire, an upper classman, had purchased an ornately beribboned box in the belief that it belonged to the much sought after Leota Callahan. Disappointed when the name inside was that of a less popular, less attractive young woman, Palmer sneaked behind a group leaving the hall, carried the meal into the shrubbery of a nearby house, and ate it all himself.

The young lady vainly sought her supper mate, cried broken-heartedly at his heartlessness, and enlisted the aid of her parents in publicizing the name of the miscreant. Palmer was reminded of his error wherever he went--until he moved out of the community and became a brakeman on the Norfolk & Western Railroad in Columbus, Ohio.

Lee, in expectation of one spring box supper festival on March 31, had a less despicable plan in mind. He spent most of a day devising an elaborate practical joke--preparing the menu, printing the owner's name, and wrapping the box in gaudy red, green, and yellow tissue. He topped the box with a huge white rosette.

Upon arrival at the school where the event was to be held, he sent 13-year-old daughter Pauline to stealthily place his entry in the center of the pile while he spread the rumor that a striking red, white, blue and yellow decorated box was being offered by the attractive new teacher hired to replace the pregnant Mrs. Kerns. The new teacher, the story went, was interested in making friends of the more presentable males in the area.

Lee had doubled his anticipated enjoyment of the event by providing an unusual supper of cold sausage patties on corn bread, six dried prunes, and a cup of sour cherries--plus the ornately lettered placard which read, "April Fool."

He sat back to await developments. Box after box went to eager buyers. "Mine will have to be next," he kept saying to himself. As the auctioneer called for bids on the final offering, it dawned on him that something had happened to his prize effort to make box supper history. "Pauline," he started, "did you--" and, glancing at his wife, realized he did not need to complete the question. Maude had instructed her daughter to place the box in the car and was quietly enjoying having put one over on the practical joker. The matter wasn't mentioned again.

THREE

For days after Lee and his hired hand had finished cleaning out the lower level of the barn, the heady smell of animal manure permeated the neighborhood. Everyone in those days used manure as fertilizer. Commercial blends of nitrogen, phosphate, phosphorous and other nutrients came later--promoting more intensive farming methods, hybrid plants and vastly increased yields.

Removal of the partially rotted straw that had bedded Lee's small herd of six dairy cows, four horses, and 20 or more swine, required at least two weeks of strenuous work. The manure was allowed to accumulate for seven to nine months and usually was about six to eight inches deep throughout the sheltered area of the barn.

Lee and his hired hand (whoever it was--he had eight to ten in his lifetime) used a four-tined pitchfork to load the material into the hopper of the horse-drawn manure spreader.

After reaching the field, the operator engaged a lever and the conveyor platform moved slowly toward the revolving blades at the rear. They were slanted to tear apart the slabs of manure and scatter the pieces evenly on the field.

When the spreader broke down--as it often did, the manual labor was almost doubled. The workmen had to fork the manure onto the flat bed of a wagon, then unload it by hand in the field as the horses pulled the vehicle slowly along. The four-tined fork had to be given a special twist at the conclusion of each swing, thus scattering the lumps. Arms, legs and stomach muscles got a workout. Lee and his helper became accustomed to the pungent smell that clung stubbornly to clothes and body.

Less work was involved with the advent of commercial fertilizers. They could be applied more evenly and resulted in vast increases in crop yields, especially after plant engineers developed hybrids.

Lee said a national record of 100 bushels of corn per acre was set in the early 1930s by Hardin County farmer Ira C. Marshall. Other farmers were hard-pressed to attain 70 or 75 bushels per acre, so his feat on a 20-acre tract was praised by farm implement dealers who presented him with the latest in planting, cultivating and harvesting tools. Then they advertised that their implements were being used by the national record-holder.

Marshall had an advantage--his land was of rich black loam in the heart of the fertile Scioto Marsh, west of Kenton, and he was able to improve its fertility by spreading over it a layer of manure.

Lee said Mr. Marshall let the modern farm equipment given to him by the dealers sit out in the weather during the next few years and it rusted out. Commercial fertilizers and the cross-fertilization that produced hybrid corn made Marshall's record short-lived. Farmers now produce more than 100 bushels of corn per acre in poor soil. In 1992, the average yield per acre nationwide was 131.4 bushels--a far cry from Lee's top yield of 50 bushels.

FOUR

When neighbor Beryl Wallace called Lee to tell him one of the Williams' cows was in his pasture, the two decided to replace the line fence between their two farms.

The fence had been trampled down before, and hogs had rooted their way to forbidden ground by digging under the bottom strand of wire. It had been patched up repeatedly and now would have to be replaced.

Under their agreement, each man would be responsible for labor and material on one-half of the 1,600 feet of fence separating Lee's cultivated field and Beryl's pasture land. Custom dictated that each farmer was responsible for the half of the fence to his right when he faced the other's tract. In this instance, Mr. Wallace would build the north half, Mr. Williams the south portion.

The two went to the farm equipment store together so the fence they built would be the same height, have the same number of wire strands of the same gauge (No. 9 for top and bottom wires, No. 7 for the other horizontal strands, and perhaps No. 6 for the up-and-down lines linking the various strands).

They purchased 125 wooden fence posts eight and one-half feet tall (five and one-half feet to be above ground, three feet to be sunk into the ground). Posts at that time were about 30 cents each. The men tried to buy chestnut or pecan, which lasted longer. They acquired eleven 50-yard spools of fence (at a cost of 10 cents a foot), 1,600 feet of barbed wire, which came in 500-foot rolls, costing approximately $12 each, and metal staples at 4 cents per pound. When completed, the fence would cost the farmers a total of $250 and the labor of four men, part-time, for a month or more.

On that late September day in 1915, Lee and his hired hand Ross, and Beryl and his hired hand began the work, rushing every operation with a view to getting the fence up and stretched before the November snows.

The children came to watch after school and on Saturdays. But none expressed a desire to become a fence-builder. The work was back breaking, too strenuous for their young bodies. But they might be sent on errands, like fetching water for the sweaty men.

First, the men distributed the spools of wire along the fence row, and began sinking the first of 125 post holes. The post holes were three feet deep and were dug slowly and laboriously. A hand-operated digger--two curved blades facing each other and manipulated by opening and closing a forceps-like handle--was battered into the soil time after time, propelled downward with brute force. Whenever it stopped, the operator spread the handles apart and closed the claws with their burden of earth, to be lifted and deposited on the ground outside the hole. Later, the dirt would be tamped around the post to hold it upright.

The four men "rested" by placing posts in the newly dug holes, tamping earth and rocks around them. Using spade and shovel, they excavated for three anchor posts, one at each end of the fence row and one in the middle. These posts were heftier and required deeper holes. Rocks and earth kept each anchor post upright until concrete was poured into the hole to form a permanent base eight inches thick.

The final job--after the line of posts and anchors stretched straight and true--was the unrolling of the spool of fence wire and stapling of the fence to its supports. The eleven 50-yard rolls were joined by splicing and braiding the wire ends together with heavy pliers--effecting a solid union. The top wire was stapled to every third or fourth post to hold the fence upright during the stretching operation. Staples were shaped like modern staples but were of heavy gauge iron and had to be pounded in place over the wire with a hammer--a good chance to smash a thumb.

The stretcher, about six feet high, was a form that clamped around every strand of fence so that the entire height would tighten uniformly. Pressure was applied by two men, using a pull and ratchet technique. When every kink had been straightened and the wire was taut enough to issue a distinct hum when struck with a metal tool, the hammer wielders took over. They pounded staples to hold the top and bottom wires--and two or three in between--to every post.

Finally, barbed wire was strung along the top and tightened with the stretcher. The barbed wire was to prevent the horses and cows from reaching over fences to graze, and to keep more active animals, like young colts, from jumping over.

Lee cautioned the children not to climb over the fence, ever. Repeated climbings made the fence break down, and it was hard work even to do the repairs. "Go to the anchor posts or, better yet, go around one end or the other," he urged.

After that, Lee had repair jobs, one or two short stretches of new fencing on his own farm, and even one 200-foot span of rail fence he had to fix with lengths of hickory saplings cut in the farm woods. But that was the last line fence Lee helped replace in his lifetime.

FIVE

Right after Thanksgiving in 1917, the Williams family decided to make the best of an early snow and take a bobsled ride to the home of Lee's sister, 12 miles away. The children, then 8, 10, 12 and 14, went along.

The family made it a real celebration by picking up Lee's parents, Ross and Sarah Williams, and two other sisters, Margaret Newell and Alice Marmon. The countryside was a grandeur of shimmering white, with four inches of fresh snow on the ground and a bright winter sun. The adults and children talked and sang, or got out and walked beside the horses at times.

The gaiety ended shortly after the group had dined at the Amanda and Hutson Smith home, south of West Mansfield. Grandpa Ross, who had arthritis in his knees, complained of mounting pain and, using his vaunted weather forecasting ability, warned that a major storm was on the way. There was no thought of staying overnight. The Smiths couldn't accommodate 16 guests--and besides, the farm couples had to get home to care for the livestock.

Clouds had taken over the sky and a north wind was hurling particles of snow as the men got the sled ready for the return trip. More straw was scattered over the floor for protection from the cold. Blankets were stretched across the top of the sideboards and anchored. Winter clothing, which had been removed during the sunny early part of the day, was donned. Those who had boots put them on.

Then the horses' noses were turned north to face the storm. Lee and his father, aided by Forrest Newell, husband of Margaret, took the driving seat. Women and children huddled together in the straw-covered bed of the sleigh, tarp and blanket pulled over them to keep warm.

Stung by the icy, wind-driven particles, the men guided the horses, peering ahead, intent on getting the group home safely. Vision was impaired from the start and became worse as night-time approached. There was no traffic--"No other fools were abroad," Lee said.

The blizzard, rated as perhaps the worst early winter storm in local history, pounded the horse-drawn conveyance all 12 of the miles back. No one could face that 30-knot north wind for long. One at a time, Ross, Forrest or Lee would climb into the sheltered part of the sled to get warm, then return to take his turn at the reins.

Maude remembered this visit to the Hut Smith home as the most grueling four-hour experience in her lifetime. Luckily, the heroic drivers escaped with only frostbitten ears and numbed fingers.

The winter of 1917-18 was the snowiest and the coldest of all the winters, Lee thought. The storms started in mid-November and continued until late February. The temperature dropped well below zero, day after day. Even the children conceded that there were just too many blizzards, too much drifted snow, and took to staying indoors where they "never had anything to do." They missed several days of school that year.

The Williamses remembered that wintry season more vividly because John Marmon, the neighbor's son who drove the school wagon, died in late January, 1918. His burial was delayed several days because of the severe cold and the deeply frozen earth.

Sometimes, Lee said, he was so tired of the snow and cold he almost welcomed the spring thaws that broke up the thick slabs of ice on Rush Creek and piled them against the bridge. The thaws could be frightening.

Fed by the cold spring rains, the huge blocks of ice moved downstream. Flood waters spewed the ice floes over adjacent pastures. Masses of ice tore out fences and water gates the length of the creek--from Mountain Lake in Logan County to its junction with the Scioto River near LaRue. The lane could be under water for a week at a time.

One spring, the flood waters were particularly high. The lane was impassable. Water was flowing a foot deep over the bridge floor, and was even higher at the bridge on the Mt. Victory-West Mansfield pike, over which Lee had to pass when he went to Mt. Victory.

The family was marooned--and they ran out of food. They were not in danger of starving; they had milk and eggs. But no flour to bake bread, no rice, beans, or rolled oats. Only a bit of salt pork was left of the butchered meats and a can or two of Maude's canned tomatoes. So Lee wore his tall boots, took a burlap bag, in which to carry groceries, trudged a half-mile across the water-covered fields to the Beryl Wallace home (on the same side of Rush Creek) and bummed a ride to town--saving himself two more miles of walking each way.

Beryl and Carrie Wallace were glad to give their neighbor a lift. Besides, they also needed provisions. They assured Lee they'd drive him home after going into town.

They were too optimistic. The bridge floor near the Wallace home was still under water after the shopping trip. So Lee had to return the back way on foot, slogging through the muddy fields and climbing fences, with his tightly packed burlap sack on his back (bearing flour, sugar, soup beans, rice, rolled oats and canned goods sufficient to last a week).

During a particularly devastating early thaw--it may have been after that 1917-18 winter--ice piled 20 feet high against the 35-foot bridge that spanned the creek. The structural steel span was shifted on its abutments before frenzied efforts of workmen (hired by the county) diverted the flow around one end. The bridge had to be realigned but was so weakened that the Logan County commissioners authorized the rebuilding of supporting abutments and the bolstering of beams, cables and framework with welds and new material.

The work of making the structure safe took a crew of four men almost an entire summer. They brought in a gasoline-powered concrete mixer and various tools to move the heavy slabs in the abutments. All the activities were closely monitored by the Williams children.

Maude recalled that her youngsters talked at length about an electrocution they witnessed. During the job of restoring the badly damaged east abutment, workmen discovered that the water inside the concrete forms contained "water dogs." These reptiles had the appearance of black catfish, with legs.

The operator of the concrete mixer had a particular aversion to them and enlisted his fellow workers in a game of catching them in wire nooses and touching their wet toes to the spark plug on the gasoline engine. They summarily dispatched 22--all they could find--and during one of the operations, the children were fascinated observers. They termed it cruel and stayed away from the project until curiosity brought them back.

Lee and Maude laughed about another incident related to the reconstruction of the bridge. Nephew Ross Engle, Lee's hired man that year, was 18 and in the midst of a turbulent love affair. He would work hard all day, take soap and towel to the creek for his bath then don his finery, make ready his horse and buggy, and drive off in the growing dark to visit his love.

One night Ross overestimated his endurance. After visiting his girlfriend, he went to sleep on the way home and awakened at 6:00 A.M. the next day.

He was still in the buggy. His horse had brought him safely home but was standing, with drooped head, the buggy stranded in a huge mound of sand the workmen had piled at the east end of the bridge. When Ross reached the house, he had time only for a hurried breakfast--and a change to work clothes. "It should have been Sunday, a day of rest," he said ruefully.

Ross Engle became almost a second son during the three years he helped Lee with the farming. He became a favorite with Maude too, although she sometimes frowned on the example he was setting for the kids.

One Saturday evening when the older folks were gone, Ross took 14-year-old Mardo with him on a melon raid. They sneaked to the back end of the Rob Richardson farm a half mile distant. The choicest melons soon were ripped from the vines and, after eating as many as they could, the miscreants carried two burlap bags of cantaloupes home with them.

By that time, Ross was hungry again and the teenager tried to keep up with him. They ate several, piling the rinds onto the grates of the kitchen range where Maude found them the next morning when she tried to start the fire to cook breakfast.

Ross stashed away the few remaining melons and would speak of how delicious they were just to see his cousin's reaction. Mardo's enjoyment had paled significantly, however, for he developed a bad case of diarrhea and a lifelong distaste for muskmelon.

That, plus the scolding he got from his mother, dissuaded him from making any additional nighttime excursions of a criminal nature. The Richardsons never spoke of the loss and their good friends, Maude and Lee, never let on that their son was one of the marauders.

Mardo ran into disfavor a little later the same summer. Ross and Lee were cutting corn by hand on a particularly hot early September day. They were opening the field for the binder and were laboring adjacent to the woods where trees blocked any breeze, and the sun bore down. Mardo had been instructed to fill the jug with fresh well water and deliver it to the workers in mid-afternoon.

Just before the allotted time, one of Mildred's close friends arrived. She had driven three miles by horse and buggy to share secrets, which might be interesting to a growing boy. Hazel Predmore was exceedingly attractive and this was an opportunity that shouldn't be missed.

The result, Maude said, was that Ross and Lee were forgotten. Parched and sweat-stained, they marched up the lane to the house two hours before their normal quitting time. Glowering at the boy playing in the coolness of the porch, they paused at the well to splash water on their arms and face, and drink deeply of the cooling draught.

"I bet you caught it last evening," were the first words Ross said when he met Mardo the next morning. The curious thing was that only a minor reprimand had been given. Lee and Maude had talked it over and concluded that the presence of a pretty girl was sufficient to cause forgetfulness in a normally reliable youngster. The parents were very understanding of the foibles of youth.

"The grown children told me once," Maude said, "that they never remembered getting spanked by either of us. I guess we used threats and withdrawal of benefits to teach right from wrong. And we always tried to set a good example by the way we lived."

The lack of corporal punishment was more than made up for by reassignment of duties. A serious infraction of conduct could result in a week's labor dusting furniture or washing the linoleum floor, the washing and drying of dishes by yourself, the daily pumping of water and transferring it to the kitchen--bucket by bucket--for all the household uses. If the infraction was at the expense of a sister or brother, the offender took over the chores (or some of them) for the offendee who gained free time and was not averse to doing a little gloating in plain view.

The children also agreed that they never heard their parents raise their voices to each other in anger. If there were arguments, they must have occurred in the dead of night and been conducted in a whisper. Despite their desire for privacy, the doors were never entirely closed to their bedroom or any of the bedrooms.

When the children left home, the older ones sometimes wondered if they might have been sent on errands just to provide their parents with needed privacy.

Mardo remembered his dad chuckling about the Joneses, a family with 12 children and altogether too much togetherness. Each Saturday night, Bill Jones told Lee, he went to town and purchased a pound of hard mixed candy. He counted the number of pieces, scattered them in the high, never-mowed grass of the front lawn on Sunday morning, and sent each ambulatory child outside in a candy-seeking contest.

"Don't come in the house until all 120 pieces have been found. The one with the most will get to eat the candy in his or her container, and will also get a nickel (sometimes a dime) as the winner," he told his youngsters.

Lee said the plan worked well as child after child joined the family. But Bill Jones spoiled it for himself. In order to assure the needed privacy, he told the contestants there were 131 pieces when there were only 124 (or some such disparity). They would search vainly for three hours or more-- or until he called them in and awarded the prize on the basis of pieces in hand.

He learned, too late, that the children could be just as tricky. They trooped in that Sunday to claim their prize and found their parents in "a compromising position." The oldest boy had held out enough candy from the previous week to meet the number father Jones said had been distributed.

"We never suspected that Mom and Dad needed to be alone," Mildred commented after she was married in 1923. "We were in and out of the house and with our parents off and on throughout the day until we started school."

Lee and Maude maintained their own brand of privacy throughout their lives. They never showed affection in public and would look askance at those young couples who boldly held hands or kissed while walking in town or in the presence of others.

SIX

When Maude and Lee moved into their new home in 1903, the creek that meandered to within 60 feet of their front porch provided a kaleidoscope of beauty. It flowed majestically around three sweeping curves within the ten-acre front pasture. The stream was lined with willow trees. It had only two extremely shallow places, over which the water barely moved during the summer droughts. No spot was deeper than five feet. It was an ideal setting for a tryst--or a swimming party.

Persons who view that portion of Rush Creek now would never believe what it had been. The dramatic change came in the 1920s when the Logan County commissioners agreed to a dredging and straightening project designed to curb flooding of adjacent farm lands.

The flooding was controlled to a certain extent. The water still came rushing past in times of heavy precipitation--all the way from Mountain Lake near Bellefontaine. Its passage was swift. The unimpeded, straighter flow sped the crest into the Scioto River near LaRue. The environmental impact was ignored. No thought was given to the possibility of erosion or the effects on water life and creek-side vegetation that would follow eradication of crooks and dips in the stream.

During the next two years, the appearance of that formerly scenic pasture land changed dramatically. The willows were the first casualty. The old channels started to fill in and in 1926 enough gravel was removed from one to rebuild two miles of the road that passed the Williams residence. A dozen or more nearby farmers used their teams of horses and special wagon beds to convey the stone from creek bed to road surface, where other workmen spread the material. Logan County paid the farmers for loading and transporting the gravel. Lee got 25 cents a load as his share for permitting removal of the flood-deposited substance.

Now the shallow creek runs straight through the almost treeless tract. The house is gone from the crown of the slope and a pre-manufactured house stands nearby. The barn and other buildings have been razed. But the windmill still stands, more rusted now. The fan stands out to steer the flow of wind and the wheel turns ponderously--and squeakingly--to pump water to the livestock for more than its 100th year.

Maude, in her old age, remembered only the earlier creek--the one the children played in and where they learned to swim, turn over rocks in their hunt for crawdads and fish with home-made tackle tied to a makeshift pole.

Mildred and Mardo taught themselves to swim when they were seven and nine years old. Then they instructed the others, with emphasis on water safety. They gamboled in a stretch of placid water that was just around a curve from an undiscovered pool. When a fisherman plumbed its depth and bragged of the big one he had caught in ten feet of water, it became a swimming hole for nude bathers--prized for its depth.

It was "males only," and not for the shy. They could be seen from the roadway, 400 feet away. A near tragedy occurred one evening when Bud

Endsley, on his first visit to the swimming hole, heard an automobile approaching and made a mad dash waterward. He leaped from the bank and made an almost perfect dive to the center of the creek.

Cheers of the onlookers turned to cries of concern as his unconscious body floated to the surface. He had made his spectacular dive into three feet of water at the shallow end of the swim area.

Friends pulled him to shore, carefully covered his nakedness and took him to his physician in Mt. Victory. He had suffered a slight concussion and injured his spine. For four weeks, he wore a neck brace. When he returned in early September for the last swim of the season, he made his way cautiously--ignoring the warnings that a carload of beautiful women was fast approaching on the roadway.

The waterway with its crooks and turns--and despite the alternating floods and droughts--was a magnet to young and old. "When I couldn't find the youngsters, I knew they were along the creek," Maude said. They entertained themselves by hunting crawfish and mussels, trying to catch small fish on bent pins, watching for water snakes or just lying on the bank to watch the fleecy white clouds. One of them would visualize an image in the formation above. This would signal the start of a competition to see animal, bird or other cloud-woven pictures in the sky.

Once the children came dashing to the house during a light shower. They were convinced they had brought on the rain. They had been lying on the bank looking upward when one started reciting a poem in which the clouds were asked to send someone to play with these lonesome youngsters.

"It immediately started to rain," Mildred reported. Her belief in her supernatural powers was diminished when she shouted another poem, "Rain, rain go away," without result.

One particularly disagreeable creek-related occurrence was due, Maude thought, to a child's affinity with mud. The children had been squishing the moist stuff between their toes. One had started making mud pies. But Mardo had found a deeper deposit, in which he could sink his legs to the knees.

He started pulling one leg or the other from the mud, enjoying the sucking sound each made as it left the ugly muck. "It's a sinkhole. I'm being pulled under," he yelled.

His sisters responded to the thought of all that fun. They were starting to wade in when Bea warned them that Mardo's legs were covered with black worms.

He had uncovered a colony of leeches. A number had taken advantage of the invitation to a free meal and attached themselves to his skin in all exposed places. Maude pried loose a dozen after Mardo was unable to dislodge them. He lost a little blood, had a few abrasions and never regained his appetite for playing in the mud.

Maude didn't find much pleasure along the creek inasmuch as she never learned to swim. Lee knew how and frequently joined the neighborhood swim parties. He convinced the younger ones to practice his "frog" stroke in which both arms were used at the same time to propel the swimmer forward by spurts.

And he initiated the "running the rapids" game. Two or more persons would line up facing each other and push their hands through the water in opposite directions to create a turbulence. The swimmer passed between them. The more people creating the waves, the more turbulent became the water and the farther the swimmer had to confront those man-made waves.

Rough games of all kinds were forbidden during the family swim parties. Smaller youngsters might get splashed or inadvertently pushed under water. And most of the women, who came in their house dresses, didn't want to get their hair wet. They attended under protest and only to get cooled off. Their dresses clung to them when they waded ashore, and they blushed in embarrassment when the men whistled.

Swim parties were canceled during drought, when the stream became so slow moving that moss formed at the water line. There was no voiced warning of typhoid fever although some may have thought of that danger.

One summer the children were enamored of a raft Lee had constructed and anchored near the bridge. Kids from all around fished from it, leaped from it into the water and, reclining on boxes, dreamed that they were on an ocean liner steaming to exotic places and fabulous adventures.

The craft broke from its mooring and was swept away by the winter ice jams or flood waters of the next spring. No attempt was made to replace it. The children had lost interest in being "Huck Finn," or Lee just didn't have the time to rebuild.

Not long after the raft episode, Lee was tempted into breaking the law. Someone, probably George Keller, a neighboring young man, had made all the arrangements for a different kind of fishing expedition. A seine, 30 feet long and four feet high--adequate to cover wider areas of Rush Creek within a two-mile distance--had been assembled. All residents in that area had been notified, advised to dress for the occasion, and bring along the buckets to carry the fish home.

A dozen men--and some boys--congregated along the banks just east of the Williams farm on the designated night. All were novices but they were strong and willing. They entered the water and found their places along the seine--eager and optimistic. When they completed the long drag four hours later, they were tired and disillusioned.

Lee reported that no one knew how to obtain the best results, efficiently. So someone unintentionally let the net dip under the surface, another jerked the seine off the bottom, and still another stumbled away from the bank to permit an end run.

"Altogether we may have lost as many fish as we caught, even after going over the same stretch of water again," he said. The greatest disappointment was in seeing the largest fishes leap the net in nonchalant disdain of the gallantly struggling seiners.

The harvest was all too meager. Each participant brought home fewer than 50 edible fish--all scrawny and full of tiny bones. The wives, who had to scale and gut the fish, convinced their mates not to try it again. One threatened to call the game warden and the sheriff if another foray was even broached.

The creek was the setting for other memorable events. Lee's only brother, Herman Williams, was a strong swimmer so he couldn't resist the challenge to cross the flooded stream after a summer storm.

Three others had already swum the muddy, bank-full torrent so Herman knew it could be done. He gave a short run and leaped as far as he could, then struck out for the other bank. He was sucked into an eddy and spent his strength trying to pull himself across the midstream current.

Realizing he was a candidate for drowning, the swimmer turned downstream to float with the flow. He husbanded his strength and, as he neared the bridge, made a desperate surge upward. His outflung hand scraped the under-structure before grasping the tie rod binding the bridge together. Hand over hand, Herman weakly pulled himself shoreward, where other swimmers grasped him and helped him to safety. He said he never over-estimated his prowess again--at least not when the potential for death was present.

Flood waters were always a hazard, whether from storm runoff or the back-up from ice floes. Lee had undergone his own ordeal in high waters earlier.

A two-year-old neighbor boy had been playing near the water's edge in front of his home. His foot slipped, or he attempted to do a little wading. Anyway he was caught in the swirling water as it swept down an abandoned channel. Lee, who was nearby, dashed into the flood, grabbed the child and carried him to safety.

"It was nothing to talk about," he said, discounting the potential threat to himself in wading chest deep in the turbulent water to effect the rescue.

There were other mishaps for the Williams children, like going home soaked after breaking through the ice, or walking into a depression in the bottom of the swimming area and finding oneself suddenly under water.

Only the males used the creek as their bathtub during the summers. There was no privacy, the women said, and no one knew who might be peering from between the willow trees lining the bank!

"Dad knows best!" Mardo decided after ignoring Lee's suggestion that he take his bath upstream from the cows, who stood near the water's edge, chewing their cuds and lazily brushing the flies from their backs. Mardo had just started shampooing his hair with Ivory Soap (it would float at his side) when the water became discolored. Wiping the suds from his eyes, he realized two of the animals had relieved themselves. He chased them from the creek, waded upstream past where the cows had stood, and carefully re-shampooed.

The creek, which was making memories for each member of the family, contributed in another way to Mardo's economic welfare and education.

Muskrats were present along its banks, and there were skunks, raccoons, and mink for the taking. Their pelts were valuable. A buyer made periodic rounds so their selling would not be a problem. But they had to be trapped, skinned, stretched on wooden shapes and dried sufficiently to keep mold from forming on the pelt.

When Mardo discussed the project with his father, he was told the rules. You will have to get up early enough to check each trap daily. You will have to kill the trapped animals humanely, preferably with a hammer blow. You will have to skin them, shape a board on which to stretch the pelts, and seek out the runways or dens where you place the traps.

The 13-year-old boy, who had not realized the effort involved, started learning. He read about habitat, eating habits, where to place the traps, and how to stake them to prevent the trapped animal from chewing off its foot and escaping.

When he thought he was ready, Lee bought four steel traps for him-- with some further admonitions. "You still have your chores to take care of. Trapping is ended if you don't keep your grades up. And, above all, you must run your trap line each morning before school and on week-ends. No animal is to suffer needlessly because you are delinquent."

Mardo eventually extended his trap line by adding eight traps. He learned how to skin his prey with the least damage to the pelt. He stretched each skin carefully on a board of the proper size for the pelt (rounded on one end to conform to the head portion). And he sold his stock one or two times a year.

The largest one-season return was $43. He never caught a raccoon but he trapped one skunk (a broad-striped one which brought him $1.25 and a lingering stink) and a mink which sold for $7.

The best price he ever received for a muskrat was $2.25, but Mardo delved into his trapping experience to send a message. One winter day when he was a senior at Ridgeway High School, he surreptitiously placed the severed tail of one of his quarry in the pocket of a coat belonging to Geneva Ansley, a fellow student.

It was an overture comparable to dipping your first love's pigtails in the ink well, or shyly throwing pine cones at her from behind a hedge.

Geneva launched an investigation. Sister Mildred tattled on the culprit, who was duly repentant. But Geneva, a lissome, blue-eyed beauty, at five feet, seven inches tall and a slender 125 pounds, forgot her anger at finding the hairy tail in the pocket of her best coat, laughed with her tormentor, and started a lifelong love affair with the young man who was almost two inches shorter than her and weighed only twelve pounds more.

Part VIII:

Lee Gets a Chevrolet, Maude Gets the Vote

ONE

*A*fter the turn of the century, when Maude and Lee were married, they subscribed to the *Old Farmers Almanack*, followed the "Hints for the Household," "Facts for the Farmer," weather and astronomy predictions, and its menu of poetry, anecdotes, conundrums, wit and humor. Church & Company was advertising Arm & Hammer baking soda, Colgate was promoting its soap, Singer, its sewing machines, and Hires, its root beer.

Lee and Maude also read *The Ohio Farmer*, which in an issue printed in the early autumn after Maude's graduation from Mt. Victory High School, detailed a procedure to speed the fattening of hogs for market-- using a variety of grains plus milk (for protein). When Lee tried it, early in his marriage, he said he was able to sell his hogs within six months. Never before had neighboring farmers been able to produce a marketable hog in less than eight months.

The couple added the *Cincinnati Weekly Times* and *Saturday Evening Post* to their subscription list, later bought *The Youth's Companion* for the youngsters and *Ladies Home Journal* for Maude. Rogers silver plate, Eastman Kodak cameras, Elgin watches, Remington typewriters, Natural Foods (Shredded Wheat) and Parker pens were nationally advertised.

The public debt was less than one and one-half billion dollars in 1883 (the year of Maude's birth)--and had been decreased by some $257 million from the preceding year. The import duty on opium was $10 per pound. There was no income tax. Two cents bought a stamp for first class mail. *The Ohio Farmer*, in its September, 1902, issue quoted apples at 45 cents per bushel, choice baled hay at $13 per ton, cattle at 7.75 cents per pound, hogs at 7.95 cents per pound and sheep at 4.5 cents per pound. The weekly paper carried a running notice that it accepted only reliable advertisers and insured its readers against fraud.

"Everything was a bargain in those days," Maude said, "if you only had the money." At the end of the nineteenth century, when the farmer of 100 acres was earning about $750 a year, ladies suits were being advertised in the *Saturday Evening Post* for $5-$10. Burpee's (the seed company) offered 20 packages of seed for 10 cents and Enameline was being pushed as a polish for the Kalamazoo wood/coal-burning range which graced every farm kitchen--and that of many town sisters.

Columns in magazines and newspapers emphasized health and comfort. People with weak eyes were advised to bathe them, using a basin of soft water to which a pinch of table salt and a teaspoon of brandy had been added. Dr. George W. Jacoby, in 1898, warned that "worry destroys the human intellectual apparatus and the physical structure." And Arthur Twining Hadley, Yale University president, complained in the *Post* "there are too many lawsuits."

In 1900 vendors started selling hamburger and "hot dachsund" sandwiches, a rolled waffle was fashioned to introduce the ice cream cone, jigsaw puzzles became popular, and safety razors went on sale. A Chicago company developed the first self-contained electric clothes washer and called it "Thor." At the end of the decade, pajamas were beginning to replace the nightshirt as sleepwear and the "V" neck appeared on certain articles of clothing to protests that "it is a threat to health and morals."

In 1906, an earthquake destroyed more than four square miles of downtown San Francisco with a loss of 700 lives. By 1910, some members of Congress started criticizing government spending. Expenditures had doubled in the preceding 10 years, to $1 billion annually.

About this time, Uneeda Biscuit started a nationwide campaign to protect foodstuffs from outside elements when it took its biscuits out of the barrel and put them in a closed package. Until that time, virtually every manner of food was displayed in open barrels around the store. The customers themselves could dip into the containers of crackers, cookies, beans, rice, sugar, flour--even pickles, Maude said.

An Ohio city, Cleveland, got its name in the history books by becoming the first to use red-green lights to regulate the flow of the burgeoning auto traffic (1914). A Tennessean started a national merchandising trend when he introduced the "supermarket" method of displaying and selling groceries (1916). The second decade was important to all seamstresses with the advent of the zipper (1913) and to the style-conscious with the perfection of the first modern bra (1914).

In 1913, income tax started, but Lee and Maude never made enough money to pay taxes--until after Lee died and Maude sold the farm.

Every decade had its highlights. The third decade of the 20th Century had an exceptional impact on Maude's life. The "Roaring Twenties" started with an economic upswing, the enactment of Prohibition and the ratification of the women's right to vote (which had been put before the Congress every year since 1878 and turned down every year until then).

Maude's first vote was cast for Warren G. Harding in 1920. He was from Marion, Ohio--almost a neighbor--and had a reputation for honesty. President Harding could do no wrong, she thought.

When his administration was caught up in the Teapot Dome Scandal (1923), she was his champion--he couldn't be a party to the fraudulent leasing of Naval Oil Reserve lands attributed to his appointees in the U.S. Departments of Navy, Justice and Interior, the Veterans Bureau and the Alien Property Custodian.

Albert Fall, his Secretary of Interior, and three other members of the government were convicted of bribery, and the oil leases canceled in 1924 by President Calvin Coolidge. President Harding had died in 1923 at the height of the investigation.

A player piano (not available in the early part of the century) sold for $475 in 1920--three years after the Williamses had started playing theirs.

Kraft cheese was 38 cents a pound, bacon was 70 cents and round steak 42 cents. Maude said milk was 17 cents a quart and eggs were selling for 68 cents a dozen. She and Lee had no reason to purchase any of these items--and frowned on buying chickens at 47 cents per pound. They bought few doughnuts at 19 cents a dozen but liked their coffee, even at 47 cents per pound. Prices were rising at the start of the 1920s. The cost of many products remained outside the Williamses' $1,300 yearly income.

But the 1919 bumper harvest of oats and corn allowed Lee to buy a new Chevrolet. It cost him $490.

"I don't think any of us ever entered a train after Lee bought his new car," Maude said. "We were so proud of it that we arranged a week-end trip to visit my folks in Toledo." The car was a two-seat, four-door, open touring model, similar to the one that Lester Bird had driven on his record speed run between Mt. Victory and Kenton. Its fabricated cloth top could be folded back or left in place, attached by clamps to the windshield. Removable side curtains had windows of isinglass sewn into the fabric. The car was black, as were practically all automobiles of the day.

Although Arthur and Nora Allen had moved from Toledo to a rural community near Woodville, Ohio, about 90 miles from the Williamses, Lee was confident he could find their new home. "They had sent us detailed directions, with street and road names. We started about 8:00 A.M., sure we could take our time, eat a fried chicken picnic lunch en route and arrive Friday afternoon before 5:00 P.M.," Maude remembered. "We would have all of Saturday and part of Sunday to catch up on the news."

The family thought of putting the top down but wondered if they could get it up in time if a sudden storm materialized. Also the car would have to sit in the sun and dew--if not rain--for the week-end. Getting the side curtains on and buckled would present enough of a problem without the added effort of erecting the top and locking it to the windshield supports, they decided. The top was left as it was, and the Williamses took off.

The car had a hand crank starter, a clutch pedal and a gear shift (as opposed to the Ford Model T, which changed gears solely via the clutch pedal). The transmission was not synchronized with the gearshift mechanism so only the most skillful driver could change from first to second speed, second to third, or place it in reverse without sending out a spine-tingling screech of clashing gears.

The gas-feeding lever was placed inside the car near the steering wheel. Clutch and brake pedals were located under foot, and every auto of the time had a hand brake at the right hand of the driver.

On its journey to Toledo, the car ran perfectly (even if the gears did grind horribly at almost every shift). Lee had no trouble with engine, carburetor, or tires. Directions sent by Maude's folks were easily read and apparently correct. The problem was the lack of road signs, their illegibility or their placement behind trees and shrubs or in out-of-the-way places.

Lee got lost twice. Even when he was on the right route, he had to stop at farmhouses to make sure. The kids became so restless that the picnic, under a tree at roadside, was staged early--at 11:00 A.M. Grandpa and Grandma Allen had a nice supper ready at 6:00 P.M. and had to place it in the warming closet. Their guests arrived two hours later. Apologies were made. Everyone ate a warmed over dinner and bragged on how delicious it was. And the Allens admired the new auto with its new car smell.

Lee felt lucky no punctures had occurred during the Toledo trip. When that happened, as it did frequently, the tire had to be pried from the rim, the inner tube removed, and the repair made by the motorist. Lee would pull the puncturing nail from the casing, lightly sandpaper the hole in the tube, apply some tire cement, attach the patch, and replace the still deflated tube in the casing. He used a hand pump to re-inflate the tire enough to stand high under the weight of the car.

Sometimes an inner tube was patched several times before being replaced. Life of the badly worn casing could be extended by placing a sleeve (or boot) between the tube and inner surface of the casing. The repair job sometimes took three hours or more--one of the more distasteful tasks related to owning a car. Discarded inner tubes could be inflated as swimming aids or appropriated--as Mardo sometimes did--to be fashioned into slingshots.

Most future trips in the car were to nearby communities where Lee knew the way. On one such trip (in the mid-1920s), he drove to a field near Zanesfield, Ohio, parked on a hillside, and for four hours the family watched a series of make-believe battles between Indians and Indian-fighters. The pageant was billed as "Isaac Zane Among the Wyandots," and had been planned by the Zanesfield community and historical groups for 18 months.

Hundreds of volunteers played the milling tribesmen, soldiers, and Indian scouts. Professional actors took the roles of major Indian chiefs and of Isaac Zane, famed Ohio Indian fighter after whom Zanesfield was named.

Thousands paid the 25-cent admission fee and lined the two facing hills to watch the epic unfold in the valley below. A commentator explained the action from a centrally located platform, his sonorous voice roaring through the strategically placed movable megaphone that he swiveled from side to side.

Audiences were swept into the action as the drama unfolded--as settlers battled Indians, as fires destroyed homes, and as captured scouts somehow survived "running the gauntlet" and the threatened "burning at the stake."

Some spectators were like Joe Early, a neighbor and friend of Lee's. He was so thrilled by the pageantry that he remembered pertinent details for months. Until late the following winter, Lee said, "You could not meet Joe--in town or on a rural roadway without being greeted by a stentorian, 'Isaac Zane among the Wyandots,' in almost exact duplication of the commentator's voice."

Each winter having a car presented its own hardships. Lee parked his first auto in the granary, keeping the side curtains on it. Otherwise, he said, he might go out one morning and find the passenger seats full of snow. Winds blew through the granary and under the doors.

Severe cold caused the oil to congeal in the crankcase so, despite Herculean efforts, he might be unable to turn the engine over. When he did succeed, the engine might backfire, tearing the crank from his hands. Luckily, he never suffered a broken hand or wrist bones as many did.

If the spark lever (manually operated) was advanced too far, the car wouldn't start; if not advanced far enough, the engine would backfire. So Lee made markings to make sure he got the spark lever right before he took hold of the crank.

One winter, the gas line froze. He had purchased some bad gasoline or the unpredictable weather variations had created condensation within the tank. He took the tubing from the car, heated it in the kitchen until he could blow freely through the line, then re-installed it on the car.

After every snowfall of four inches or more, he had to hitch his horses to the drag and clear the 500-foot lane--just to make sure his car wouldn't get stuck in pockets of snow (in the event he got it started). The county roads over which he traveled to and from town were just as hazardous, so he installed tire chains with the first snow and left them on until late February.

TWO

All-purpose tractors had gained acceptance by 1920. Lee obtained his one-cylinder Titan the next year and treated it like a cherished toy, Maude said. He would come in from the fields at night, exhausted by the ordeal of guiding the awkward-looking appliance around the rutted field.

The Titan was capable of pulling a gang of three 14-inch sod-breaking plows through all but the toughest jackwax (black clay). Its uniformly spaced out "chug," "chug," "chug" could be heard all day as Lee fought the manually operated steering wheel.

All wheels were of iron and steel. The front ones had ridges of metal circling the circumference so that when turning each corner, the wheels dug deeply into the soil. Supreme effort was required to change direction.

Lee became adept at lifting the plows and dropping them to resume plowing a few feet away, thus leaving the unplowed strips at each corner to be completed when the remainder of the field was done. He could plow three times as much land in a day as with a team, and the Titan replaced horses by pulling discs and harrows in the soil conditioning that followed.

Maude recalled the day he came stumbling to the house with blood on his hands. "I feared the worst," she said. "I thought he'd been badly injured." But it was their cherished collie dog--a second "Pal," named after the dog Maude had so loved during the early years of her marriage--that had stumbled beneath the tractor wheels in the newly plowed earth. The animal was crushed and died at the scene.

THREE

When they were married, Lee and Maude had no idea of the problems they would face, the troubles that would develop or the way that hardships would keep mounting. Like the young people of today, they had no experience on which to draw, yet their confidence never wavered.

Hardships became pleasures in disguise--"a challenge to our patience, thriftiness and ingenuity," Maude said. "We had everything we needed, and no indication there ever would be more."

When they added up the experiences, they found that they totaled a lifetime of living and loving.

"Sometimes just the living was almost too much. The children came too close together--17 months to 28 months. They had illnesses that left us tired and ill-tempered. And we had difficulty finding clothes for them all. The younger ones complained that they had to wear hand-me-downs and the older ones said they had to wear their clothing for too long a time," Maude recalled.

Things had to be worn out. Nothing was thrown away. Corduroy trousers and denim overalls were acquired for the males because they were long lasting. Toboggan caps, shapeless coats and knitted mittens were winter fare for all.

Maude remembered the time Mildred received the wrong tam from Montgomery Ward. It was returned three times before the purchase was righted. And Mardo thought he would be a style-setter at school with his white sweater from Sears. But when he donned the garment, it stretched to his knees. He got a replacement but it was almost as bad. Still, he wore it because nothing could be thrown away.

During one of the sieges of illness, five-year-old Mardo began walking in his sleep. Feverish, he walked into his parents' bedroom and announced, "I want some nails to fix the house." Earlier the family had been discussing the drafty house and wishing Uncle Forrest Newell had fixed some of the rattling windows and ill-fitting outside doors when he had done the other extensive repairs.

Luckily, few of the family's illnesses required services of a doctor. They were treated with home remedies and poultices. Horse liniment was good for sprains and muscle tension.

Ross Williams, Lee's father, swore that the root of slippery elm trees controlled periodic bouts of constipation and also helped regulate the digestive system. Strips of sarsaparilla root were boiled each spring to make a tea that acted as tonic to the winter-lulled body. Ross used both religiously and was never without a piece of the slippery elm in his mouth. It had a slightly bitter taste and could never be compared to the Wrigley chewing gum that was later to become so popular.

For years after Maude's hysterectomy, she plied herself with patent tonics and antacids for relief of what she said was a persistent stomach ache. She used an elixir from Hartman's of Columbus which was about 30 proof alcohol, Lee thought. Geritol became a standby, and at one time in 1921 she was using an over-the-counter product called Adler-Ika.

Mardo said he remembered the latter product vividly. The sixteen-year-old had obtained his father's permission to use the family car for a date with a neighbor girl. He was under heavy questioning by his sisters who insisted they had a right to know who the "unfortunate" girl was, inasmuch as the family auto was being used.

Mildred was persistent. Bea and Pauline argued that "we'll know eventually--why not now?" Their brother refused to answer. It was no time for such discussions while they were eating supper. Then he gave in. "Her name is Adler-Ika," he announced.

They found out later that his date was with Norma Kerns, daughter of a farm couple who lived three miles away. But for the remainder of the school term, Norma became Adler-Ika--to her mystification and Mardo's embarrassment.

Maude's reliance on stomach medicines eased off as her health improved. Still much in evidence in the Williams' larder were products that had been advertised during the latter part of the 19th century and would continue in use throughout the 20th century--castor oil, Lydia Pinkham's, Philip's Milk of Magnesia, Bayer Aspirin, Mentholatum and Vicks Vaporub.

The children had survived corduroys, button shoes, long underwear with drop seats, all the prevalent illnesses and home made remedies. They had experienced treatments with lard and kerosene compresses, castor oil, and asafetida (the latter an evil smelling concoction which was hung on a string around the neck to drive all germs--and friends--away).

They left behind such childish things as playing in the leaf piles, making clumsy kites (with thin strips of wood, rags, newspaper glued over the framework, and hoarded string), and watching the tumble bugs roll little mud balls down the lane.

The slingshots made with tree forks and rubber from the automobile inner tubes were being laid aside as were the make-believe flutes, fashioned from tender shoots of the willow tree. Winter evenings under lamplight in the living room with the family, popcorn, apples and a good book would never be forgotten, but would never hold the attraction they had as the children progressed through their teenage years.

In the early 1920s, the older children Mildred and Mardo went farther afield for their amusements--sometimes as much as 20 miles! Autos were still the butt of jokes. Their engines were unpredictable. The tires were inclined to puncture easily when they passed over nails (with deflating results). Many roads were of stone or gravel, and all were poorly marked.

Their parents agreed it wasn't unusual for a high school kid to leave for Russells Point or some other amusement center on a date and end up "lost" as many miles away in an opposite direction. The youngsters--bent on dancing, roller skating or riding the roller coaster--might have to be content with necking alongside the little traveled highway.

Mildred and Mardo and their dates liked especially to go to Russells Point on Indian Lake, 20 miles away. A carnival-like atmosphere prevailed. There was the roller coaster where for 10 cents a ride, the amorous young man could hug away the terror of his screaming companion as they plunged down the 40-percent grade. One could knock over the milk bottles to win her that coveted teddy bear. Or maybe show off manly strength by swinging a 10-pound sledge so forcefully as to ring the bell at the top of the tower.

If you tired of the games of chance, and still had some money, you could take a motor boat ride around the lake, or stop off at the bathing pavilion a mile out--with water all around. During holiday weeks and on other week-ends, young couples (like Mardo and Mildred and their dates) who couldn't afford the admission fee stood outside the dance hall and listened to the music of the era's big bands--Guy Lombardo, Glenn Miller, Tommy Dorsey--muffled somewhat as it was filtered through the building's boarded up windows.

Promoters were reluctant to let non-payers see or hear. What if they decided to dance for free on the rough pavement outside the hall? (Some did!)

A poor cousin of the Russells Point operation was that at Lake Idlewild, just two miles north of Kenton on the much-traveled State Route 31. A private side road, little more than half a mile in length, led to the pavilion. For a nominal fee--usually 50 cents each, $1.00 per couple--a person could dance all evening long (until after midnight) to some of the best local dance bands of central-northern Ohio.

The dance hall stood alone on a plot just east of the small lake which, during part of each day, served as a swimming and diving pool. The building was approximately 80 by 120 feet, with a walkway along both sides and one end. Wooden panels could be raised for cross-ventilation, lowered to block cold winds or rain. When open, as they often were, couples without the admission fee, or those with romance in mind, could park the car nearby and listen uninhibitedly.

Whenever dance hall operators Henry Pfeiffer and Harry Duckham advertised a dance, they were assured of a crowd. They had acquired a reputation for providing good music. And the hardwood dance floor was always in tip top condition--with no waxy buildup or stickiness.

Maude said her children also learned to roller skate when a rink was established in a large barn in Mt. Victory. The owner built an oval hardwood floor, stocked a supply of rental skates, and opened with a fanfare. Bea was less adept than the others, due to weak ankles, but all got much enjoyment out of going around and around, falling down now and then, and learning to sidestep the pileups.

"It looked pretty monotonous to me--all that exercise to wind up in the same place," Maude said. "But each of them saved their pennies and when they had collected 25 cents, they spent it at the roller rink."

Other activities of the teenage set took them to each other's houses to play charades, take part in sing alongs, compete in word contests, play games of the hostess's choosing (sometimes spin the bottle or post office--

kissing games at which some of the more strait-laced parents frowned). Birthday parties were infrequent, due as much to the large number who would have to be invited, as to the refreshments that might be expected. At most impromptu parties, invitation was by word of mouth; refreshments were popcorn, apples, and either lemonade or cider.

Mixed square and round dancing on the spacious Armory floor in Marysville (24 miles distant) and colorful masked balls in Kenton (12 miles away) several times a year were events that attracted all members of the family, with everyone making the trip in Lee's car.

The masked balls were a spectacle, Maude said, attracting 2,000-3,000 onlookers who came to gape at the 300 or so costumed persons who paraded around the large Armory Hall. The Logan sisters usually won first prize. They always came as a pair. One Valentine's Day they came as cupid and his quarry; one Halloween, as a witch and her cat.

In the 1920s, when the family drove up to Toledo to visit Harley Allen and his first wife Lydia, Lee and Harley would go to see the Toledo Mud Hens, a professional baseball team in what was then the American Association. There was no night lighting so every contest in the 10-team league was played during the afternoon. Rare double-headers might start at ten o'clock in the morning.

One Saturday, Lee and Harley walked in the door of the Allen home on Vinton Street after a four-mile hike from the Mud Hen stadium. It had been an important game near the end of the season and the stands were filled with noisy supporters of the home team. It was hot and fans verged on the violent as Toledo fell behind in the eighth inning. When the Mud Hens scored two runs in the last of the ninth to win on a walk, double and single, enthusiasm soared to near hysteria.

The outpouring of fans filled the available waiting street cars. There would be a long wait before others would arrive so Harley suggested he and Lee walk home. "It's not far," he said. "We'll follow the street car tracks and when one approaches, we can board it." But the loaded street cars passed them by--and the road home stretched ahead interminably, Lee thought.

He was accustomed to comfortable work shoes and his new store-bought shoes were tight across his instep. He loosened the strings, then the shoes rubbed up and down on his heels. He accumulated blisters, which burst. Maude treated his hurts, he swore off all physical activities during the remainder of the weekend, and nurse Lydia (Harley's wife at the time) bandaged his heels lightly before Lee and family started the drive home.

Lee had followed the careers of some of the legendary baseball greats, many as they worked their way up. Babe Ruth became Lee's favorite topic as "the Sultan of Swat" hit 54 home runs for the New York Yankees in 1920.

Lee grieved with fans when eight Chicago White Sox players were banned for life from playing professional baseball (1920). Commissioner Kenesaw Mountain Landis took action after critical grand jury evidence mysteriously vanished.

Players and gamblers, who'd been charged with "fixing" the outcome of the 1919 World Series between the favored Sox and Cincinnati, were acquitted. But Landis, the newly appointed baseball czar, thought it was a miscarriage of justice.

He reviewed the evidence and the day after acquittal, the eight, including "Barefoot Joe" Jackson, then were outlawed from the activity that the Commissioner said was "more than a game." He warned that when suspicion destroys a boy's faith in the honesty of baseball, "you have planted suspicion of all things in his heart." Lee agreed.

The family also journeyed to Kenton to see the Kenton Reds basketball team. For drama, Lee said, nothing held a candle to those games in the team's peak years, 1918-1924. The players were rough and tough. Their home games took place on the fenced-in ground floor of the armory. There were no time outs, no out-of-bounds, and spectators watched every act of wrongdoing from seats that circled the playing area.

Kenton had been leading the league of small city cage teams year after year, due to a combination of skill and violence--with perhaps some aid from the home town referees. Ralph (Joner) Jones was the captain and, at six feet, four inches and 280 pounds, a domineering figure under the basket. He relied on Ackerman, a compactly built former professional wrestler, to help in the back court. Every team member was adept at ball-handling so Lee (and even Maude) enjoyed seeing the running, dribbling, and passing.

Violence was a crowd-appealing bonus. Fouls were called infrequently, but always when a player had to be carried off the floor. Lee said the point-getting play might involve sending Ackerman (the former professional wrestler) down court to temporarily disable an irritating defender, or double-teaming the ball carrier against the encircling fence-- much like today's hockey players.

Joner Jones would sweep a path to the basket and, if he didn't score, one of his teammates--wading through the fallen bodies--would do so.

"The winning team usually had the biggest, toughest, most brutal players--unless that squad was made of fumblers and poor shooters," Lee said to his wife. Maude went with him a time or two, then found an excuse to say "no." The violence made her too nervous.

Today's games would be considered wishy-washy by the fans of yesterday--with too many whistle-blowing interruptions.

Part IX: The Children Leave for the City

For the first time in history, city dwellers outnumbered those living on farms.

ONE

*P*erhaps Maude's brother, Eugene, had given his nephew Mardo the incentive to try city life, the idea it was to be preferred over the rural environment. In 1915, he had promised that the 10-year-old would eventually get the college education of an electrical engineer. Eugene himself had electrical experience but no degree. He felt it was the coming thing and, in the meantime, had set up a board of battery-operated gadgets (transformer, telegraph key and switches) for Mardo's education and enjoyment at home.

The possibility of higher education was not mentioned after Gene died in 1918. Mardo wasn't interested in becoming an electrician although he welcomed the chance to leave the farm for Toledo that first autumn after his graduation from high school in 1922. His Uncle Waldo Allen had contracted to wire a number of houses for a builder and thought the 17-year-old could work with him to learn the trade, or determine that this line of work was not for him.

It became the first of a series of jobs that were used by the young man to save money during the winters and spend it during the summers, when he labored for free for his dad on the farm.

For four winters, he tried a variety of jobs--winding armatures at Electric Auto-Lite, wet-grinding transmission parts for Chevrolet, assembling Willys-Overland autos, and operating a punch press at Acklin Stamping Company--and liked none.

The time spent in Toledo dragged interminably for Mardo. He lived with grandparents Arthur and Nora Allen. Nora was quiet and retiring. Arthur seemed to take more interest in the young and, puffing on his corncob pipe, sometimes tried to carry on a conversation with Mardo, who had no young friends in the city and no inclination to bowl or go to the movies alone. He paid for his room and board, then tried to save as much of the remaining money as he could for the next summer's pleasures--with Geneva Ansley.

After the muskrat tail episode, the teenagers found they had much in common. They enjoyed life. Each had a good sense of humor. And Geneva had a rare trait of describing places and events in colorful language. Once, she tried vainly to recall the name of a businessman friend of her dad's. "You know him," she declared. "He walks like a duck."

She was right. The man, an electrical contractor in Kenton, hobbled around, leaving the impression that both feet had been cut off at the ankles (her description).

Mardo waited for Geneva's letters, wrote her in return, kept a semblance of romance going from 80 miles away, and disproved the skeptics of their time who insisted that "absence makes the heart grow fonder, of someone else!"

During the fall of 1924, he welcomed a break from the tedium of factory work when his uncle Harley invited him to a Ku Klux Klan rally and picnic near Monroe, Michigan. Mardo had read newspaper exposes about the Klan's reign of terror in Louisiana, the lynchings and the beatings of marked victims, and he went to the rally out of boredom and curiosity.

He wrote to his sweetheart describing the Klan bigwigs in full regalia, and the sense of relief he felt that Harley and his railroad friends (and some 2,000 more men) wore only their work clothes.

Harley seemed to be in charge of refreshments for his group and manned a grill to cook the hot dogs. Klan officials gave no long-winded speeches and made no serious efforts to enlist the non-members.

The Ku Klux Klan, founded in 1866 to oppose reconstruction and terrorize blacks and their friends, had been reorganized in 1915. It was active against minority groups (Blacks, Catholics, Jews, and immigrants) as well as against birth control, pacifism, Darwinism, and the repeal of prohibition. By the mid-20s it had four to five million members and contributed to the 1928 defeat of Presidential candidate Alfred E. Smith, a Catholic.

Mardo never knew if Harley was a Klan member or just a visitor to the 1924 gathering. After the Michigan rally, Mardo expressed an aversion to the Klan's activities. Harley made no attempt to enroll his nephew, nor did he propose another Klan event.

Harley wanted Mardo to become a railroad man like himself and insisted, on what was to be Mardo's last employment in the Lake Erie port city, that he seek a job with the New York Central Railway. There were no openings for firemen, switchmen or brakemen so Mardo became a boilermaker apprentice at the roundhouse, a menial job, despite the title.

The giant locomotives were sent to the roundhouse at the end of a certain number of operating miles, placed on the turntable, and routed to an unused area adjacent to water, steam, and compressed air lines. While the skilled boilermaker did the more interesting jobs, Mardo or another apprentice worker would enter the firebox, from which the ash and clinkers had been removed, and clean the series of pipes that surrounded the combustion area.

These pipes extended from one end of the firebox to the other. They passed through the boiler, transferring heat from the fire to the water. The steam would build up 90 pounds of pressure, or 150 pounds, or the recommended pressure to drive the engine, propel the train at the desired speed, and operate safely.

When soot lined the flues--as it always did after a certain number of operating hours (fewer when a poor grade of coal was used)--the heating efficiency went down dramatically. The fireman had to shovel more coal, and more frequently, to maintain the necessary steam pressure.

Controlled air pressure was used to rip soot from the walls of the flue. It spread a black dust throughout the enclosed area. Mardo wore a kerchief over his mouth and nose, a hat on his head, and a long-sleeved shirt. He rode the street car home, looking like an old-time minstrel man, and was shunned by the other passengers.

Harley and his wife Lydia, with whom Mardo stayed, never complained about the black ring on the bath tub or the occasional smudge on the clean sheets. But after Mardo quit his job that spring to return to the farm to help his dad, Uncle Harley didn't ask him to try out for another New York Central position.

TWO

Twenty-year-old Mildred married John Perry in 1923, right after John's 21st birthday (August 20). The couple moved to an apartment in Marion, Ohio, where he had recently started factory work as a machinist.

Mildred was much like her father, Lee. She was a smaller replica, a sprightly waif with brown eyes, dark complexion and a tendency to laugh at the most absurd things at inopportune times. She liked a joke--any joke. She thought life was a game that should be played with enthusiasm, even when the outcome could be deadly serious.

Her husband John was more solemn. He was darker-skinned than his wife; his eyes were almost black, as was his hair. They were each the foil of the other, became the perfect hosts--even of those who tried to take advantage of them.

Mildred told of one such incident. She and John had taken Robert Hill and his girlfriend of the moment to a movie in Kenton. John reached the ticket window to order tickets for the party of four--and found that Bob had made himself scarce.

Young Perry paid for the tickets, even hauled Bob and his date back to Ridgeway at the end of the evening. "We skipped supper after the show," Mildred laughed. "I was afraid we'd have to pay for their meal as well."

Neither Mildred nor John liked living in Marion. They had no friends there. Mildred became homesick and had to return to the farm each weekend. John developed a mystery illness. He blamed the fuzz on some peaches he had eaten, until his wife's physician said husbands sometimes were stricken with the "morning sickness" during early weeks of their wife's pregnancy.

The young couple moved back to Ridgeway, the little village that straddled the Hardin-Logan County border, close to parents and lifelong friends. John returned as a mechanic to the Ellza Limes Ford dealership and garage. And son, Harold Eugene, made his debut on April 17, 1924.

Mardo was the next member of the family to leave. He and Geneva Ansley were married on September 15, 1926. They joined her father, Morton E. Ansley, in a four-bedroom house on Kenton's South Main Street. The town, population 7,000, was 12 miles from the Williams' farm. Geneva had just quit her job as secretary-typist at the Runkle Candy Co. Mardo was working as carpenter's helper at the Toledo & Ohio Central car shops in Kenton, where railroad boxcars were rebuilt. Geneva's teenage sister Eunice lived with them and attended high school.

Car shop operations shut down in January 1927, and Mardo lost his job. Married for only four months, he was looking at four blank walls, with a wife to support. Geneva decided to take advantage of his unexpected availability by doing a complete house cleaning. And husband, looking for a way out, answered an ad on the front page of the *Kenton News-Republican*, a county seat newspaper.

In essence, the request was for a reporter. No experience necessary, it said. Knowledge of English was mandatory and some experience in typing would be helpful. So Mardo, with enough typing skill from his brief night course at the Tri-State Business College in Toledo to bolster his confidence, applied. He was hired at a starting "salary" of $8 per week (with no fringe benefits). He reported for work at 7:00 A.M. the next day.

The city editor, who was the son of the publisher and had never been on a reportorial beat himself, took Mardo to the courthouse, told him the Sheriff's office, the Clerk of Courts, and Probate Court would be primary sources of daily news and left him to carry on. "Just pick up what news you can," he said, "and come back to the office to type it for submission to the composing room. I'll make any necessary revisions."

Mardo soon extended his rounds to every office in the courthouse, sought personal news as well as public news. He wrote of decisions in Probate and Common Pleas Court cases, property transfers, marriage licenses, arrests, civil suits and criminal actions.

Once in 1927, during his early weeks, he was present for the assignment of cases in the new term of court. In a hurry to meet the 3:00

P.M. deadline for the four o'clock press run, he made a mistake which went--uncorrected--through the city editor. He was mortified when the publisher, who had the added role of proof reader, stopped him. He displayed galley proof and news copy reporting the "assignation" of cases and, with a sly grin, questioned his embryo reporter just how that was to be accomplished.

As Mardo became more proficient in typing out the basic lead of "who," "what," "when," and "why," he expanded his daily rounds to City Hall, the police and fire departments, the funeral homes, and the Chamber of Commerce. Because he was the only reporter, he assumed the responsibility of covering the bi-weekly City Council meetings and the monthly Board of Education sessions.

Of course, with only one reporter, the paper was missing stories and everyone was eager to tell him about it. He was sometimes scooped by Karl McElroy, the reporter on the rival *Kenton Daily Democrat*, who was one of the first to gloat. Mardo was happy when Karl accepted a job on the neighboring *Marion Star*.

During Mardo's first few months, he found it an ordeal to go out, introduce himself, and then write a story that was not always approved by the person interviewed. When he reported that a prominent farmer had committed suicide, he alienated his widow and daughter for life. The fact was correct, but the surviving family had an aversion to the word "suicide." They thought that "ended his life" would have been kinder or, even better, just the notation that he "died."

One day when feeling disappointed with his progress at the Kenton paper, Mardo received an unexpected compliment from Frank C. Ransdell, the superintendent of Ridgeway public schools when Mardo was a student there. "You're in the right profession," Ransdell told him when he saw him on the street. "Your description of a make-believe Keel's Island during your senior year was the most vivid writing I have ever read."

Mardo covered the Scioto Marsh onion laborers strike, the train wreck at neighboring Dunkirk which killed 14 passengers, the fiery crash in which five prominent Kenton women, returning from a luncheon in Lima, sideswiped a truck they were attempting to pass. One victim was the wife of Judge Hamilton E. Hoge of Hardin County Common Pleas Court.

Mardo was on call for all emergencies. His name was listed with law enforcement agencies and the fire department so he was sometimes called out of the house at night to cover breaking local stories. He became a stringer (correspondent) for every metropolitan newspaper in central and northwestern Ohio (including the Columbus *Dispatch, Citizen*, and *Journal, The Toledo Blade, The Cleveland Plain Dealer, The Lima News*, and *The Marion Star*), and for one wire service, the International News Service (now defunct). He was even pressed into service to set his own type when he wanted a larger headline or a style that couldn't be set on the Linotype machines.

When Lee asked his son how he liked newspapering compared with farming, Mardo said he appreciated the independence of farming but he'd grown to love news reporting for the opportunity to meet the people who make things happen, the feeling that he was among the first to know about accidents, scandals, and intrigues in the community, and the knowledge that he could write a better story about the incident than anyone else could! (You'll notice that modesty wasn't one of his shortcomings!)

He was a reporter in its various aspects, copy desk, travel editor, featured columnist--for nearly 44 years. Even when he returned to the factory for three years during World War II, he continued to work four hours a day at the *News-Republican*. He was employed on the late afternoon-evening shift at the Lima Tank Depot, worked through the night when rush orders for tanks and armored vehicles came through--and never missed a partial day of work at the newspaper.

When he was called to Columbus in August, 1945, to interview for a position on *The Columbus Dispatch*, he was earning some $130 per month from outside sources as a stringer--more than he had ever made at the Kenton newspaper.

He started on the *Dispatch* at $60 for a five-day week. When he argued that figure was too low, the editor agreed he would be paid an additional sum for working Saturday nights to help get the Sunday edition to press. He may have been the last reporter without a college degree hired by the *Dispatch*

Mardo told his parents that the change to "Ohio's Greatest Home

Daily" was not nearly as traumatic as his Kenton debut where he had to learn to write newspaper-style (concisely, graphically, and without editorializing), seek out his own sources of information, and develop stories through interviews and legal records. In Kenton, he had never received "canned" information or public relations handouts about a company, club activities, or personnel changes as he did in Columbus.

At the *Dispatch*, he observed, he would not be able to set up his own headlines on the Ludlow machine--as he had done on rush days at the Kenton paper. The *Dispatch* labor agreement prohibited any composition work by a non-union employee.

Editor George A. Smallsreed, Sr. started him on the Copy Desk, the proving ground for experienced newsmen who might later be moved to other positions. There would be no beat--no legwork, no assignments, an activity he missed more and more as he specialized in editing another's articles and writing headlines.

He used those first months to study manuals on various facets of the newspaper, learn its writing style, and improve his ability to tell the major message of the story in skeletonized English at the top.

Later, the role of travel editor was added to his duties and, in 1954, he became a reporter on a business beat, instructed to write articles about the city's growing business and industrial establishments, develop personality sketches about their chief executives, and compile a list of contacts.

He became a stringer for the *Wall Street Journal*. He substituted for Business Editor Robert N. English when Bob had a day off or went on vacation. And he developed his own daily business-financial column, with picture and byline, in which he was allowed to make editorial comments about business trends.

He wrote about major established firms, their operations, products, and personnel, and "covered" many trade organization events. Yet, he told his parents, he never felt as much "in the know" as he did in Kenton. However, he never considered going back. He had rejected an offer in 1946 from the new publisher of the *Kenton News-Republican*, Edwin S. Rutledge, to return as his next-in-command.

THREE

In 1927, when Mardo joined the Kenton paper, he had no idea it would be a lifelong career. He needed the work. Money was in short supply. Geneva's father paid the $30 a month rent for the house they shared. The young couple paid $10 a month for milk as their part of the household expenses, and Geneva did all the housework.

Their living standard was helped two years later when Mr. Ansley was elected sheriff. Daughter Geneva was appointed matron of the Hardin County Jail during his two terms (1929-32), was paid a salary and gained a small return from feeding the prisoners at 25 cents per meal. She and Mardo lived at the jail-residence for four years and received their board and room "free."

Bea became the third child to leave the Williams farm home. In 1925, she had headed for Toledo and a secretarial job with the Ohio State Life Insurance Co. Wilbert A. (Buck) Deerwester, a schoolmate, was working in Toledo at the Acklin Stamping Company. They had been close friends at school, were contemplating an even closer relationship.

Beatrice, the prettiest Williams, had blue eyes, dark blonde hair and a peaches and cream complexion. She was a slim five feet, five inches tall. Husband Buck was swarthy. His weight varied between 180 and 200 pounds on a five feet, ten inch frame. Bea was friendly and helpful in a quiet, unassuming way. Buck could be affable, even flamboyant. But sometimes he was moody, envious of another's good fortune. He was protective of Bea and frequently complained the rest of the family didn't really appreciate her.

Bea and Buck decided they should get married, pool their pay envelopes, and purchase a home. They were married without fanfare--no close relatives were invited or even notified that a wedding was in the offing. And on their wedding day--January 21, 1929--they later told their friends they were in both the Hardin County Home (a home for the aged, where Buck's parents were superintendent and matron) and in the County Jail (where Bea's sister-in-law Geneva was matron). They were just visitors--part of a surprise visitation to notify relatives of their marriage. Maude felt hurt that the child she had coddled during her illness-plagued childhood had not told her in advance. After all, she could have kept the secret!

Pauline, the youngest, left the farm for Kenton in 1929 to help her sister-in-law Geneva with housekeeping and cooking duties at the County Jail. A quiet service on June 18, 1930, united her and Sonny (Lauren) Ansley, son of the Hardin County Sheriff. Pauline became the fourth child to wed a Ridgeway schoolmate. Maude wasn't present at the ceremony but at least she knew about it.

Sonny and Pauline made a striking appearance. She was dark, with brown eyes. He had blue eyes and a ruddy complexion. He was almost six feet tall, thin as a whip in his younger years; Pauline was five feet, two inches tall and, although she usually weighed less than 115 pounds, looked rather buxom. It was her body type. She felt she always had to diet.

Sonny was the dominant one, certain he was always right, and somewhat of a daredevil when he drove a car. Pauline danced a good Charleston. The bobbed hair, the long waists and short skirts of the Flapper Age suited her. Like her dad Lee, she was a people-pleaser.

In late June, Lee hosted an after-the-fact bachelor party for his newest son-in-law. The two collaborated. Lee cleared the woodshed, set up the table, provided the accessories and arranged for Maude to make a supply of her cottage cheese, known as the finest in the county.

Sonny brought luncheon meats, cheese, and a keg of beer. Prohibition wouldn't be terminated until 1933, but Sonny, who was commissioned as a special deputy sheriff, had made the necessary arrangements with an illegitimate supplier of the illegal beverage.

About 40 uncles, brothers, brothers-in-law, cousins, and close friends (all males, of course) congratulated the newlywed, ate his food, drank his beer--and after the keg was empty, made a boisterous exit.

When Lee began to clean up the mess the next day, he found porch furniture overturned and lawn chairs high in a pear tree. He knew that Sonny's brother-in-law, Norris Richardson, had done it--his reputation had preceded him. When Lee next met Norris, he told him the furniture was still up in the tree and requested his help in getting it down!

Sonny operated back-to-back service stations on the parallel Kenton streets of South Main and South Detroit. During the second year of his marriage, he decided that low volume gasoline service stations would remain unprofitable for the small operator. He took a job as mechanic's helper at the Ohio Machine Tool Company in Kenton and learned the machinist's trade.

He and Pauline made almost weekly trips to the farm to help Maude with the cleaning and Lee with necessary repairs.

With the children all married and gone, Lee and Maude began to socialize more. Maude, in her late forties now, dressed up for these events, usually wearing simple dresses with straight skirts ornamented with a belt and a string of beads. She liked to wear a wine turban-like hat that rested jauntily to one side. With her high cheekbones and deepset eyes, bobbed hair, the hat gave her an air of mystery, a look like Garbo.

Maude and Lee were frequent guests at the jail-residence. They regularly played Euchre at the kitchen table there with Lee's sister Dawn and her husband Roy Ansley, brother of Sheriff Morton Ansley.

Roy was the perfect foil for Dawn's acerbic wit. He was good-natured. His response was measured, as befitted a ponderous man who weighed twice as much as his spritely spouse. And when he made a point, his rolling laugh invited all to join in.

They loved each other and, in good voice, were the life of the party. She would attack; he would respond. They aired many of the plaints of married life, without getting angry. She told of clothing scattered about, he of soiled dishes left in the kitchen sink. No one took the blame for the stain left in the bathtub or lavatory. One or the other would let the children run wild, fail to set out the bottles for the milkman, lock the door so the iceman couldn't deliver his product.

They argued about the muddy tracks across the just-cleaned kitchen linoleum, the doors left open to the flies in summer and the cold in winter. They had rehearsed a routine, as much for their own enjoyment as for entertainment of their listeners, and everyone recognized some of their own failings as they listened.

Dawn and Roy were best friends. They were inseparable. What troubled one affected the other. Lee and Maude thought them the ideal couple and joined them whenever possible--for dances, cardplaying, picnics or simply conversation.

Eight-year-old Maude with brother Waldo (approximately 1891)

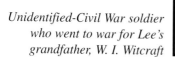

Unidentified-Civil War soldier who went to war for Lee's grandfather, W. I. Witcraft

Maude Williams
at 28 years old.

Lee Williams at age 20, when he was attending Ohio Wesleyan University

Lee's parents,
Rawson and Sarah Williams (1912)

Maude's mother,
Lenore Wilson Allen
(approximately 1920)

Lee and Maude Williams with children: Mardo, age 3; Mildred, age 5; and Bea, age 18 months

Mardo, age 5; Pauline, age 1; Mildren, age 7; Bea, age 3 (approximately 1910)

Mildred (standing) and Bea (on pony)

Farm of Lee and Maude Williams where they lived their entire married life. The house, the first non-log cabin in the area, was built by Lee's maternal grandfather, William Witcraft in 1854

Ross and Sarah, the 7 children and their spouses (about 1917): Front Row (left to right):Roy Ansley, Dawn Williams Ansley, Lee Williams, Alice Williams Marmon, Blanche Manson Williams, Herman Williams; Middle Row: Margaret Williams Newell, Neola Williams Engle, Sarah Williams, Maude Williams, Rawson Williams, Amanda Williams Smith, Hut Smith; Back Row: Forrest Newell, Harry Marmon, Will Engle

Reunion, fall of 1909 at the family home of Rawson and Sarah Williams (Amanda and Hut Smith family not pictured); Front Row (left to right): Ross Engle, Bill Engle, Lucille Ansley; Middle Row: Herman Williams, his wife Blanche, Dawn Ansley (wife of Roy) holding Ronald; Back Row: Will Engle, Neola Engle, Velda Engle (In front of Neola), Forrest Newell.

Reunion photo, continued. Front Row (left to right): Mildred Williams, Clare Engle, Ralph Engle, Bill Newell, Mardo Williams. Middle Row: Maude holding Pauline, Alice Williams (married Harry Marmon later), Margaret Newell, Roy Ansley. Back Row: RawsonWilliams, Sarah Williams, Lee Williams, holding Bea.

Students and parents in front of Spice Wood Glen School (approximately 1910). Pictured left to right front row: Ross Engle, Ralph Engle, Mildred Williams, Velda Engle, Edith Williams, ?, Stewart Richardson, ?, Beatrice Williams, Mardo Williams, ?, ?, Teacher, Bessie Hill. Center row, standing: Will Engle, Jr., Clare Engle, Ruth Richardson, ?. Back row: Grandpa Ross Williams, Harley Allen, Maude Williams, Lee Williams, holding daughter Pauline, Alice Williams, Grandma Sarah Williams, ?, ?, Neola Engle, ?, ?, Blanche Williams, ?, ?, Herman Williams, ?, ?

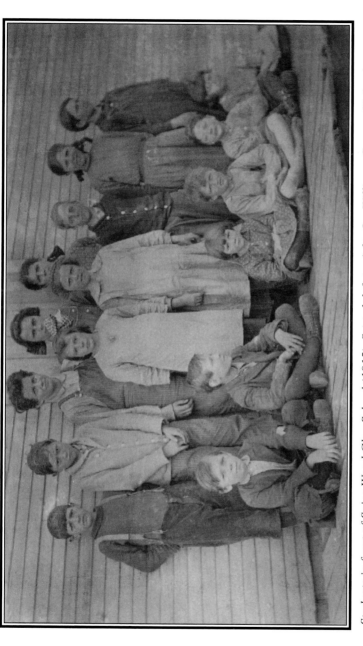

Students in front of Spice Wood Glen School (1915). Seated, left to right: Ira Williams, Stewart Richardson, Pauline Williams, Glenn Keller; Mardo Williams, Beatrice Williams; Standing, center row: Mildred Williams, Velda Engle, Charles Marmon, Jr., Bertha Fields, William Engle, Jr.; Back row: Paul Fields, Olen White, Clare Engle, Isabel Marmon, Iva Fields

Graduating class of 1922, Ridgeway High School: Back row: Mardo Williams; Teacher, Mrs Schwartz; LaMotte Mayle; Ethel Hatcher. Seated: Mary Krouskop, Oten White, Mildred Williams, Bob Hill and Marie Whetsel

Lee, age 41, and Mardo, age 18, in oats field (1923)

Lee and Mardo (on the hay), Bea (driving the team), Pauline (standing) (1923)

*Campfire Girls:
Mildred Williams, Vyrtle
Keller, and Geneva
Ansley (1920)*

Bea Williams and Geneva Ansley at Indian Lake (approximately 1924)

*Geneva Ansley, Buck
Deerwester, and Bea Williams
in Toledo (1925)*

*Mardo Williams and Geneva
Ansley in Toledo (1925), the
year before they were married*

*Pauline Williams Ansley (with Eddie), Geneva Ansley Williams, Bea Williams
Deerwester relaxing on Rush Creek (1932)*

*Mardo Williams
and Geneva Ansley
(1925)*

*Pauline Williams
Ansley (1930)*

Sonny Ansley (1930)

Bea Williams Deerwester (1929)

Buck Deerwester (1929)

Lee and Maude at home (1928)

Bea Deerwester standing by their first car, a Model A Ford with rumble seat (1929)

Alice and Harry Marmon (recovering from TB) en route to the Williams family reunion (1932)

Maude and Lee Williams in front of their farm-house (1932)

Dawn and Roy Ansley (1929)

Art Conaghan and
Lucille Ansley (1929)

Dawn and Lucille
Ansley (1947)

Morton Ansley,
taken while he
was sheriff (1930)

*Eunice Ansley
Held (1935)*

Eunice (1990)

Four generations: Rawson Williams with son Lee, granddaughter Mildred, and great grandson, Gene (1928)

Four generations: Sarah Williams (holding great grandson Eddie Ansley), with son Lee and granddaughter Pauline (1933)

Williams family (1934): Mardo, Bea, Maude, Lee, Mildred, and Pauline

Grandchildren (1944): Front Row-Joe Ansley, Jerri Williams; Back Row-Eddie Ansley, Kay Williams

Family Reunion: left to right: Mardo Williams, John Perry, Mildred Williams Perry, Pauline Williams Ansley, Maude Williams, Lee Williams, Geneva Ansley Williams, Lauren Ansley, Bea Williams Deerwester. Grandchildren, left to right: Ed Ansley, Gene Perry, Kay Williams, Jerri Williams. Joe Ansley is seated in front between Gene's knees (1942)

Maude and Lee's five grandchildren: Joe and Ed Ansley, Gene Perry, Kay and Jerri Williams

Maude and Lee Williams
at age 60 and 61 (1943)

Lee and Maude, Phoenix visit (1948): Gene Perry, Lee, John Perry (Mildred's husband), Mildred, Maude, Isabel (Gene's wife)

The Perry's: Gene, Mildred, Maude's Great-Grandson Billy, John, and Gene's wife Isabel (1950)

The Williams' family: Mildred, Pauline, Mardo, Maude, Lee, and Bea (1952)

Harley and Norma Allen, Maude and Lee Williams (about 1954)

Brother Harley with Maude at her 100th Birthday party (1983)

*Maude at 89
(1972)*

*Brother Waldo Allen
at 84 (1972)*

Maude, in her 110th year. Antique chiming clock in background.

Maude enjoying her 110th birthday party, despite the pain from her broken leg. Granddaughter Kay Williams is beside her.

When Lee and Roy won at cards--which was frequently--they were inclined to kid their wives unmercifully. On this hot summer night, the two couples were seated around the kitchen table in the jail where they were visiting Geneva and Mardo. The men had divested themselves of all unnecessary clothing and were mopping their brows. Roy commented that this was the hottest room he'd ever been in. It was tough being in jail, he laughed.

They had exhausted repartee about the lack of fans and cross-ventilation when Lee added the final touch: "Yes, even the cupboard doors are closed." The two men laughed uproariously, as Lee opened the cabinets to get more air. It was a wonderful joke, or maybe, as Dawn and Maude thought, it was more humorous because the men were two-thirds of the way to inebriation.

Sometimes son Mardo received free passes from the Kenton *News-Republican* to wrestling and boxing matches. They were staged every two or four weeks during the fall-winter season in the Hardin County Armory at Kenton.

Maude accompanied her husband to Kenton and visited with daughter-in-law Geneva while Lee and Mardo watched the fights (or the grappling) from ringside. Roustabouts set up the squared circle in the center of the ground floor during the afternoon of the evening match. Each performance--and they were viewed as performances by Lee--attracted 400 to 500 spectators. They surrounded the ring, or sat in bleachers on each side.

The boxers were not as good, or as big, as the heavyweight greats like Jack Dempsey, Jess Willard, Max Schmeling, Jack Sharkey, and the other world champs up to that time, but they provided a lot of drama.

"Dad seemed to enjoy watching the fans as much as the action by the paid principals," Mardo told his mother. Alex Simms, a welterweight from Canton, Ohio, was his favorite boxer. He wasn't afraid to mix it up, carried the fight for the eight-round or 10-round distance, usually won and was re-booked with another contender. And Lee was there to cheer him on.

Simms was so good at his role that fans got involved on the sidelines. They would feint, swing arms, or grimace--all to Lee's huge enjoyment.

His favorite spectator was a little, gray-haired, 70-year-old woman. She fought as violently as any boxer, twisted so intensely that she almost tied herself in knots during the wrestling matches--and probably was tired enough, when the overhead lights faded, to drag herself home to 12 hours of sleep.

Lee finally learned the name of his favorite fan. She was M.A. Littleton, the owner-operator of a two-story boarding house on South Main Street, Kenton. He never met her, but in his mind she became "Ma" Littleton.

The boxing-wrestling matches ended with the bankruptcy of the promoter.

FOUR

Maude's brother Harley continued to seek Maude's counsel long after he'd wed Lydia Freund, the nurse, whom he'd met in 1918 while a patient in a Toledo hospital for treatment of an infection. Harley and Lydia for a time were constant visitors to the farm. They would arrive on a Friday night and stay until Sunday--enjoying Maude's cooking and Lee's repartee.

They frequently brought some libation, which pleased Lee. Maude would kill a fryer and express regrets that she had nothing different to cook--a hint that went over their heads. After all, she served what they were looking for--fried chicken, mashed potatoes, pan gravy, and coconut pie with hot rolls, coffee or iced tea.

When Lydia and Harley divorced several years later, she accused him of being subject to drinking spells which placed his job as New York Central Railroad fireman-engineer at risk.

Harley thought she was seeing other men. They had been bickering for years. He would miss work and was reprimanded once for drinking intoxicants on the job. He would come home to find her visiting with a male attendant from the hospital where she was employed.

FIVE

After Geneva and her husband Mardo started living at the County Jail in 1929, Harley and Lydia found Kenton a nice stopping off place on the way from Toledo, and it made for interesting conversation with Harley's railroad friends and Lydia's nursing associates. "We spent our week-end in the Hardin County Jail," they'd say.

One time Harley convinced Geneva it would be a treat--and he would pay for the entire meal--if she would just roast a raccoon for him. He would acquire and dress the animal and provide her with an approved recipe.

She consented, against her better judgment. After all, Harley was goodhearted--and persistent. Meantime, he had another conversation with Frank Arter, the Kenton fire chief who was a sort of gourmet cook. Arter had been cooking a variety of meals for the firemen when they were on 24-hour duty and recently had been acclaimed for his raccoon dinner at the firehouse.

Arter agreed to purchase the 'coon from a hunter friend, have it dressed, then provide Harley with a sure-fire recipe. On the Saturday of the feast, the raccoon arrived in the jail kitchen only half cleaned--and it looked very unappetizing to the chef.

The meat was dark. The carcass, without fur, looked like a small dog. But Geneva cut it up, marinated the pieces, and when ready for the oven, applied a flavoring sauce, tenderizer and a blanket of sauteed onions. The cooking fragrance filled the big brick residence area and adjoining jail offices and cells.

"When we sat down to eat," Geneva remembered, "only Harley bragged about the meat, and even he refused a second helping. It was black and stringy, with a strong gamey taste. Most of it was left. Even the prisoners said, 'No, thank you,' when offered a portion of Harley's gourmet delight."

Maude's brother gave Geneva no more suggestions. The family returned to eating the same foods prepared for the jail inmates, basic meat and potatoes dishes--with the addition of desserts or special dishes Geneva arranged solely for the sheriff's table.

The Hardin County Jail was two stories tall. In the front were the sheriff's living quarters, with four bedrooms on the second floor. Mardo and Geneva shared one, Pauline and Sonny another. Morton Ansley, the Sheriff, took the bedroom at the top of the stairs. The fourth bedroom was occupied by Mort's youngest daughter, Eunice, then 18 and a senior at Kenton High School. Also on the second floor were a large living room and bathroom.

At the back of the building was the jail, with two floors of cells, a detention cell for women and juveniles, and a holding area for prisoners in isolation. Geneva and her assistant Pauline did the cooking and laundry for residents and prisoners alike--a hectic undertaking, but not dangerous. Most prisoners, arrested for drunkenness, burglary and passing bad checks, were not violent.

Inmates usually complimented the jail matron and her assistant on being wonderful cooks, but one man, being held on a burglary charge, found fault. He remembered the meals he was served while growing up in the mountainous area of Kentucky and demanded that lard be substituted for butter or margarine. Another asked for raw onions with every meal.

The Williamses recalled some humor from jail experiences via the son and daughter-in-law. Geneva swore it was untrue but the story went around that when an escaping prisoner dashed past her through the partially opened steel door, she shouted--even as he crossed a schoolhouse yard 300 feet away:

"Come on back. You're going to miss your supper!"

Sheriff Mort Ansley, her father, was unconcerned. He said the escapee was being held on a minor charge and would have caused major expense if he had gone to trial, or if the county had been compelled to pay his way back to the hills of Kentucky.

The sheriff effected a comparable savings during that same summer, Maude and Lee were told. A laborer in the Scioto Marsh onion fields near McGuffey (a resident of the mountainous area of Kentucky, as were many of the marsh workers) was awaiting trial on a multiple intoxication, disturbing the peace, and resisting arrest charge.

Mort had been trying to talk him into going back to his home state, thereby saving Hardin County the cost of the trial. The evidence was marginal, and the prisoner was demanding that the county pay for his return.

Sheriff Ansley solved the stalemate to the satisfaction of all. He instructed a deputy to fill the gas tank of the man's junk car and park it along Carroll Street at the side of the jail--with keys in the ignition. Then he sent the man out to mow the jail lawn, unsupervised.

The law officer looked out a few minutes later to find the lawn uncut and the car missing. Luckily, the escapee left the lawn mower behind. Like the man who fled earlier, he also missed his supper.

The eldest child of Lee's sister Dawn and Roy Ansley liked to visit her cousins in jail. Lucille was a voluptuous young woman, five feet, five inches tall, weighing 120 to 125 pounds. She was dark complected, with flashing brown eyes. She could never refuse a dance invitation, liked to play cards, was generous to a fault, and had a kind word for everyone.

She and Art Conaghan had been an item for five years. He was an inch shorter than Lucille and weighed only 115 pounds. Despite his smallness, he was an ebullient Irishman.

A perpetual joker, he once arrived for a date with "Janie"--his pet name for Lucille--and told her with a straight face that his one-hour delay was because of having to open all the chain letters he'd received. He brought two with him to show the $1 in each, and bragged that he was due to become very rich.

One time Art and Pauline's husband Sonny Ansley, the sheriff's son, decided to cross-dress and surprise the women. Lucille was visiting her cousins, Geneva and Pauline, at the jail. All were duly impressed by Art's debut as a woman. He had shaved closely and was of a slender build, able to wear Lucille's dress and fall coat.

Sonny was less presentable. The two men agreed to take a chance and attend the afternoon movie in their costumes. All went well, seemingly. They had returned to the jail and discarded their feminine attire when Police Chief Oliver D. (Doc) Sheldon stormed in. He told them they had broken the law, threatened to throw them in a cell and, finally, warned them not to attempt such a prank again.

The Chief may have recognized the culprits from the movie house's first report of the "suspicious characters" and decided it was a good opportunity to make a point with the young set.

There was no animosity. The Chief and the Sheriff remained on good terms, due to the friendly temperaments of both.

Sheriff Mort was neighborly, Maude said. Anyone who called at the jail residence at meal time was invited to sit down and partake of food--whatever it was or how little of it there was.

His daughter, the matron, might protest that he became more like his father James R. Ansley every day but it had no effect. James R. was known in his early 80s for that same trait--and for planting a big garden, harvesting more than five families could eat, then distributing the surplus among all the widow women of Ridgeway.

One fault Geneva found with her father was his inability to discard the "lucky" older things for the new--especially when it came to clothing. She would confer with Sheriff Mort before going through the clothing in his closet, then toss away the unneeded things.

"Mysteriously, they would always be back when I started to clean house the next time," she said. "If Dad didn't bring them back from the incinerator, his trusty, Bud Banks did."

The sheriff had a particularly decrepit looking top piece which he termed his "lucky hat." "I slipped it out to the incinerator and lit the fire," Geneva recalled. "Before I got back to the house, Bud had rescued it. When Dad saw it on Bud's head, he reclaimed it. I gave up," Geneva said.

During Sheriff Mort's tenure, Lee and Maude heard one story about the Kenton jail which may or may not have been true. The contraband seized during the prohibition years--from illegal distilleries and from vehicles transporting the alcoholic beverage--was stored in the basement at the sheriff's jail-residence as evidence. After each case was tried, Common Pleas Judge Hamilton E. Hoge would order the bailiff to pour the liquor down the drain.

Somehow, the story went, the county's riff-raff learned that hundreds of gallons of moonshine whiskey were being destroyed. For a time, no one knew why a dozen men--and a woman or two--were lined up along the bank of the Scioto River. Then investigators determined the group was at the spot where the jail's storm drain emptied into the Scioto River. They were waiting with empty containers for a draught of the potent water.

SIX

Prohibition, which endured through the 1920s and ended in 1933, was welcomed by some, resented by others. It never was very successful. There were too many loopholes and too many opportunities to cheat. The drinker might convince his doctor that he had to have his before-dinner highball or a little dollop just before bedtime to ease his worries, let him get a good night's sleep. And the physician could prescribe a pint of commercially distilled liquor for medicinal purposes once every week or two. The prescription was filled and filed, the pharmacist never questioning the doctor's judgment.

During this period, rum-running became big business. Organized mobs controlled transportation and distribution--even some of the production--as the public made a game of sneaking into illegitimate clubs for illegal drinks. Al Capone's gang took over the Chicago trade and held on violently until federal agents put Al away for tax evasion.

Makeshift distilleries proliferated--one went up in a farm building eight miles from Lee's and Maude's farm--and prospered until Sheriff Morton Ansley raided it, demolished the still, and arrested the operator. Sheriff's deputies watched the highways for autos so heavily loaded that their tires were almost scraping the body. Approximately one of every three cars stopped under those conditions was loaded with moonshine, the sheriff told Lee.

Stills were operating full tilt in the mountains of Kentucky in 1929, with much of their output being sent north to bootleggers in Toledo, Columbus, Detroit, and Cleveland. Kenton, at the intersection of south-north Route 31 and east-west U.S. Route 30, was a popular rest stop for autos loaded with moonshine until word was sent out to avoid Hardin County because of over-zealous law enforcers.

Locally, prohibition made little difference in the lives of most farm people. They had no money to buy the refined product (distilled in a commercial distillery), even if they could obtain a doctor's prescription, didn't like the taste of the cheaper white mule (a corn liquor from the bootlegger), and would never set foot in a nightclub.

Kenton and Hardin County law enforcement agencies sometimes had to pool their forces to quell intoxication related disturbances. Even staid citizens seemed to relish the idea of breaking the law that they considered undue restraint of their rights. Police and sheriff's deputies moved in only when celebrations got out of hand, or neighbors called to complain about the noise or fighting.

A few of the more boisterous were arrested week after week. They would congregate each Saturday, pool what money they'd been able to earn from odd jobs during the week, purchase rotgut whiskey or cheap wine, and wind up in jail that night. Most would promise to do better, make arrangements to pay court costs, and go free on Monday (to do the same thing that next weekend).

Al Lightner, one of the repeat offenders, seemed to take an arrest as a challenge to his manhood, Kenton Police Chief Oliver D. Sheldon said. The result frequently resulted in a scuffle between him and the law enforcement officers. One time, Deputy Sheriff Wilbur Mitchell made the arrest, brought Al to the Hardin County Jail, and led the muscular, 190-pound man to the cell block--where Al concluded he didn't like the idea of being locked up.

Jail matron Geneva Williams watched nervously as Mitchell and Al wrestled back and forth on the 12-by-20 foot apron leading to the open jail door. The lawman assured her he could handle it, no need to call for help. The contest between the two evenly-matched combatants raged for 30 minutes or more before the breathless deputy sheriff pulled his blackjack and threatened to knock out his prisoner if he didn't pass through the jail door on his own two feet.

"I'll never do that again," the deputy told the matron--and the interested inmates, who had watched the struggle through their jail bars. "If I have to bring in a prisoner alone, and he resists, I'll coldcock him first and drag him through the jail door."

Another frequent resident during those boisterous times was Bud Banks. The 220-pounder would be arrested about once a month on a misdemeanor charge of drunkenness or disturbing the peace. His fine was small--but he never paid it. He liked the food at the jail, and the aura of trust that always greeted him. The sheriff installed him in one of the women's detention cells and welcomed his help in serving the meals to prisoners and overseeing the housekeeping in the cellblock.

Very few locals patronized the only known nightclub in the area, which offered illegal booze and gambling. It operated on the second floor of a downtown Kenton commercial building--until agents arrested five out-of-town racketeers during a poker-playing week-end, with thousands of dollars on the table. The resultant publicity forced the closure of the establishment. Its poker tables, roulette wheels, crap table and other equipment were confiscated.

Shortly after that, another gambling enterprise was discovered in a remodeled barn on a farm six miles east of Kenton. The operator was arrested and the gaming accessories ordered destroyed.

During the summer of 1930, as Sheriff Ansley began his campaign for reelection to a two-year term, rumors spread that slot machines were making their appearance in the outlying villages. Adding to the concern was a report that a Kenton High School teacher was going into debt playing the one-armed bandits at a cigar store-poolroom in McGuffey, west of Kenton.

When sheriff's deputies investigated, they could find no evidence. The operator, if there was one, had picked up the machines and vanished. Store owners denied any knowledge of any slot machine activity.

The rumors persisted during the election campaign. Prosecuting Attorney M.B. Underwood, running for re-election, told the sheriff that he thought the innuendoes should be answered. Time after time, Underwood denied knowledge of any criminal activity. His protestations engendered distrust--where there's smoke, there must be some fire, his critics thought. He was defeated at the polls in November.

Sheriff Ansley ignored the issue as being raised by persons with an axe to grind--by the opposition party with a view to electing its own officials. Wisely, he refused to react, explaining, "It's like s---! The more you stir it, the worse it stinks." He was reelected for a second term.

The fourteen years of prohibition created a sense of rebellion among the youth, who experimented with the banned product. It was a wonder that more did not die from imbibing the illicit liquor that poured from makeshift stills, operated by ignorant persons, with only immediate profit in mind.

Mardo drank some white mule once, on a trip to the summer resort town of Russells Point, on Indian Lake. Pat Lane, a school mate at Ridgeway, had bought a half pint from someone's favorite bootlegger, and passed it around to his friends in the car. Each took a swig--Pat, Ed Perry, Bob Hill, and Mardo--then another drink, to keep from being the party pooper. The four teenagers (all were 18) never tried it again. It was too bitter, and the boys had just heard about the man who died after drinking a similar distillation--it had been laced with wood alcohol, a poison when taken internally.

Drinking raw corn whiskey and smoking were linked in Mardo's mind as illicit but not much fun. He had once sneaked out of the house with matches and smoking materials--corn silk and newspaper wrapping--and lighted up. He concluded that even with real tobacco, smoking would never be a favorite activity.

SEVEN

Maude recalled that her son and daughter-in-law were giving a lot of thought in 1932 about leaving the jail-residence. Sheriff Ansley's term would end in January, 1933, and he was prohibited by law from serving more than two terms. Geneva would lose her role as matron, with its salary, room and board. "Dad was more concerned about us becoming homeless than we were," Geneva said at the time. "And he did something about it."

The Great Depression was well under way so the sheriff started watching for distress sales of properties that were being auctioned to satisfy mortgage claims. Finally, he made his recommendation. A two-story house in the near-downtown of Kenton, only a short block from Mardo's job at the News-Republican, might be a bargain.

The place had some disadvantages. The lot was very small, with little space for lawn. The New England style, two-story house, with its pillared porch, was solidly built but was in a state of disrepair. It needed a new roof, and paint inside and out. It had no garage. It was too large--with four bedrooms, a bath and a sun room upstairs; a formal dining room, large living room (12 by 20 feet), huge kitchen with no cupboards, and a laundry room downstairs. The basement held only the coal-burning Farquahr furnace with its five-foot long firebox.

"It's a good time to buy," the sheriff told the couple, "and it's being sold at auction to satisfy a debt to the Home Loan Savings Company. There may be no others who can come up with the cash payment required and you'll get a bargain," he argued.

So they entered a bid, obtained the property for $2,000 cash and assumption of the $100 past-due real estate tax, and took possession late in 1932. When they moved the following April--after Sheriff Wilbur Mitchell had designated the new jail matron--contractors had installed a new roof, hardwood flooring over the rough pine boards, a wall and paneling over the open stairwell at one end of the living room, and a small garage in an open area between the street and the glassed-in laundry room.

Plumbing fixtures were added--toilet and laundry tubs plus a new kitchen sink downstairs, and a completely new bathroom upstairs where a wall had been moved to enlarge one of the four bedrooms. The kitchen also boasted of a new work-bench with upper and lower cabinets along an entire wall.

"Geneva and I stripped the interior walls of wallpaper and did all the painting, to save money," Mardo remembered. "When Kay was born on November 3, 1933, we convinced ourselves it was a new home, especially built for her arrival." It had cost $2,100 to buy and almost $2,500 for materials and labor to improve it.

The young Williamses were living in it when Jerri was born on May 4, 1938, and left it on November 11, 1945, to move to Columbus where Mardo was embarking on a career with "Ohio's Greatest Home Daily." They pocketed a gain of nearly $3,000 when they sold it and were able to buy a three-bedroom home in a suburb of the Ohio capital city.

EIGHT

The Volstead Act, which was designed to wean an entire generation from the harmful effects of John Barleycorn, had been of doubtful value. Critics blamed it for creating a multitude of lawbreakers.

In 1933, with the Act repealed, the nation's citizens established a perfectly legal industry of brewing their own beer for home use. Mardo bought equipment and supplies--so did his dad. The operations were modest--each sought to bottle a case (24 bottles) or less at a time. "We were never able to produce a palatable brew," Mardo said. "It was too strong of malt or hops, so yeasty that the cap had to be removed very carefully to keep the sediment at the bottom of the bottle from spreading throughout. More often than not, the bottle was opened above the sink so the pressure-driven overflow would not stain the carpet or upholstery."

He has forgotten the recipe but it involved malt (a thick, molasses-like mixture sold by the can, usually bought from Blatz), a leaf or two of hops if you wanted a lighter-textured brew, plus yeast, a teaspoon of corn syrup to speed fermentation. An earthenware jar and bottle-capping equipment also were needed. Mardo used the two-gallon size jar and said he could rely on 18 bottles of product despite losses from skimming flotsam off the top, or an occasional bubbling over as the mixture "worked."

"You could not dip the brew and funnel it into the bottle without stirring the sediment," the home-based brewer noted. Any agitation would result in a cloudy mixture so full of spent yeast that additional fermentation might tear away the cap, or even break the sturdy glass bottle.

So every two-gallon jar in which the nutrient-rich liquid was fermented had a spigot inserted about a half inch above the bottom. Through it, each bottle was filled to within one and one-half inches of the top a day after the "brewmaster" had failed to find foam atop the mixture. That indicated the yeast had completed its task.

The filled bottle was topped by a metal cap similar to those used on soda bottles. The brew "cured" in the bottles and was ready to drink in a week or ten days. The taste improved if kept longer.

Geneva never liked the home-made brew; Mardo considered it of inferior quality--so difficult to make and to drink without imbibing unwanted yeast that he discontinued his production after five batches. Before that, however, he served it to a group of young people at his and Geneva's house-warming party in 1934. A dozen guests congratulated him on the unique taste of the brew, which he took as a compliment until he followed Charlotte Ansley (wife of Ronald) into the cold night air and found her vomiting into the shrubbery at the side of the porch.

An after-effect of the brewing venture was the publicity engendered. Five-year-old daughter Jerri, who wasn't born until 1938, blatantly told her Sunday School teacher, Mrs. Ollie Magann, an ardent Prohibitionist who had just warned about the evils of beer and all intoxicants: "My dad drinks beer. My mother drinks beer. My sister drinks beer. My whole family drinks beer."

Geneva said the family hadn't had an intoxicant in the house since Mardo had abandoned brewmaking in 1935. His one attempt at producing wine was a failure, she noted. The sticky mass of crushed Concord grapes, sugar and water had boiled over during fermentation, the soured foam at the top had spread an irritating aroma throughout the house that lasted for two weeks, and the resultant wine was both bitter and sour.

"We should have realized we had no taste for wine," Mardo commented later. "We had tried the dandelion and grape wines produced by Geneva's father, and never liked them."

The couple crossed wine off their shopping list, and beer was "partaken of" only at the St. Nicholas Hotel where a combo played soft music in the evenings, and where cousin Jim Ansley, Roy's and Dawn's son, was a temporary bartender.

Part X: Hard Times

"Some will rob you with a six-gun,
*Some with a fountain pen."**

ONE

*I*n April, 1928, Maude was called to Toledo to be at her mother's side during her last illness. Nora Allen had been treating a chronic stomach illness, but this was much more serious. The doctors discounted the possibility of cancer and determined, after her death in May, that near the last she'd suffered internal hemorrhaging from a ruptured blood vessel. She may have had an aneurysm for years, Maude was told in an effort to ease her feelings of guilt that she might have done more to make her mother's last weeks more comfortable.

Maude remained in Toledo to help brothers Waldo and Harley arrange for burial of their mother at the side of her son Gene in Forest Cemetery. Maude had been gone a little more than six weeks. When she returned home, Lee had trouble adjusting to her changed appearance.

She'd been a 45-year-old brunette with a gray hair showing here and there when she left to nurse her mother. Now she was an attractive white-haired woman. The ordeal of taking care of the pain-stricken woman who literally starved to death in those final days had taken its toll.

*PRETTY BOY FLOYD

By Woody Guthrie

© Copyright 1958 (renewed) by FALL RIVER MUSIC INC.

All Rights Reserved   Used by Permission

This was the beginning of a 12-year period of heartache for Lee and Maude. One tragedy followed another. The Mt. Victory bank failed just before the disastrous New York Stock Exchange debacle in October, 1929. The bank closed its doors in the midst of rumors that the officers had been guilty of mismanagement, making loans to each other without collateral, and even actual fraud.

Lee's father, Rawson W. Williams, became a land-rich pauper. His life's savings were in that bank--money that the 81-year-old farmer had hoarded to assure peaceful security for both him and his 79-year-old wife in their later years. When the bank was liquidated two years later--with the depression fully under way--he was repaid 15 cents on the dollar. He got less than $1,800 for the slightly more than $12,000 he had saved.

Lee said the amount his father lost would have constructed in the early 1930s the finest three bedroom, six-room brick house with full basement in the area. "And it would have been fully furnished." A modest six-room brick house in the area today (1995) would cost between $100,000 and $115,000, without furnishings.

Ross was devastated. He had known--and done business with--those bankers for 50 years or more. Henry J. Dickinson, the president, was a personal friend. He defended them, termed the closing just a mistake, and insisted that "Henry will make things right."

But Henry was indicted, went to trial and served a term in prison, as did some of the other officer-directors. There was no deposit insurance in those days and no adequate way for depositors to collect their losses from directors or stockholders.

Franklin D. Roosevelt would attempt to correct some of the banking system's failings in the early years after he became President. The first move came in March, 1933, when he ordered all banks closed, the financial condition of each studied, and only those which met the criteria permitted to reopen. Hundreds were forced out of business until they could reorganize with adequate resources. Some never made it.

Another development increased Maude's and Lee's woes. In January 1929, 25-year-old Mildred contracted a severe head cold and sinus infection. It held on stubbornly. This was long before antibiotics. Her nose was so stuffed up, she found it difficult to breathe. The Mt. Victory doctor said he didn't know what to do. A popular remedy at that time for chest colds was a mixture of kerosene and lard applied to the chest (without the lard, the kerosene was corrosive and could blister the skin). The doctor finally suggested Mildred pack her nostrils with kerosene-soaked cotton. She followed his prescription. She regretted it the rest of her life.

The infection spread to her bronchial tubes and lungs. Unable to clear it up, the country doctor advised the couple to seek a warmer, drier climate. His mandate: Leave Ohio's miserable fall and winter weather or run the risk of Mildred's early death from pneumonia and congestive heart failure.

Her condition became worse during the next year. Bronchiectasis was brought under control but she developed an asthma that left her struggling for breath. So in October, 1930, the three Perrys, John, Mildred, and six-year-old Gene, loaded their Ford touring car with all the possessions they could haul.

They left their Victrola with Lee and Maude, wept a little and started West. They liked Denver, but it was too cold, too damp, and too high. They ended up at Phoenix. Only later did Mildred realize that the kerosene had drained down her throat and vaporized in her lungs, inflaming her bronchial tubes and causing irreparable tissue damage and scarring.

While Mildred and family were en route to Phoenix to seek relief for her illness, Maude and Lee were stunned by the murder of Roy Ansley, the husband of Lee's sister Dawn. It was October 26, 1930, and they were at the Ross Williams' home for the family reunion when they heard the news.

The day had been planned as an important occasion for Ross and Sarah, marking their 59th wedding anniversary (October 26); Ross's 82nd birthday (October 10); and Sarah's 80th birthday (October 12). Roy and Dawn had planned to be there.

The news was incomplete. It spread a pall over the gathering. Was Roy the victim of a robber? He was such a friendly, compassionate man that no one could visualize him as victim of a planned assault. The bountiful covered dish dinner went largely untouched. The group disbanded somberly. Lee and Maude took off for Kenton to comfort the widow and see if they could do anything to help.

"We learned that no one could have anticipated the events that led to his death," Maude said.

The night before the murder, Roy's daughter Lucille had been at a loose end. It was Saturday night. Her boy friend, Art Conaghan, was in Tiffin, Ohio, visiting his parents. Lucille knew her parents, Roy and Dawn, would be dining out that evening--and "people watching" around the busy downtown area of Kenton, where they frequently met Mardo and Geneva Williams.

Roy Ansley and his niece Geneva, Dawn and her nephew Mardo were more than relatives. They were close friends. They enjoyed each other's company. On these occasions, the two couples always window shopped and socialized with town and farm families from throughout Hardin County. The four often walked home together, since Roy refused to drive his two-seater Ford touring car downtown and take up a space that should be reserved for out- of-town shoppers

Lucille, on her way to meet a woman friend at the Sugar Bowl--a popular soda fountain-confectionery just off the square, thought she might see her mom and dad and Geneva and Mardo sitting on the low balustrade that surrounded the courthouse, which occupied the entire square formed by Columbus, Franklin, Main, and Detroit Streets. It was a convenient place to rest and converse. She didn't see them and didn't seek them out, but hurried on to meet her friend.

As she did so, Roy and Dawn, Geneva and Mardo idly chatted. They sat in front of the courthouse and watched the passing parade. Roy was laughing about having been in the Les Howe meat market when one of the employees playfully "goosed" another, and the victim almost jumped over the counter. Roy said he couldn't resist the temptation. He made the clucking noise that usually preceded the act, then joined the other customers in laughing as the over-sensitive man leaped a foot off the floor.

Roy was a little shame-faced when he ended his story. And Dawn didn't show any mercy. "You should go back and apologize to him. He has to put up with that kind of treatment from fellow employees--he shouldn't have to fear the customers."

Taken aback by the onslaught but not completely cowed by his critical wife, Roy replied with a sharp rejoinder: "Mom is starting to show her age," he said. "You know, she's in her 50s and I'm only in my 40s." She was born May 19, 1880, and he was born the following February. She had passed her 50th birthday five months earlier and, understandably, was a little sensitive about it.

This jolly, slow moving man and the vibrant little woman couldn't remain angry with each other for long and were laughing when the four separated to continue home.

In the meantime, Lucille and her friend, a Miss Ramge, had window shopped, discussed the latest news on who was getting married, who divorced--and then decided to take in a movie if management had a replacement for the one they'd already seen.

Lucille's choice of that evening's activities was the most momentous decision she would ever make. It would change her life as she had known it, terminate her vivacious, fun-loving attitude and transform her into a fearful, guilt-ridden woman. For the present, she was happy and carefree.

She and her woman friend greeted acquaintances, looked in the store windows, found they both had seen the movie but bought a bag of popcorn anyway. As they were debating their next move, a car pulled into the crosswalk in their path. They were only casual acquaintances of the two men, but accepted their invitation for a cruise around town.

What could go wrong? This was an era of innocence. Families left their doors unlocked. Children were not experimenting with drugs. For most, it was a time of abstinence--liquor was illegal. And criminal activity in rural areas like Kenton was virtually unknown. Besides, there were two of them, the women must have reasoned. They could fend off any unwanted overtures.

So the four took off in the early evening of October 25--two unmarried young women in their mid-20s and two personable young men of the same age who, it became known, had previously been arrested (one for auto theft). A sense of unease developed as the pleasure ride proceeded. The young men, at first covertly, then openly, drank from a bottle of bootlegged whiskey.

Apprehension mounted as John Johnson, the driver of the car, drove recklessly through the crowded streets, while his companion Jimmy Willis, spoke of plans to commit a robbery in the nearby town of LaRue.

"We thought at first they were joking--just trying to get a rise out of us," Lucille said. "Then we saw the handle of the revolver Jimmy was carrying. I started thinking of some way to escape."

They were hostages. The men insisted the girls accompany them on the crime spree; refused to let them leave the car. It was about ten. Lucille knew her folks would be home preparing to retire. So she agreed to accompany them if they took her home to tell her parents she would be out late. It was a ruse that almost worked.

As Johnson slowed the car to a halt in front of the Ansley home, Lucille tumbled out, ran terrified through the unlocked front door, and dashed up the stairs, warning her dad that Jimmy Willis was outside and he had a gun. He helped her through the bathroom window to a hiding place on the roof. "Stay out of sight no matter what happens," he warned as he prepared for whatever was to come.

The *Kenton News-Republican* wrote that after Miss Ansley left the car, Jimmy Willis forced Johnson to accompany him into the Ansley home at 317 East Ohio Street. Johnson called to Lucille to come down, that Jimmy wanted to talk with her. Johnson, testifying that he was frightened, dashed up the stairs, through the bedroom and out the window. Before leaping from the roof and fleeing, he warned the family that Jimmy had been drinking and he had a gun.

Roy asked Dawn and son Jim to enter a bedroom and shut the door. Then he met Willis near the top of the stairs. They struggled for the gun and Ansley was shot in the hand, in the abdomen, and near the heart. He died at 7 A.M. Sunday, October 26, the day he and his family were to have attended the anniversary celebration for his wife's parents. Dr. R. G. Schutte, who operated in a vain attempt to save his life, said death was due to internal injuries, shock and loss of blood.

Willis, who had been wounded in the leg by one of the bullets from his gun, hobbled down the stairs and drove Johnson's car away. Miss Ramge had fled on foot when the gunfire started.

Roy had been a bluff, good natured man--30 or 40 pounds overweight--who delighted in teasing his diminutive wife Dawn. She was barely five feet, four inches tall, weighed 115 pounds, and secretly enjoyed the joshing while sternly reminding her 225-pound mate he was completely out of line.

Dawn also liked to hear off-beat stories--frequently told them herself. She had a sly sense of humor, and a way of needling her closest friends. This became more apparent in later years, as demonstrated when her husband's niece, Geneva (Mardo's wife), proudly displayed her new mink stole--a gift from her husband of 35 years.

"What has he been up to now?" she demanded. Everyone laughed.

"We were stunned when we heard of the shooting," Geneva said. "Mardo and I had just left Uncle Roy and Aunt Dawn an hour earlier." The message had been called to her father, Sheriff Morton E. Ansley (brother of the victim), within minutes afterward. Geneva, as matron of the county jail, was then left alone to answer the phone, steer complainants to the proper law enforcement agency as other crimes developed throughout that night.

Her husband Mardo and Sonny Ansley, her brother, who also lived at the jail-residence, were sworn in as special deputies to aid in the investigation.

"No one was certain where he'd fled after the shooting," Mardo said. All five members of the Kenton police force were on the streets by 11:00 P.M. that Saturday, seeking the two men (Willis and Johnson) or the get-away car.

"Officer W. H. Thomas and I were sent to the E.M. Willis home (Jimmy's parents) on East Carroll St.," Mardo told his wife later. "I didn't know anything about self-protection so I stood directly in front of the door as Patrolman Thomas knocked. He then stepped aside, but I was unarmed and a perfect target if the gunman had fired a shot through the door."

Luckily, the parents answered the police order to "open up," and led officers to the bedroom where Jimmy lay semi-conscious with a bullet hole through his leg. The charge that had passed through Roy Ansley's hand had also penetrated his assailant. An ambulance was called and the man--later to be charged with murder--was taken to Kenton's San Antonio Hospital, under police guard, and treated.

Geneva had endured the long night with only her teenage sister Eunice and sister-in-law Pauline at her side. She was notified shortly after 7:00 A.M. that Uncle Roy had died in McKitrick Hospital. As soon as breakfast was served to jail inmates, she and Pauline led a small contingent to the

Ansley home. "We didn't want Dawn, her daughter Lucille, and son Jim to return to a blood-spattered home," she said. So the group washed down the bathroom, sponged off the walls upstairs, and mopped up the floors.

The furniture, which had been upset or shoved around during the struggle, was rearranged. "When we finished, there was no indication that this had been the scene of violence," Geneva said.

Roy Ansley was held in high regard throughout the community. A newspaper headline read: "Entire Community Bows in Respect to Slain Citizen." Hundreds of relatives, friends, and Roy's fellow employees of the New York Central Railroad thronged the First M.E. Church, where his body rested. The church overflowed with baskets of flowers. Hardin County commissioners ordered every office in the courthouse to close on Tuesday afternoon, from 2:30 to 3:30, the hour of the funeral.

Three days after the shooting Willis was released from the hospital to the custody of Sheriff Morton Ansley, the victim's brother. He was placed in a special cell after Sheriff Ansley received a warning the murderer might be physically harmed by other prisoners. The sheriff transferred the defendant to the Allen County Jail at Lima, Ohio, when he heard rumors that friends of Roy were planning to rush the jail and lynch the prisoner.

When that died down and he was returned to the Hardin County Jail, Jimmy told his defense attorney, Roy Warren Roof, that jail personnel were intentionally harassing him by banging the metal food utensils against prison bars. Mr. Roof decided against introducing that complaint at the trial since it might put Willis in a worse light.

Court habitues said they had never witnessed a speedier prosecution. George LeRoy Ansley was shot about 10 P.M. Saturday, died at 7 A.M. Sunday. A special grand jury was seated Sunday and returned indictments that afternoon.

Arraignments were held the following Wednesday and both defendants pleaded not guilty--Willis to two counts of first degree murder (one for premeditation and one for killing while committing a burglary); and Johnson for burglarizing an inhabited dwelling (a lesser charge because he would testify against Willis).

A deal was made with Johnson. For his testimony against Willis and a guilty plea to a lesser charge, the prosecutor would recommend to the judge that a lighter sentence be imposed.

Willis, "who had been in several scrapes with the law," according to the *News-Republican*, appeared at the arraignment proceedings on crutches, and with his right leg bandaged. His defense centered around the premeditation charge as well as the burglary charge. "It was an accident," maintained Defense Attorney Roy Warren Roof. "Jimmy had no intention of killing anyone--he just wanted to be with Lucille, with whom he was entranced."

In his words, Willis contended it was all a mistake. "I went to the home simply to see Lucille for I was crazy about her." There was no criminal intent--"I just wanted to talk to her," he reiterated.

Jurors determined otherwise after a week-long trial. He was found guilty on both counts and sentenced to life imprisonment. He died in 1993.

The trial did not end Lucille's trauma. This tragedy led to the break-up of the romance between her and her longtime friend Arthur Conaghan and made her fearful that some sort of reprisal would be made for her role in the conviction of Jimmy Willis for murder.

Lucille never married. She told Art she could not desert her mother, who'd just been widowed. And she became the "mother hen" for a group of older women--making plans for them, hauling them in her car to social events and carefully making sure that no one was left out. She wore her sadness quietly. Mother and daughter lived together until Dawn died at age 89--the specter of the dead husband and father always between them.

TWO

"The 1930s were a bad dream," Maude said. "One year worse than the next." Still mourning the murder of Roy, Maude prepared to welcome Arthur Allen, her sick father. He'd been living with Waldo in Toledo most of the time since his wife's death. Now lonely for his daughter, and ill with what he thought was colitis, he returned to the rural environment from which he'd sprung--expecting miracles.

He fished in Rush Creek through the summer of 1932, helped as he could with garden work, and ignored as far as possible the increasing pain in his lower intestine. When he died on a bright October day that same year, Lee and Maude attributed his death to compaction of the bowels, kidney failure or anything except cancer of the colon--which it might have been. For cancer was of unknown origin and anyone who died of cancer in those days was an object of suspicion.

Arthur Allen's death triggered the only major rift in the Allen family. Maude and Lee, with her brother Harley agreeing, made arrangements with the Mt. Victory undertaker for the services. Waldo, the older son, made a surprise visit to the mortuary, loaded the body of his father in an ambulance and took it back to Toledo. He left it up to the Mt. Victory undertaker to notify Maude and her younger brother Harley of the drastic changes being made in their funeral plans.

Maude didn't attend the Toledo services. Neither did Harley. Waldo said he had legitimate reasons for his action. Arthur had requested he be buried beside Nora, who had died a few years earlier. And Waldo had maintained a small insurance policy on his father, adequate to pay for burying him beside his wife.

Maude was shocked by the arbitrary way in which Waldo disrupted plans for the service. Brother Harley was so angered he carried a grudge for the rest of his life. Both conceded their father should be laid to rest at the side of his wife, but they resented the older brother's failure to notify them of his plans as well as the way he engineered the surprise "snatching" of the body.

"He never called to tell me of his sorrow or his decision to hold services and burial in Toledo," Maude said. "We knew nothing until the funeral director asked us if we wanted to hold memorial services anyway. We said no. And started notifying friends and relatives of the change in plans."

Waldo said he never thought his action would be so disruptive. After all, he would use his father's insurance to pay for the burial; the gravesite was paid for; and Arthur Allen had spent most of his life in Toledo where many of his friends and some of his relatives resided.

The estrangement between Maude and Waldo lasted for over 30 years.

THREE

Ross Williams, who'd lost most of his life's savings in the Mt. Victory bank failure, felt betrayed by his friends there. He lost much of his vitality, his interest in life. He became bedfast in 1933, with Rose Summerfield as his live-in nurse. He died that year at age 84. His wife, Sarah, followed him two years later.

Although a large part of their substantial land holdings had come from Sarah's parents, the Witcrafts, Sarah had spent her life in the shadow of her husband. She was a quiet little woman about five feet, five inches tall and weighed 108 pounds at the most. She was self-effacing, helpful and generous, Maude said of her mother-in-law.

"I recall one hospitable gesture you could rely upon. In her first words, she would offer you a cup of coffee, which I learned to refuse." The beverage came from the large gray granite coffee pot which always sat on the back lid of the wood-burning range. She would add coffee and sometimes egg shells to the grounds in the pot. This was supposed to save coffee, which cost 48 to 50 cents a pound, and enhance the flavor.

The pot was cleaned once every five or six weeks, and the cycle started over. "She was a wonderful lady," Maude declared, "but her coffee was just too bitter."

FOUR

Some prices plummeted during the Great Depression to levels below those of the early 1900s when some cuts of beef sold for 10 cents a pound and ground beef, when available, was three pounds for a quarter, Maude remembered. The new autos were being sold for from $500 to less than $1,000, according to make and style.

"If we needed them," Maude said, "we could buy eggs for 44 cents, milk for 14 cents, bread, nine cents, bacon and round steak each for 42 cents per pound." Usually, store-bought products were paid for with Maude's butter and eggs.

A Hart, Schaffner & Marx men's suit cost $29.50 in 1931; Old

Granddad Whiskey was $2.99 a fifth in 1935; Libby's baby food, three cans for 25 cents in 1936; and if you chanced to be in New York City in 1937, you could get double cocktails at Rockefeller Center for 25 cents each or have dinner and entertainment at Billy Rose's Cafe Manana for as little as $1.00.

Maude and Lee, who contended their life was much the same during good times and bad, marveled at depression prices, yet had no available cash to take advantage of any bargains.

Hard times didn't daunt the inventors or the entrepreneurs, she said. The jet engine was invented. Tractors with rubber tires were introduced. Instruments were perfected to guide planes taking off, landing, and while in flight. Spam was developed. Nylon stockings replaced silk ones. President Franklin Roosevelt's "New Deal" placed its alphabet agencies in operation to provide both work and direct relief to the unemployed.

Drought beset rich farming areas of the Midwest and Northwest. Winds tossed the rich dust high in the heavens and spread a pall across much of the nation east of the Mississippi River. It was so dense in spots that the sun shone through only dimly.

During one of the more difficult periods of the depression-era drought, prairie farmers sent out a call for harvest hands. The wheat crop was at risk from Missouri and Kansas to the northern Dakotas. Laborers were needed who would follow the combines from south to north, from start to finish.

Francis Perry, Ridgeway, the brother of John Perry (Lee's and Maude's son-in-law) had returned from one such harvest with the resolve never to go again. It was too hot, too dusty, too few amenities, and too little rest for the makeshift crews trailing across the limitless flat lands. He was single and unemployed so when another appeal for workers was made, he reconsidered.

Francis hitchhiked out of Ohio in the summer of 1934, according to brother John. The next word came from law enforcement officials in Kansas City, Missouri. Francis had been picked up as a transient and placed in a holding area atop the Kansas City jail. During the night, he fell five stories to his death.

There were few details. A banker friend said there were suspicious circumstances surrounding the tragedy and suggested that a member of the family investigate. Francis's father was dead, his mother ill, and family members scattered. No one had the money for the trip so simply requested that the Hardin County sheriff make inquiries.

The only elaboration: Perry had no luggage, no visible means of support. He had swarthy skin, wore a heavy beard. His clothing was soiled and torn. He had been picked up with the intent of sending him on his way the next morning. Was he tossed over the railing during the night by others in the holding pen? Did he fall accidentally? Was it suicide? No one learned anything.

Maude said, "He was not a troublemaker. He'd never threatened to take his own life. We didn't think anything like this could happen to someone we knew."

At that time, more than half the states in the U.S. had laws to keep out the unemployed. The International Workers of the World, termed the "I Won't Work" Party by its detractors, was trying to organize farm workers and there was a fear that people in America were thinking of revolution.

Farmers were getting next to nothing for their grains, a condition aggravated by overproduction. Crop subsidies were authorized in the 1930s, to the quiet opposition of Lee and Maude and many smaller operators. They viewed the program as just another political ruse to aid the large farm owner with work-free cash for land he already was leaving unplanted.

"It will saddle the government with another costly agency, with its complement of bureaucrats who can't make a living elsewhere," Lee told Maude. "They will tell us what to plant, when to plant it, how to harvest it, where to store the product, and how much we will get for it.

"The program will tend to create ever larger farms by ever richer people to make possible ever larger payments," he contended. "It will spell the eventual elimination of the small farmer and our right to make our own decisions."

Lee was led into the crop subsidy program, protesting all the way. The agricultural agent, who measured his fields, insisted he had to comply if he wished to sell his crops to the grain elevator. Twelve of the 53 acres on his farm currently under cultivation were to be set aside--eight in the tract that was being planted to corn; four from the proposed wheat field.

"I couldn't leave a 12-acre tract fallow," Lee said. "The agent insisted that one parcel had to be from the corn field, the other parcel from the wheat field. It would have been too simple to combine the two in one plot." So he swallowed his misgivings, agreed to sow legume crops (hay) on the idle land, and signed the agreement. The subsidy payments would vary-- from $5 per acre that first year to $10 or more as grain surpluses mounted. So he had much more hay than he could sell, or give away. He let the fields lie fallow and used them as pasture land.

"I found myself waiting for the subsidy check, planning in advance what I would do with the lump sum $60 or $100," he said later. By the time he went on Social Security, the payment for not planting corn or wheat almost equaled the yearly profit from planting those crops.

He was lucky, he noted, that he didn't have any pigs to get rid of during the wholesale slaughter authorized by Secretary of Agriculture Henry Wallace in the mid-1930s. The little pigs were sacrificed to curb the mounting surpluses that had sent the price of pork to record lows. Lee didn't like the idea of killing animals not used for the production of food.

The subsidy programs, inaugurated as a relief measure, were continued in an effort to control crop surpluses and eventually became a profitable source of income for absentee landlords. Farmers were paid to shift corn and wheat acreages to hay crops, or let a portion of their land stay idle.

Lee had been long buried when some Congressmen started to question expense-laden features of crop subsidies, wanting to effect changes but fearing political repercussions from the most prosperous farm operators. "Farmers have become accustomed to it," Maude said to her son Mardo in the eighties. "This is another 'temporary' operation that is becoming permanent."

Lee's efforts at farming slowed down during the 1930s, Maude remembered. He rented the fields, letting the share-cropper do the necessary plowing, cultivating and harvesting of those areas not under the subsidy program. He shared the costs of seed and fertilizer. He helped as needed on a daily basis.

"We planted a bigger garden and we sat on the porch, drinking iced tea or lemonade, during the mid-day summer heat," she said.

The children were gone. The couple read the books of all the popular authors--tales of romance, adventure, mystery, and of the Wild West so recently tamed. They borrowed many, bought some.

The few volumes they retained were by Ellery Queen, Booth Tarkington, Zane Grey, Gene Stratton Porter, Bret Harte, Jack London, Louisa May Alcott, Charles Dickens, Hawthorne and Longfellow. One or the other liked Charlotte Bronte, Anna Sewell, Herman Melville, Edgar Rice Burroughs, Erle Stanley Gardner, Mark Twain, George Eliot, and Horatio Alger. They had read, with the children, all the books assigned for high school classes. A favorite of all was James Fenimore Cooper's *The Last of the Mohicans.*

The couple liked word games. Once, Lee "opined" that Maude was a "likely" (attractive) lass and touched off an afternoon of linking some of the time's most colorful words and phrases.

Hundreds of graphic terms were in common usage, like *tuckered out* and *not up to snuff, willy nilly, on the lam, live wire* and *longhair, cap the climax, sourpatch* and *rotten egg, raise the roof,* and *watch my smoke.* Colorful and dramatic sayings created descriptive pictures in the mind of the listener: "I'll jerk a lung out of you as long as a wagon tongue," "you walk like the dead lice are dropping off you," "you're as cross as a bear with a sore behind."

You might use "shank's mare" (your feet) to get to town; "cat got your tongue?" might prompt a reluctant child or adult to speak; "turkey gobbler on your lip" could coax a smile from a pouting youngster. Phrases encompassed a whole menagerie: *the biggest toad in the puddle, knee high to a gnat, crazy as a bedbug, on your high horse, till the cows come home, no spring chicken, pigheaded, go whole hog, snake in the grass, hold your horses.*

Maude and Lee knew them all. They had heard the language spoken, in its variations, by their parents and grandparents, friends and neighbors, all their lives. Some words and phrases became popular carryovers into later times.

On this particular afternoon, as the two sat in their chairs on the breezy porch, Maude could have asked Lee to "mosey" down to the road and pick up the mail. Lee no doubt would reply, "I'd rather 'skedaddle' to town for a spree." And Maude, entering into the spirit of it, might have challenged, "You're the apple of my eye, but make no bones about it, if you come apart at the seams or come home high as a kite, you may find you have no place to hang your hat."

To which Lee most likely responded: "You said a mouthful. I'm just a hayseed who has been behind the eightball all my life. On the off chance that you will turn a deaf ear to any suggestion that I have been asleep at the switch, I'll learn the ropes, quit my fence-sitting, go on the wagon, and eat crow."

When they had depleted their vocabularies, they must have asked themselves, "Why beat a dead horse?" So they stepped lively and made tracks to the kitchen where Maude took her own sweet time preparing supper.

FIVE

"We were well off, compared to many during the depression," Maude recalled. "We had vegetables and milk." Lee had sold all but two cows when he quit sending milk to the Ridgeway processing plant. He said he could meet the sanitary requirements for the milking area but was having trouble keeping the milk at the proper temperature in summer and winter.

Also, the milk man was insisting the cans be at the roadside, 400 yards from the barn, when he passed the farm. He was never on time--having stopped to pass the time of day with farmers down the way. "If our milk spoiled in summer or froze in winter, we were the loser--not the processing plant," Maude explained.

"Milk prices were so low," Maude remembered, "Lee thought we would be as well off financially with fewer cows." Their DeLaval cream separator was in good condition so their dairy efforts centered around that. Cream was sold to friends and the skim milk added nutrition to the slop fed to the hogs.

Mardo's wife told them they were selling too low, even for the depression years. "They brought us a quart of 40 per cent cream and would take only 50 cents for it," Geneva remembered. "We had whipped cream on everything for a week." They asked a higher price when they sold outside the family, Maude said. And she used most of the cream to form one-pound blocks of butter which she could trade to the grocer for needed staples.

The children began helping more, despite their meager incomes. They joined Lee and Maude in acquiring a dozen sheep, then a prize Shropshire ram to upgrade the flock. Bea and her husband (Wilbert "Buck" Deerwester) bought eight small pigs which Lee fed and sold. During those lean years, they also fattened and butchered a beef cow or two--with the meat going into the couple's larder.

"We read about the plight of the truly needy and felt extremely lucky. We were still scrimping, making each dollar go a little further, but we were no worse off than we'd been in the previous quarter century. We never went hungry. We had a roof over our heads. We still had our health-- and a conviction that things would get better.

"And as we were congratulating ourselves," related Maude, "we got another death message--Lee's brother Herman, in a fit of despondency, had shot and killed both his wife and himself."

He left behind a son, 19-year-old Austin, who was asleep in the house as his father roamed the halls, rifle in hand; and two married daughters, Edith Epps of Marysville and June Cleveland of Columbus. A rambling note explained his actions. Dated January 3, 1939, it blamed financial reverses and dread of reporting the next day to work on a WPA project.

"I have shot my wife, not because of anything she has done but because I did not want her to know the ruin to which we have come," he confessed. In the next sentence, he blamed himself for being a poor manager. "She did not realize to what straits we were come."

He insisted again that Mrs. Williams (the former Blanche Manson) had no role in his decision to kill them both. "She and I have lived harmoniously together, so it is not her fault."

He asked Judge Hazen to appoint either Richard Thrall or Clifton Carlyle to straighten out his tangled affairs. "There isn't much left--only the little property in Mt. Victory," he wrote. "There is a bank book somewhere but I can't find it." And he spoke of a metal box containing receipts.

"So many things there are that belong to the children," he wrote after earlier expressing concern about their welfare. "But I do not know what will become of them anyhow," he said of his inability to smooth the way for them.

He expressed deep prejudice against the Works Progress Administration, termed it a thinly disguised handout. He believed such work would only pinpoint his inability to support his family. "I dread to think about going to the WPA job" and "Beware of a WPA job, everybody, as it is just a step to hell."

The WPA had been established in the mid-1930s by the Roosevelt Administration to ease the drain on direct relief funds by steering the unemployed to improvement of roads, drainage systems and small structures. Thousands were employed and preferred the jobs to charity. But Herman apparently held a view of men leaning on their shovels, never doing any work, and was not impressed.

"I am now going to shoot myself and God have mercy on the children and, if He will, on me."

He looked in on Austin twice and in a "my son, my son" protest before his final act repeated, "if I had tried deliberately, I could not have made a more ruinous mess.

"It is about midnight, I suppose. I will now go to my place....No one knew what I was going to do and I did not do it until midnight."

"I do not suppose the children will ever forgive me and I am sure God will not." (Signed) H. H. Williams.

Herman Williams, next to the youngest of seven children born to Rawson Welch and Sarah Witcraft Williams, would have been 50 in less than three weeks. He was born on January 20, 1889, at the farm home of his parents. He farmed for a period after he was married to Blanche Manson, then moved to Mt. Victory.

Herman received a temporary teaching license by taking classes at the Bowling Green Normal College. He taught an elementary grade from 1912 to 1917, then lost the position under new teacher accreditation rules. There was some favorable publicity in May, 1932, when he and his daughter, June, graduated together from Mt. Victory High School.

Thwarted in his ambition to become a school teacher, he may have been secretly disappointed that his parents did not provide him with an opportunity to attend college as they had done for his brother. Lee thought his own "dropout" may have influenced Ross and Sarah against attempting to finance another college education.

One summer--it may have been the same year he lost his teaching job --Herman was badly injured in a handcar accident on the Big Four Railroad (CCC & ST. L). He was working as a laborer on the right-of-way and was on his way to a new work location when the handcar overturned. He was pinned under it with a badly crushed right leg. He limped thereafter and felt that his handicap prevented him from employment in roles for which he was fitted.

The move to Pottersburg, where he ended two lives and disrupted the lives of several others, was designed to promote new opportunities, encourage new friendships. It failed miserably.

Lee mourned his only brother, whom he had seen only rarely over the previous few years. Herman's wife, Lee remembered, had been discontented in Mt. Victory and eager to seek new opportunities in another community.

They had moved within the last two years to Pottersburg, a small Union County village 25 miles distant, and Lee had not seen him since. "Maybe if I'd known he was despondent, I could have done something to cheer him up," he told Maude, "let him know he wasn't to blame for having nothing, that millions of people were in the same straits."

SIX

"During the 1930s we lost Lee's parents, his brother, sister-in-law and brother-in-law, and my father," Maude said, "but we gained four grandchildren."

Eddie was born to Pauline and Sonny Ansley on July 23, 1932; his brother Joe on June 2, 1939. Mardo and Geneva gave her her only granddaughters--Kay on November 3, 1933, and Jerri on May 4, 1938.

They joined Gene Perry, Mildred's only child, born April 16, 1924.

Mildred, John and Gene had been established in Phoenix, Arizona, for nearly ten years when Maude's youngest grandson was born. Their emergency trek across the country in late 1930 was almost forgotten.

Mildred had corresponded with no one except her mother for the first few months. Then she started writing to her Uncle Harry Marmon. She had known him as her fourth grade teacher at Spice Wood Glen and her seventh-eighth grade teacher at Ridgeway Junior High School. They progressed to exchanging poems.

Her favorite was one he penned to her on July 5, 1932, entitled, "Down to Old Arizona."

Recovering from tuberculosis, he spoke wistfully of the hot, disease-fighting desert air. "From out the swiftly passing air, I draw a long, deep breath, And with a sneering laugh, I'd say good-bye to Old Man Death."

Mildred thought it was a wish for both of them. He was battling his illness and she was seriously ill with asthma.

Mildred's husband John had endeared himself to Maude and Lee because of the way he took care of Mildred, moving from Ohio to Arizona, to start a new career there. He had worked for a time in a Phoenix auto repair shop, taking advantage of ten years' experience in the Ellza Limes dealership in Ridgeway, Ohio.

Then he became an insurance adjuster in the Southwest, once being assigned to New Orleans, Louisiana, after a hurricane struck the Gulf Coast. They had begun paying back the money lent them by family members at the time of Mildred's health crisis.

But despite the dry Arizona air, Mildred's asthma had worsened so that she was taking both inhalants and heart stimulants under her doctor's supervision. She must have thought often of the Mt. Victory doctor and his kerosene "cure" for her sinus infection.

During the depression years, no one enlisted the services of the doctor unnecessarily. It cost too much, and no one had money for such frivolities. Lee often erred on the side of caution. In the early fall of 1940, he battled what he thought was an upset stomach by taking spoonful after spoonful of baking soda. He sought a physician's advice only after he developed severe abdominal pains.

He was rushed to McKitrick Hospital, Kenton, where Dr. R.G. Schutte performed emergency surgery. The appendix had already burst, spreading infection through the intestinal tract. He almost died before sulfa drugs brought the inflammation under control. He was in the hospital two weeks and had to take things easy for four weeks after returning home. The surgeon's bill: $55.00.

His illness was the final event of a devastating 12 years. The couple dismissed the depression years as an aberration. The 1940s, they agreed, would be better. There surely couldn't be another comparable period in which they'd experience so much heartache.

Part XI: The Forties--Traditions

ONE

*I*s the ice cream freezer on the porch? Has Grandpa been to town for ice? Will I get to turn the crank? might have been in the mind of every child at those Sunday dinners for which Grandma Maude was famed. The tradition was that she had to provide the ice cream dessert, just as Lee was relied upon to get the ice. If he failed, the earliest arrival went to town for any missing supplies. No mid-day Sunday meal during the summer was without ice cream. Maude started the custom when the four children entered their teens, continued it after they were married and had children of their own.

Farm dinners were at noon; the evening meal was called supper. *Lunch*, if anyone used the term, took on the meaning of a snack in the minds of farm folk. Once, in the early 1920s, Lee and family were invited to dinner at a friend's house in town. They arrived promptly at 12 noon, only to learn that the meal was scheduled for early evening--to the mutual embarrassment of hostess and guests.

Thereafter, Maude made it perfectly clear that "*dinner* will be at noon time," and no one was late. If the meal wasn't served until one o'clock or later, the children would urge their grandma to hurry up because they were starving. Year after year, the Sunday dinners were a magnet that drew three generations together in fellowship.

Grandpa made a contribution to the festivities by putting the children to work, turning the crank of the ice cream freezer. He eliminated arguments over whose turn it was. Grandson Gene would be first--if he was visiting from Phoenix with his parents, Mildred and John. Gene was eight years older than his oldest cousin Eddie Ansley. Eddie would follow Gene at the crank, then Kay, next oldest, would take a turn, then Jerri, and Joe.

The freezer was an object of awe to the youngsters. The container, embedded in ice that had been sprinkled with rock salt, held the tasty liquid. As the crank was turned, a paddle inside the container slowly agitated the concoction. Self-adjusting scrapers on the paddle prevented the ice cream, as it hardened, from caking on the walls. The more it froze, the harder the crank became to turn, so Grandpa or one of the fathers had to take over. Finally, the paddle was removed and salt-laced ice was packed over the top of the container to keep the ice cream hard until it was served.

"What will we do with the paddle?" Lee always asked the children, as if he didn't know. "It has all this delicious goo clinging to it, which might drip on the porch and attract flies." The grandchildren solved that problem. They carried it into the yard and fought over it until the last flavorful lick.

Maude said they started with a one-gallon freezer, but at one Sunday dinner the children were still hungry after devouring the entire output. She hurriedly whipped up a mixture of cream, eggs, sugar, milk and vanilla--which couldn't be frozen because the ice had melted. "We had no alternative--we had to get a larger freezer," she said.

She experimented once, used the same basic flavorings, added a spoonful of flour, and substituted milk for cream. She brought the mixture to a boil, let it cool, and poured it into the ice cream container for freezing. It was good but not as delicious as that prepared with fresh eggs and 40 per cent whipping cream from the DeLaval separator. She went back to her original recipe. Not one "no" vote was cast.

The youngsters drifted away when Lee tried to explain the mechanical details of the freezer. They were not interested in the fact that the stainless steel cylinder holding the mixture was anchored in a metal cap at the bottom and in meshed grooves at the top (to permit its turning with a minimum of friction), or that the delicious dessert could not be frozen with ice alone. "We need salt," he proclaimed. "It causes the ice to melt, driving the temperature down to as low as 10 degrees above zero."

"And," he continued, to no one in particular, "if the mixture is too soft when you remove the paddle, you can firm it up by piling ice and salt over the top and letting it set for an hour or so. If there's one thing I like hard," he concluded, "it's ice cream."

On the morning of the dinner, Maude chopped the head off the chicken, letting the blood drain completely away before dipping the carcass in near boiling water and stripping away the feathers.

The method of execution was always the same. Maude grasped the fowl's legs tightly in her right hand, dragged the upper body across an upright block of wood, and struck the outstretched neck just below the head with a sharp axe. As the head fell to one side, Maude would fling the body onto the grassy plot at the rear of the woodhouse. When the reflexive jumping ceased, the chicken--usually a young rooster--was prepared for the frying pan.

The skin was carefully scraped for she'd discovered early in her married life that nothing turned Lee off like a pin feather in chicken skin-- or a loose hair of any kind in his food! He was particular--even finicky-- about everything he ate. One time a neighbor butchered a large turtle and gave a chunk of it to Maude. When she prepared it, it looked like steak and Lee devoured it hungrily.

When she told him what it was, he immediately threw up! Luckily, she said, they were home alone. She never tried to foist a surprise food on him again--even refrained from cooking leg of lamb--because he said he didn't like any kind of meat from sheep.

Lee should have been a cattle rancher in the early Wild West, his wife often commented. He not only didn't like to eat lamb chops, leg of lamb or mutton, but refused to have sheep on the farm. It wasn't until the early 1930s that he relented, and then only at the insistence of wife and children.

"The pasture along the creek in front of the house was becoming choked with weeds and small shrubs," Maude remembered. Wild grass was rampant in the yard and around the farm buildings. The lane to the woods was overgrown. And the woodland itself could use the grazing impact of a flock of sheep, she told her husband.

The daughters, son and their mates concurred and agreed to help Lee buy a dozen Shropshire sheep from a neighboring farmer. A year later, as members of the flock started to drop their first lambs, Lee acquired a purebred ram. He was quick to admit that he was wrong to have allowed his aversion to the meat influence him against use of the animals as gardeners *par excellence*. He praised their efforts as he accepted compliments on the changed appearance of the "crick" pasture and the grounds surrounding the house.

He said he never got friendly with the male sheep. He warned the smaller grandchildren not to venture along the creek if the ram was loose. "He's unpredictable," Lee said.

The youngsters forgot, as they are wont to do, ventured into the pasture to wade in the creek, and on that Sunday afternoon, were heard calling for Grandpa. When he rushed to the scene of the commotion, he found grandson Eddie holding the ram by the horns and granddaughter Kay gripping it by the tail. They had urged Jerri and Joe to safety but now were trapped--unable to let go.

Lee replaced Eddie at the horns, smacked the pugnacious sheep on the nose and herded it to the barn.

This peril may have added to the thrill of the grandchildren's weekly visits. Nothing they would do ever approached the entertainment they experienced at the farm on the banks of Rush Creek--not the movies, nor the county fair, nor a trip to the ice cream parlor. They all would congregate to watch Grandma Maude cut the head off the chicken meant for the Sunday dinner, fascinated as the headless bird ran crazily in circles.

After the cooking commenced and the tantalizing smells wafted through the screen doors, the children hovered in the porch swing until, too hungry to wait, they sneaked inside and snatched pickles and olives from the table, or scooped up fingers full of the home-churned butter and ate it like candy.

At last the food arrived and everyone stuffed themselves full of fried chicken and home-made noodles, mashed potatoes and gravy, corn on the cob, green beans, pie and ice cream. The grandchildren argued over who would get to wish on the wishbone.

While the women did the dishes in the antiquated kitchen, the men dozed. The children wondered how they could sleep when there was so much to do.

They dug for fishworms in the garden, the younger ones refusing to pick up the slimy angleworms they needed. Then they fished in Rush Creek with makeshift poles fashioned from small tree limbs, discarded wrapping cord, and bent pins, the line kept afloat with a well-dried corncob. They swam in the creek, caught minnows and frogs, marveled at the way the crawfish scooted backwards, and were attacked by the leeches (like Mardo, years before). They ate juicy red apples from the tree, plump red tomatoes snapped from the vine. They roamed the woods behind the house, looking for berries, nuts and wildflowers, stained their hands with the juice of black walnuts.

More than once, they garnered a memory that was enforced by two weeks of itching and scratching. All would suffer from chigger bites and sometimes a case of poison ivy. After being stung by some angry bees, they concluded the farm posed hazards for which they were unprepared.

They rode the hay wagon, played in the hay mow, laughed at the pigs as they squealed in the mud behind the barn, and helped Grandma bottle feed the orphan lambs named Eddie, Kay, Jerri and Joe.

When the weather was bad, they rummaged in the mysterious upstairs attic--finding relics from the past, an old Civil War rifle with the bayonet in a scabbard at its side, the antique cradle and spinning wheel, and a treasure trove of old picture postcards with faded messages scrawled years before.

Grandma's brother Gene had given the family a player piano in 1917, the year before he died of influenza. The grandchildren especially liked "Don't Leave Your Gum on the Bedpost Over Night" and pumped the pedals as fast as they could to make the music play in double time.

They listened to records on the hand-cranked Victrola Mildred and John had left behind, made fun of the old-fashioned sounds of Rudy Vallee and Al Jolson. All were excited when in 1942 Lee and Maude added a modern record to the collection, a song about Hitler, "Last night I had a dream that Schickelgruber passed away, They put him in a pigpen but the pigs all ran away." They liked to let the Victrola wind down, so the song would get slower and slower, stopping on a drawn out moan, "Yes, the pigs refused to stay."

They read the books moldering in the bookcase, *Les Miserables*, Horatio Alger, other sentimental "rags to riches" tales, and discovered a cache of modern reading, the lurid *True Detective* magazines Lee kept on hand.

Each Sunday at five o'clock Jerri and Kay sat in their Dad's Buick and listened to "The Shadow." Grandma and Grandpa didn't have a radio.

For two or three summers during the early 1940s, the four grandchildren stayed a week at the farm. It was an adventure, a vacation for them (unlike when Mardo and his sisters lived there and toiled at their daily chores). Maude cooked the fresh eggs the children gathered for breakfast, made pies from the blackberries they picked.

They soon found out they had to eat all the food they ladled onto their plates. "A clean plate or no pie," Grandma told them.

They trailed behind teenager Gene Perry when he was there. As the oldest, he was trusted to look after the four. He taught them to stand behind him when he fired Grandpa's 22-caliber rifle at targets, and even how to shoot the gun themselves.

Kay still remembers a thrilling and terrifying horseback ride, with Gene holding her in front of him as the two galloped bareback across the pasture. She was eight years old, he was 17. He was the cowboy, she was the maiden he'd just snatched from under the feet of the stampeding herd. When Gene grew tired of the juvenile play and dozed off in the rocking chair, Eddie or Kay would stick him with pins until he woke up and masterminded other adventures.

Granddad Lee could be counted on to fascinate and entertain the grandchildren. They watched enthralled as he removed his teeth and held them in his hand. He showed them how to fold sheets of newspaper into boats. He told them tall tales--fables about Paul Bunyan or someone he'd once met--told as the truth but with a twinkle in his eye. Like any actor, he loved to get a reaction--the louder the better. Grandpa wasn't like any adult they'd ever known. He could be maddening and childlike--just like them. He could make them feel important--almost like adults.

The children grew to tolerate Grandpa's teasing. He did it so innocently and in such good humor that it would have been a crime to take offense--though sometimes a child might lose patience with his apparent dimwittedness. He always greeted Jerri as "Rachel" and Jerri always responded with indignation, "I'm not Rachel, my name is Jerri." She wondered how her granddad could forget her name from week to week.

Joe was the youngest grandchild--a cute youngster who was always trailing behind, anxious to get into the action. Grandparents Lee and Maude remembered one time when he was out in front--as a first-rate story teller. His parents (Pauline and Sonny Ansley) said he had learned the tale from a five-year-old neighbor boy and was anxious to pass it along. Actually, he may have been coached by his father!

There was this family of moles which dug under a house and came up under a worn wooden floor, much like that in Grandma's and Grandpa's kitchen, the little boy said. They were very hungry so when they spotted a hole in the flooring, they climbed up to investigate, with Papa Mole in the lead, Mama Mole next in line, and Baby Mole in the rear. Papa sniffed loudly and said, "I smell pancakes"; Mama got the aroma and said, "I smell pancakes"--Baby Mole, from the bottom-most position, complained, "All I can smell is molasses."

Joe, although he didn't get the implication until he was older, enjoyed the reactions of the adults, who laughed uproariously and, he thought, senselessly.

His grandparents also remembered the time he made a big fuss about sleeping overnight away from home on Christmas Eve. He was worried that Santa Claus couldn't find him. He reluctantly went to bed, slept restlessly, and arose while it was still dark. The entire household was awakened by his shout: "YEP, HE COME!"

All were worried the next summer, Grandma Maude said, when the youngster toppled from a swing in the back yard of the Ansley home in Lima. His foot became entangled in the rope and he was dragged, head down, across a sharp-edged stone on the ground beneath. The skin was peeled from his forehead in a partial scalping and he was rushed to the hospital.

Doctors stitched the loose flesh back together and applied a pressure bandage. This was a strip of cloth wrapped completely around the head and bound tightly. It restricted the flow of blood and was designed to prevent bleeding from the just-closed wound. Attendants refused to loosen the bandage, although son Joe had been in severe head pain for two days, Sonny Ansley said.

The excuse: they required the doctor's orders and he had left no instructions when he'd left town on vacation. The hospital administrator refused to intervene--until Sonny threatened to sue both surgeon and hospital. The original bandage was cut away, a looser pressure applied. By that time, a skin graft had become necessary to replace the damaged tissue. The erring health providers did the necessary repair work and made a cash settlement that would help Joe, after he married, to buy his first home.

"Our youngest grandchild became our biggest," Maude said. He grew to six feet, one inch tall and weighed 190 pounds. He developed a wry sense of humor, a delight to all.

The grandchildren, while they were growing up, were drawn almost irresistibly to the spacious barn, with its billowing hay mows above and livestock quarters below. One sultry summer evening, Grandpa was busy milking the cows when he realized that grandson Eddie, age 8, was not at his side asking questions and demanding that Grandpa squirt milk at him. Even the cats had scorned the oppressive, fly-infested milking area. So the absence of Eddie (Pauline's and Sonny's oldest) should not have triggered suspicion. But it did.

Grandpa moved to the last cow in the evening's milkathon. It occupied a stall at the side of a boxed-in stairway that led from the basement level to the barn's main floor.

Before seating himself, he carefully sprayed the cow's back with a kerosene solution as insect repellent. The flies had been particularly obnoxious that night, causing the animals to lash viciously with their tails and swing their heads in the hopeless battle.

Seated on a three-legged stool at the right side of Old Bossie, Lee grasped the two front teats and started spraying a tune into the galvanized pail. Unknown to Eddie, Lee had glimpsed him huddling under the stairs and sensed, from an earlier experience with Grandson Gene Perry, what was going to happen.

The boy concentrated on steering a stiff straw of hay through a small hole in the wall of the stairwell. When he succeeded, he gouged the stiff straw into the tender side of the cow's udder. The animal upset the milk bucket in its attempt to escape this sudden pain and Eddie grinned at the resultant bedlam. Grandpa Lee feigned outrage and, in full voice, berated the cow. "Stand still, you miserable old crowbait," he shouted. "I'll beat you with a board. I'll cut off your ears if you don't stand still."

The teasing by Eddie continued until Lee finally set the stool and milk pail aside, twisted the cow's tail over its back and unleashed such a fearsome tirade of threats that the grandson fled. Neither Eddie nor Grandpa ever mentioned the incident, each enjoying his little "secret."

The cow parlor--despite the heat, flies and strong smells of summer and the cold of winter--remained a magnet, an attraction to city youngsters. Nephews, nieces, cousins, and grandchildren, all were entranced by watching Lee, on his three-legged stool at the side of a cow, squirt a stream of milk into the galvanized pail.

Lee welcomed an interested audience too. He would have each child draw close, open his or her mouth, and direct a ribbon of milk accurately from factory to palate. When trust was established, he might spray the children's clothing or shoes, then laugh quietly as they ran to tell their mothers on him. Maude was always the one to bawl him out.

TWO

After Pauline's husband Sonny transferred from Kenton to the Lima Westinghouse plant as a skilled machinist, Maude and Lee often visited the couple's Lima home. Maude said she remembered one week-end trip to her daughter's home--not because of any special incident, just a little humor introduced by Lee.

"We--Lee and I, Mardo and Geneva--stopped to eat a picnic lunch at a small roadside park 10 miles west of Kenton," Maude said. "The oats bugs were numerous and particularly obnoxious that summer so Geneva and I were very careful about covering each dish as we placed it on the picnic table.

"Lee, of course, dipped into my potato salad and protested immediately that it was full of oats bugs." The insects are small and black. At first glance, they were almost indistinguishable from the celery seeds used in the salad.

Thereafter, Lee would bring up his wife's "oats bug" creation at every picnic or outdoor covered dish lunch. And Maude would smile, never arguing.

Lee's penchant for raw humor and his tendency to tease his children, the young grandchildren, nieces and nephews caused Maude some annoyance. She found herself biting her tongue to keep from demanding that he "stop it." His teasing was innocent, actually enjoyed by the victims. Even Maude found herself smiling at her husband's antics.

He frequently asked son-in-law Sonny Ansley if he'd like some home-fermented grape wine, a reference to Sonny having once swiped a gallon of his father's wine, which he shared with schoolmate Paul Ulrich. He had suffered a terrible hangover that left him with a perpetual distaste for wine.

Lee could ask personal questions and make impertinent observations without creating resentment. Maude said that on one occasion she thought her husband overstepped the bounds of propriety. Nephew Ronald Ansley, of Columbus, had just driven his small car up the farm lane to spend Sunday afternoon with his favorite uncle and aunt. As Lee greeted the new arrivals, he observed that their three children filled the car's rear seat and that wife Charlotte was almost ready to present Ronald with another.

Leaning over so the children wouldn't hear, Lee advised: "Son, you're going to screw yourself out of a place in your own car!" The couple laughed aloud, then accepted his invitation to "come in and have some lemonade."

Lee liked people. He made Maude's brother feel so welcome that Harley Allen brought several railroad friends for short stays each fall for several years. They shot rabbit and pheasant in field and woods.

Maude wasn't so welcoming for she had the chore of planning the meals and cooking for five to seven hungry men. They brought little food and bottomless appetites. She could recall only one instance when they brought anything--five pounds of fresh lake perch which she had to clean and cook the same evening they arrived.

During those November days, the Williamses' breakfasts were scheduled even earlier than usual. The hunters had to be ready to bag that first rabbit well before the sun rose--if there was any sun. So they ate their ham and eggs (with coffee) early, piled scores of shotgun shells into their pockets and prepared to end the tranquility of the countryside with a fusillade that would not be equaled until they returned another year.

They would line up abreast and advance across a field, flushing the game up before them. If the first shot missed, the entire group opened fire. It was a wonder that the animal didn't die of heart failure, Lee kidded them. He never hunted with them, but Mardo and son-in-law John Perry did.

John and Mardo would start at one end of the line, then slip away to hunt by themselves. When Uncle Harley wanted to know why they didn't stay with the party, they made a weak excuse. The real reason was they were frightened by the careless shooting and competition to obtain game.

One time, Mardo said, "We came over a slight rise just as a cock pheasant burst out of the bottoms. One of Uncle Harley's friends shot at it when it was over our heads. He missed both us and the pheasant, but it was close." After that, they hunted by themselves, arriving at the farm only after the Toledo party had entered the fields.

The hunting season started each November 15, unless it was a Sunday. The bag limit was ten rabbits and two rooster pheasants daily. Hunting could start an hour before sunrise and had to end an hour after sunset. The visitors never reached their limits but did kill enough rabbits to take a few back to Toledo, and have one rabbit dinner at Maude's table. Pheasants were much more difficult to locate and, when flushed from cover, went out from under one's feet with such a whoosh that the amateur hunter usually missed.

The five-day game hunt became history after a few years. Either Harley concluded that his friends were unappreciative of the Williams's hospitality or the railroaders couldn't endure the hardships imposed by sleeping two to a bed, getting up before daylight, and having to lose sleep if they wished to play poker and drink whiskey.

The crowning blow to male conviviality may have been dealt by Harley. That last year, he invited an eccentric switch tender who had a phobia against cleanliness. He hadn't had a bath since last spring and smelled to high heaven, Lee said.

The hunters had insisted shortly after their arrival that all enter a drawing, conducted by Lee, to see who would sleep with the malodorous one. Harley lost, couldn't bribe another to take his place, was unable to locate a cot, and slept on the floor the last night.

When the Toledo hunting expeditions became history, Maude found relief from those cooking/cleaning duties. Lee viewed their departure with mixed emotions. He admitted he enjoyed playing cards with the Toledoans (because he usually won) and sharing their whiskey which usually was gone by the time they left.

One year, after pondering the injustice of the affluent railroad men having access to all that liquor, Lee carefully poured a small portion out of each quart bottle each day and funneled it into another container.

Bottle after bottle received the treatment. Lee justified his act by saying that as he drank the contributed beverage he would think of his benefactors and mentally thank them for bringing such a generous supply of quality whiskey. Besides, by restricting their supply, "I may be helping them break the drinking habit," he reasoned.

Part XII:

The World Comes to Rush Creek

ONE

*L*ooking around her kitchen in the early 1940s, Maude said she was surprised at how little things had changed in the almost 40 years she'd been cooking and baking there. The corner cupboard was still standing at the entrance to the pantry. She'd repainted it, as well as the table and chairs, and the kitchen woodwork.

The only thing different was the addition of a pitcher pump that pulled the water from the cistern outside, and the kitchen sink--over which the pump was fastened. The inside pump saved Maude many exposures to the elements over the years, as she used rain water for washing dishes, laundry, and personal hygiene. She welcomed that convenience as a "first." Harry Marmon, Lee's brother-in-law, had helped install it over a sink along the east wall during the spring of 1923, leaving the outside pump above the cistern.

She recalled one interruption in the kitchen pump's operation--other than the normal slowdown during periods when rainfall dipped and water flowing through gutters and down-spout of the roof became inadequate to refill the cistern. The water crisis that time was not due to a drought--the 2,000 gallon cistern was at least half full. She pumped water and no one would use it. It had a terrible smell. Maude sprinkled a LaFrance product which was guaranteed to settle the impurities. A day later, the water was clear, but "it still smelled to high heaven," she said.

She refused to use the cistern, sent children and husband to the deeply drilled outside well for laundry water, then protested it was so hard that sudsing was impossible with any amount of soap.

Lee delayed work, impressed his farm hand into domestic service to help him find the source of the foul odor. They pumped the cistern dry. The culprit was located. A rat had tumbled into the cistern and drowned. It was in an advanced stage of decomposition--"smelly as all get out"--in the dregs at the bottom.

A complete clean-out was mandatory, followed by a scrubbing, rinsing, and sealing of walls and floor. Maude had to wait for the next rain before she could test the water and give her seal of approval to the project. She cited this "minor problem" as an indication of the amount of work entailed in solving the most simple challenges of the early 20th century.

The first water from the newly scrubbed cistern still had a trace of the rat fragrance, so it was thrown out. The next pailful was approved and went into the water reservoir at the right end of her massive kitchen range, the Kalamazoo, the same stove the couple had started housekeeping with in 1903.

After fooling around with the fluctuating oven heat for years, she said she'd finally placed a heat resistant thermometer on a shelf of the oven prior to the start of baking (with roasts, the fluctuation of the heat level wasn't too important). Even with the thermometer, success was not assured. So she had to peer in from time to time to see if one side of the cake or pie was cooking faster than the other.

Eventually, she bragged, she was able to outguess the temperamental beast and sometimes get a passable product in return. Lee and others said she was unduly modest. In fact, she had an uncanny ability to make do with nothing and end up with pies, cakes, and cookies that no one else could come close to matching, even with the most advanced equipment of the forties (according to Lee, the children and grandchildren).

TWO

Unemployment in the nation had dipped to 17.2 percent in 1939. The average wage was 62 cents an hour. A luxury Packard was being offered in 1940 for $907, but Lee said he couldn't buy one if it were a tenth the price. The Depression was abating, but slowly.

The economy began improving in 1940 and 1941, then took a dramatic leap when the United States was pulled into World War II by the Japanese attack on Pearl Harbor. "We didn't see much change at our level," Lee said, "But we were fearful what the war would do to our young grandsons and nephews."

Only two were drafted. Their grandson, Harold Eugene Perry of Phoenix, Arizona (Mildred's son) went into a tank battalion. James Ansley, a nephew (son of Dawn and the late Roy Ansley), was taken into the U.S. Army despite a major visual handicap. He served as a company clerk.

Gene Perry was unalterably opposed to the war when it was first talked of, saw no reason for the U.S. to get involved, and threatened to hide out in the mountainous areas near Phoenix to evade armed service.

But when the Japanese bombs fell on Pearl Harbor on December 7, 1941, he changed his stance. He went into service willingly when called at age 18, became a gunner in "C" Company of the 736th Medium Tank Battalion (Special), also known as the "Kiddie Battalion," since most of the men were just 18. Gene was affectionately identified by his comrades as Harold "Down-a-Hair" Perry.

"Down-a-Hair" became a nickname that everyone recognized even when the name Perry didn't register. His friends in arms said it resulted from his careful sighting-in of the tank's cannon, after the unit's commander, Captain Rogers, ordered a correction in the trajectory. Gene would tell his gunner to lower the muzzle "down a hair" and became known for the accuracy of his shots on target.

Robert F. Hall, a comrade in the 736th, cited an incident of early May, 1945, near Zerbst, Germany, that justified his respect for "Down-a-Hair" Perry. "Our two tanks were 'dug in' east of the Elbe River with only the turrets above ground when a German Tiger tank approached. Only Perry noticed the arrival of this behemoth on the scene. He opened fire, bounced five 76-millimeter shells off the turret and saved the immobilized U.S. tanks from almost certain destruction."

Hall said the German tank changed tactics, slowly backed away and disappeared in a wooded area. "All of us were alerted by that time and would have riddled the thinner rear armor of the tank with cannon fire if the driver had dared to turn around before fleeing."

Perry, who died on December 22, 1993 at his home in Phoenix, would have been thrilled by the poem Hall had penned in tribute both to "Down-a-Hair" and to the Red Cross girls who showed up soon afterward at the battle scene. "They called to us to come out [of the tanks] and have coffee," Hall wrote.

Hall, who lived near Proctor, West Virginia, died unexpectedly in 1995 while returning from a vacation trip with his wife. He had submitted this poem to the American Red Cross Overseas Association for its publication. It is entitled "The Tiger":

When you see that Tiger tank coming with his cannon 88,
*   And you know damn well you can't hurt him, I think you'll*
defecate.
With only your turret showing, I know you'll hope and pray
*   That bastard doesn't see you, hiding there in the woods and rain.*
And the trees fall like toothpicks as he fires down the rows
*   And why he doesn't see us, gosh only knows.*
Your buddy across the road sees him, lays five 76's on his bow,
*   The tiger backs up slowly, slowly--He cannot see us now.*
About 20 minutes later, when your guts have settled down,
*   And you finally have the courage to get feet out on the ground,*
You hear a "6-by" coming, blasting that familiar Glenn Miller noise.
*   It's the brave Red Cross girls, bringing donuts and coffee*
To us frightened little boys.
We will never forget them for the deeds that they have done.
They all are really heroes and we love them every one.
*   Sorry they never received the honor they deserved,*
But I know there'll be a place in Heaven for them, marked
RESERVED.

Then Mr. Hall invited those Red Cross girls, who were east of the Elbe River on that fearful day, to show up Sept. 26-29, 1994, for the Battalion's reunion in Arizona. They would be honored in person, said Hall, and Gene

"Down-a-Hair" Perry would be toasted in memory. If he'd been alive and well, Gene would have been present. He and his wife Isabel had traveled all over the country to attend past reunions. He never would have missed one in his home state. (Isabel was there. The Red Cross girls were honored in absentia. Gene was toasted along with all the other missing comrades.)

"Both Grandmother and Grandfather would have been thrilled by the praise belatedly given their grandson," Isabel said.

In one of his many battles, Gene (as gunner), with his loader Alex beside him, killed an estimated 500 Germans. "They came through a break in a hedge," he later told Isabel. "Even though they saw their comrades ahead of them being picked off, they kept on coming. They were trained never to give up." Gene's tank, the only one in the area, faced the Germans alone.

In his last battle of the war, Gene and his team had crossed the Elbe in an amphibious tank. Soon they found themselves trapped, the tank stuck on a log. It wouldn't budge. Capt. Rogers, the commander, climbed out to find help.

As next in command, Buck Rogers (no relation), popped his head out of the turret to have a look. He was hit in the head by a German shell, collapsed back down into the tank, and fell dead at Gene's feet. The shelling continued, one of the bullets smashing the log the tank was stuck on. In the nick of time, they were able to move. In the meantime, the captain had found air support, without which, Gene said, he and his tank comrades never would have made it.

Gene received two Bronze Stars for bravery and was to have received the Silver Star but, by then, the army had run out of medals. He received a Silver Star lapel pin instead. Isabel said it wasn't important to him that he never received the actual medal. The main thing for him was doing his job well, then getting out and going on with his life.

When the war ended, occupation forces faced other hazards in the defeated country. Germans sold buzz bomb fuel to the GIs in whiskey bottles. Many of Gene's comrades drank it and died, his good friend "Shug" (his tank driver) among them. Alex, Gene's loader, drank just a few sips, but still suffers from stomach trouble today. Luckily, Gene didn't drink a drop.

After he was discharged, Gene had nightmares for several months. His wife Isabel said he'd scream out in his sleep, "Oh, Alex, they got Buck." She'd have to shake and shake him to wake him up.

Grandfather Lee noted at the time that Gene's Army career was monitored more carefully because he was the only member of the immediate Williams clan to serve. The son and sons-in-law had been exempted because of their roles in defense industries or farming. Other grandsons were too young to register.

Their nephew, Jim Ansley, had been classified 4-F for deficient vision, then reclassified later in the war. He was assigned to a clerical position, probably because of typing experience as a reporter on the Kenton *News Republican*. He served in France and returned to start an insurance company.

Lee himself was to miss service in both World Wars. He had registered for the draft on September 8, 1918, but World War I ended on November 11th that same year. He was 36 years old. He was too old to register (age 59) when the U.S. was catapulted into World War II.

The second World War had one beneficial effect on Maude's and Lee's economic future. Lee was renting the farm fields so became a cannery employee, took home a weekly pay envelope, which later qualified him for Social Security benefits. He and Maude were able to buy more, do less gardening, and have more leisure time.

The "factory" in which he worked was not the industrial workplace, with barred windows and strict regulations. It was a friendly gathering of housewives and farmers, who worked with the products they had known all their lives--string beans, garden peas, sweet corn, cabbage, beets, cucumbers, and pumpkin.

The Mt. Victory Canning Company was established near the source of supply to meet scarcities created by the demands of the armed forces and defense-employed civilians. It drew on the surrounding community for both its products and its work force. Practically all of its efforts went into canning produce for the area's gardeners.

Lee said farmers and folks in town with Victory Gardens brought in baskets of freshly washed vegetables to be processed by the assembled work force. Each consignment was cooked in stainless steel vessels, then canned mechanically to seal in flavor and seal out contaminants. The cost varied--according to the product, the effort entailed in the processing, and the size of the container. For example, a No. 2 1/2 size can (almost a quart) of string beans would cost the farmer 12 cents--the expense of labor, materials and profit in processing his produce. The cannery made a profit; the farmer got his vegetables back as canned food at a minimum cost.

Occasionally, the company might credit a penniless farmer for a small proportion of his vegetables in payment of his bill, then offer the unlabeled surplus to other gardeners or independent grocers, who would pay an additional three cents per can.

Both the scarcity of certain products on the grocery shelves and the surplus of fresh vegetables from the government-promoted Victory Gardens combined to keep the cannery operating for two years after the war ended in 1945.

THREE

The porch was the focal point of Maude's canning preparations, the location for the ice cream freezer at countless family gatherings, and the resting place for tired youngsters after feverish explorations. But now --after 90 years of trampling feet, summer heat and rains, winter snows and the freezing-thawing cycle--some repairs were necessary. The wooden floor had rotted all along the south side. Boards had been replaced, but when the support beams became unsafe, there was general concern that someone might be injured.

"Our children, and then our grandchildren, had grown so attached to the old porch that its loss was unthinkable," Maude declared. She took action. With the children and grandchildren assembled for a very special Sunday dinner--of fried chicken, mashed potatoes, homemade noodles and biscuits, farm grown vegetables and the dessert of homemade ice cream with Devils Food cake--Maude broached a plan.

Lee and his hired hand would tear up the old floor and rotted beams, haul in some gravel for a base, purchase the cement and rent a portable concrete mixer if the family would cooperate by spending one or two days of a weekend to help pour a new floor. There wasn't a dissenting vote.

Lee said preparations would take two weeks and suggested the third weekend in October, 1945 as the target date. The weatherman cooperated and a dozen workers--relatives and friends--shared duties of carrying water and gravel to the cement mixer, adding cement in the proper proportions, wheelbarrowing the concrete to the site and smoothing it out. To prevent confusion, each man continued in the work to which he was assigned initially--there was no swapping of duties.

Smoothing the concrete after it was poured required both patience and skill. Two or three workers placed planks across the wet concrete. From vantage points on the one plank, one or two men roughly leveled the material. Sonny Ansley and Cuyler Smith (husband of niece Fern Marmon) assumed that chore.

The finisher followed on a separate plank. It was his responsibility to leave the surface smooth but not so slick as to be dangerous when it dried, to trowel out the air bubbles and to give the completed porch a slight slope from the wall of the house to the outside edge.

Sam Moser, a close friend, did such a masterful job of finishing that the concrete never chipped or cracked, and it sloped as planned. The surface could be scrubbed with impunity, and rain never reached the back wall no matter how strong the gust, Maude said. She ranked this project as the most satisfactory accomplishment of her life--until 18 months later when the old house was wired for electricity.

They were late with electric service for two reasons, in addition to shortages resulting from World War II. The Rural Electrification Administration was hesitant about expanding into the neighborhood because of a lack of customers. And Lee himself had been reluctant to seek the hook-up until he had the funds to pay both for wiring his house and the added cost of running the line 300 feet from the roadway.

The couple never could have swung it ten years earlier when the REA was first established.

In the spring of 1947, Garrett Brugler, recently returned from U.S. Coast Guard service, started wiring the house. He was the nephew of W.A. Deerwester, one of Maude's three sons-in-law.

Mr. Brugler was interested in making a career of the electrical training he had received in the Coast Guard. The Williams project was a challenge.

Not only were the walls of solid lath and mortar but the structural timbers of black ash and oak had become so dry in the 90 years since they were cut that a drill would become dull after boring a single hole. Each hole had to be drilled by hand, and each drill bit had to be sharpened after every use.

"I didn't have enough working tools of my own so I had to borrow from my uncle and from Sonny Ansley (another son-in-law of Lee and Maude)," Brugler noted. "I even relied on Maude's sons-in-law to sharpen each drill bit after every use. They would take them home to sharpen them on electrical grinders, then return them to me before start of the next work day."

Brugler finished the wiring in late summer by working most weekends. It was a labor of love. He made little profit but did get a number of Maude's delicious meals. And he said it all became worthwhile when he observed the thrill that accompanied the turning on of electricity.

As Maude said later, "It seemed like a miracle. Lee would go around turning on the lights. I would follow him and flip the switch to turn them off. No more cleaning chimneys, trimming wicks and filling messy lamps with coal oil."

FOUR

The couple's life underwent more changes with the end of World War II. The canning factory where Lee worked started phasing out its employees. He lost his job in 1946 and applied for Social Security compensation. The next year, at age 65, he started receiving $12 a month. A combination of boredom, advent of the long winter evenings, and the absence of farming and work demands contributed to a midlife adventurism that almost ended his marriage.

At first, no one realized anything was amiss. Maude harbored her resentment in secret. Mardo was getting established in his new job at the *Columbus Dispatch*, Pauline's husband was busy with postwar duties at Lima Westinghouse, and Bea's husband was in the process of changing careers at Toledo.

It remained for Mildred to ferret out the estrangement. She had arrived from Arizona in September, 1946, for a two-week visit. She was very thin and racked by coughing spells that left her breathless. She spent most of her time with her mother. Lee was seldom around in the evenings.

"What's wrong with Dad?" she queried. Refusing to accept evasions, she finally got Maude to level with her. Lee would rush through his evening chores, change clothes and be gone until 11:00 P.M. or later, three or four nights each week. He was continuing the same pattern he'd followed the last few months he'd worked at the cannery, her mother said. She finally learned the attraction was a 62-year-old widow and her daughter, living only four miles away.

"It's probably innocent," Maude admitted. "A number of other men are there. They play cards and drink beer." (The widow was apparently bootlegging as she had no license to sell alcoholic beverages.) Maude, who finally released her pent-up feelings, said her complaint was that she was left alone so much of the time.

Mildred was aghast. Her parents always had been so close. They did everything together. She had never heard them argue, or even speak loudly to one another. This can't go on, she decided. Maybe it's a matter of communication. Perhaps Dad just doesn't realize how selfish he's being.

"We'll discuss it with Dad," she told her mother. "If he doesn't admit this is a problem and he's ready to do something about it, you can pack some things and go home with me to Arizona." Mildred, Maude and Lee had a showdown the next day.

Lee said he didn't realize what his frequent unexplained absences were doing to his wife's peace of mind. "I enjoy being able to play cards with the men," he explained. "They give me more of a challenge. I should have thought of your feelings but you never complained to me," he protested, in an attempt to partially justify his thoughtlessness.

Maude suggested that she could learn to play the more involved card games and they could invite the neighbors to join them. "I'll serve sandwiches and lemonade or iced tea," she promised. "And I'll tell you straight out when something is bothering me. The two of us can make it right."

Maude told Mildred she'd been lying awake at night, fearing she might have to leave the man she loved and the farm that had been placed in her name when the Rawson and Sarah Williams estate was settled in the mid-1930s. She never considered asking Lee to leave. The place had belonged to his family and she had acquired title only because Lee, as administrator of the will, could not legally make an offer for it. She made the best bid of $2,300 at the estate auction sale. Lee's sister, Dawn Ansley (widow of Roy Ansley), purchased the adjoining 136-acre tract for $3,800.

The year after Maude and Lee restored their togetherness, they embarked on an automobile trip to Mildred's home in Phoenix. They permitted Clay Bealer, a neighboring farmer and lifelong friend, to accompany them (and help pay the expenses).

They filled the pre-war Ford sedan with all the home-canned produce it would hold--then spent six days making the 2,100 mile trip via Routes 40 and 66. The auto was in good mechanical condition and made only one enforced stop--for repair of a punctured tire.

They enjoyed the leisurely trip westward, staying in tourist homes along the way, enjoying the bountiful breakfasts included in the fee. Few motels existed in 1948. They were not only more costly but breakfasts would have been an added expense.

Part XIII: The Fifties

"AND the band played 'Annie Laurie-e-e-e'"

ONE

*T*he rain had started at noon on this October day in 1950. It was going to end with snow flurries, Lee forecast gloomily. "We may have Squaw Winter on your birthday," he told his wife of more than 47 years.

It had been a wonderful autumn. The first killing frost came just 10 days earlier--and daytime temperatures had hovered around 75 degrees since. "Maybe we can have our Indian Summer in mid-November or even at Thanksgiving time," Maude said.

They were sitting on the roomy front porch, rocking gently in their favorite chairs while discussing the weather, the almost completed corn harvest, and the possibility of visiting friends over the week-end. The conversation was dying for lack of topics when Maude had an inspiration --they would discuss the Allen and Williams genealogy charts they had received during the early years of their marriage and had stored in the bookcase.

"I'll bet we are related directly or indirectly to a third of the people in the United States," Maude declared. "The first Allen set foot in America in 1632, 12 years after the first Pilgrim landed in Plymouth, Massachusetts; the first Williams came a half a century later. They started populating the New World at once--Samuel Allen, Jr. with 10 children, Richard and Prudence Beals Williams with 12."

All the early settlers had large families. Their children and children's children followed suit. Cabins overflowed with youngsters. When a girl reached 16, she was married; a boy of 18, if he was not needed on the home farm, took off for a neighboring state or the little-explored Ohio Territory.

So the Williams and Allen clans exploded, traveled to distant areas, mixed their blood with that of other names like Parsons, Coffin, Gouldin, Wallace, Hunt, Branson, Hammond, Witcraft, Hiatt, Stanton, Mathews, Sullivan, Wilson, Miller, McQuade, and a host of other colonial families.

Maude told Lee that the Allens had a 50-year head start, and he countered with the indisputable fact that the Williamses had caught up by consistently having more children per couple. In fact, the Allens could count only eight generations between Samuel Allen, Sr. and Maude's birth.

The Williamses had seven generations, starting with George's arrival in Philadelphia with a wagon train of Quakers about 1690. Shortly after, he settled in Prince Georges County, Maryland. He had left his native Wales after receiving a land grant from King Charles II. Lee never learned the names of the other children George launched in colonial life; he followed only the line of direct descendants to himself.

George was followed by Richard, who was married on November 19, 1746, to Prudence Beals (12 children). Their son Silas married Mary Hunt (12 children); his son Asa married Elizabeth Branson (12 children); his son Jesse married Elizabeth Hammond (12 children); Rawson, the next generation, married Sarah Witcraft; and their son Leonidas Witcraft Williams was married on February 25, 1903, to Maude B. Allen. The population explosion started to fade with Rawson and Sarah. They had only nine children, two of whom were stillborn.

Samuel Allen Sr. came from Braintree, Essex Co., England, to Cambridge, Massachusetts in 1632 and then moved with his 14-year-old son of the same name to Windsor, Connecticut. Maude traced her lineage from those two, senior and junior, through Samuel Allen III, Joseph, Adam, her grandfather Ethan (named after the Revolutionary War hero), and her father Arthur Allen. They rivaled the Williamses in the size of their families, bested them in longevity, and Maude's grandfather Ethan even may have established a six-generation record when his wife, Susannah

Straley Allen, gave birth to Margaret Alice on March 19, 1862. She was their 15th child--a sister of Maude's father, Arthur Allen.

Both Maude and Lee boasted of some colonial dignitaries in their family line-ups. Lee pointed to Levi Coffin, Jr., the famed abolitionist who is credited with establishing a network of way stations from the deep South to the North--through which fleeing slaves were shuttled to freedom. He was the son of Levi Coffin, Sr. and Prudence Williams (one of the 12 children of Richard and Prudence Beals Williams).

He wrote in his *Reminiscences*, published in 1876, of his Great-Grandfather George Williams arriving in the New World from Wales and settling in Prince Georges County, Maryland.

He told of the hardships that his grandfather Richard and his wife Prudence Beals Williams endured when they left Maryland with their two children to come to Guilford County, North Carolina, in 1749. When provisions were depleted, Prudence, a remarkable woman, rode 50 miles on horseback to get food for the family and 50 miles back alone through a wilderness where there were many Indians.

The couple planted corn that first year and garden seed, went without bread until the corn ripened, dried it by spreading it on the ground in the sun, and then "took it on horseback to a mill about 30 miles distant" to be ground for flour. They raised flax, prepared it for the loom, wove it into cloth and made their clothing.

Levi Coffin, Jr. related that the Quaker meeting house, donated by his Grandfather Williams, was used as a hospital for wounded soldiers after the Battle of Guilford Court House during the Revolutionary War. Grandfather Williams's house was occupied by British officers; Grandfather Coffin's by the Americans, Coffin wrote.

When smallpox broke out among the British officers, "Grandfather Williams caught the disease and died. My grandmother was left with five sons and seven daughters. She lived to a good old age and died, respected by all who knew her... She was an elder in the religious society of Friends for many years."

Levi Coffin, Jr. wrote that his grandmother's brother Thomas Beals reportedly was the first white man in the vast Territory of Ohio, going there in 1795 to preach to the Indians. "At his death in 1801, he was buried in a coffin dug out of a log, there being no dressed timber available and no sawmill within hundreds of miles."

Maude told Lee that her family tree was topheavy with exploits of the sons of fourth generation Joseph Allen. Six of his sons fought in the Revolutionary War, including her great-grandfather Adam. The others were Joseph, Jr., Solomon (who rose to the rank of Major), Jonathan, Moses, and Thomas.

Solomon was in charge of escorting Major Andre to Headquarters in connection with the Benedict Arnold treason investigation. He also had a role in suppressing the Shay Rebellion. Thomas became the first minister at Pittsfield, Massachusetts, during which time he was a good friend of the Reverend Jonathan Edwards (author-evangelist and famed for the revival of Puritan idealism).

Reading from her record of the Allens, Maude told Lee that her great-great-grandfather's wife, Elizabeth Parsons Allen, was known throughout the Northampton, Massachusetts, area for her Christian character and for having been present at the birth of three thousand children--in addition to her own ten (by Joseph). She was much sought after as midwife throughout a wide area.

Maude said many of her early ancestors lived for the moment. They took chances. Some went to sea. Some followed Indian trails as the Red Man receded across the plains. Some became criminals, although these warranted but a line in the Allen genealogy charts. William Allen, a son of Captain Moses Allen, was mentioned but with only the notation that he "followed a profligate life."

Maude's mother, Nora (a Wilson), gave her a history lesson almost every day as she was growing up, telling her about her famous relatives. On the Wilson side, Maude was related to Presidents Wilson and Taft, Nora told her, though Wilson (being a Democrat) was suspect. On the Allen side, Maude was descended from Ethan Allen, of the famed Green Mountain Boys.

Ethan, a hard drinking, rough frontiersman and a second cousin of Maude's great-great-grandfather Joseph, would be remembered in history for his exploits during the Revolutionary War. George Washington wrote of him: "There is an original something in him that commands attention." He was "brave, even to rashness" wrote Hugh Moore in his *Memoirs of Colonel Ethan Allen*. He was "celebrated among his townsmen (Tinmouth, Vermont) for acts of boldness, and a perfect contempt of everything pertaining to cowardice."

Two incidents showed the reckless character of the man. The Governor of New York put a 100-pounds bounty on his head because of the intimidation and force used by his armed band of Green Mountain Boys in preventing the New Hampshire Grants (land that is now Vermont) from becoming a part of New York State.

Ethan Allen gambled with his freedom by going to Albany, New York, calling for a bowl of punch at the city's most prominent house of entertainment, then escaping back to Vermont under the nose of the sheriff.

The other event was a needless act of gallantry. He was in the home of a gentleman who, although not a dentist, "was in the habit of extracting teeth." A woman arrived. She had a badly decayed tooth and was suffering pain. She would approach the dentist's chair, then back away in fear. After several minutes of this, Ethan ordered the dentist to extract one of his teeth. "But your teeth are all sound, General," the man demurred.

"Never mind--do as I direct you." A tooth was extracted and Allen told her to "take courage from the example I have given you." The result: "Pride overcame her fears; she was soon relieved from apprehension and pain."

When Ethan Allen died of apoplexy in February, 1789, he was honored not only for his exploits during the Revolutionary War but as "a staunch friend, a good citizen, and an honest man." His Green Mountain Boys--once termed armed bandits who conducted guerrilla warfare--were praised for victories at Fort Ticonderoga and Bennington, and for the violence that prevented Vermont from becoming a part of England's New York State.

In 1834, Hugh Moore wrote of him: "To the poor, his hand was ever open; and, in behalf of the oppressed, his energies were ever directed."

"He sounds a little like my Uncle Harve," Maude said. Harve was a big, bluff, ruddy-faced man who liked alcoholic beverages. Like Ethan, he died of apoplexy.

Maude's great-grandfather Adam Allen had enlisted in General Washington's Army while a resident of Pennsylvania. Shortly after the end of the war, he joined a few other adventuresome youths and emigrated first to Kentucky, where he was engaged in running the Upper and Lower Blue Lick Salt Works.

During the War of 1812, he started to go to Detroit to enlist but hostilities were over before he arrived. He next came to Fayette County, Ohio, where he was married to his second wife, Nancy Gardner. Throughout his life, Adam was passionately fond of hunting and provided venison for the table and buckskin clothing for his family.

On November 1, 1924, the Washington Court House chapter of the Daughters of the American Revolution honored Adam with a memorial program and the dedication of a monument inscribed: "A soldier of the Revolutionary War. Entered the Army of Washington in 1776. Fought in the Battles of Monmouth and Brandywine." Adam died at the home of his son Ethan (Maude's grandfather) in 1851 at the age of 97.

"Here's something surprising," said Lee.

His wife followed his pointing finger down the genealogical chart.

"The children--Mardo and Geneva, and Pauline and Sonny--are cousins. And so are your sister Dawn and her husband, Roy."

The facts were there before them, buried in a multitude of data. Ruth Ann Williams (who had married James R. Ansley) and Ross Williams were second cousins; their grandfathers were brothers. So that made Geneva and Sonny Ansley, who were the grandchildren of Ruth Ann, and Mardo and Pauline, the grandchildren of Ross, fourth cousins of each other. Roy Ansley and Dawn Williams Ansley, as children of Ruth and Ross, respectively, were third cousins!

The couple jotted down the facts, just to convince each other and the disbelieving relatives. Both Ruth Ann and Ross could trace their lineage back to George Williams, the Welshman, who settled in Prince Georges, Maryland in the late 17th century.

"We might have been living in Barbados," Lee told his wife. He said one story that had been passed down through the generations had placed his great-great-great-great-great grandfather (the first Richard Williams to come to the New World) in Barbados. He stayed there but his son,

George, had the wanderlust. "He came to Pennsylvania and our branch of the Williams family scattered to North Carolina, Ohio, Indiana and throughout the new nation. We can blame George for having to endure the miserable Ohio winters," Lee declared.

Reading from his chart, he told Maude the name of *Williams* was very ancient, going back to Marchudel of Cynn, Lord of Abergelen in Denbighshire, one of the fifteen tribes of North Wales who lived in the time of Roderic the Great, King of the Britons, about 849.

Maude said Fitz-Alan, who crossed the English Channel in 1066 with William the Conqueror, was her ancestor.

Maude and Lee were impressed by the history they had uncovered in the lives of their ancestors. But, they agreed, there were probably more scoundrels in their families' pasts than would ever meet the light of day. They thought that it would be almost impossible to keep a record through their 300 or 350 years in the New World, detailing all the children and children's children, their births, deaths, marriages, and occupations--plus the blood lines of the men or women who added their own lineage by marrying an Allen or a Williams.

Large families were the rule, the couple decided. They differed as to the cause. Maude insisted that children were wanted--the more the merrier. Husbands and wives alike believed that "many hands make light work"--at a time when work was done by hand, the hard way. Children, too, brought the happy sounds of laughter to a home that had little to laugh about, Maude thought.

Lee, by contrast, believed that many children were born as a result of a biological urge that should have been repressed. He said that many males of the time measured their manhood by the number of children their wives bore. "They kept their mates barefoot in winter--pregnant during the summer," Lee declared. Many of the births were unintended. When night fell, parents had nothing to do; there was no television, no radio, neighborhood movie or bar.

As the two continued their friendly debate, Lee recounted the story from years earlier. A stranger was visiting nearby LaRue, Ohio, when he became aware of the large number of children on the village streets. "You must be setting a birth record for the state, if not the nation. What is the reason for so many youngsters?"

There was no orphanage nearby, the visitor was told. "What we have is an eastbound train that gathers speed on a straight run from Mt. Victory, 10 miles to the west. It goes through here at a speed of 80 to 90 miles per hour, with the engineer playing a tune on the steam whistle at every crossing."

It's pretty disruptive and is sure to create problems for schools and municipal services in the future, the LaRue resident said. "You see, the train goes through here at 5 o'clock each morning. It's too early to get up and too late to go back to sleep."

TWO

The couple, as they neared 70, entered the 1950s in an optimistic frame of mind, Maude said. There was no mortgage on their 100-acre farm, and no outstanding debts. The fields were rented, so Lee was relieved of that responsibility. Both were in good health. A neighbor plowed an acre of ground near their house each spring and worked it up, so Lee and Maude were assured of all the vegetables they could grow--and preserve. Their two cows provided them with milk and butter, their 20 hens with eggs.

They considered themselves so well off they spent several weeks in Phoenix during the winter of 1951-52. They helped grandson Gene and his wife Isabel moved into their newly purchased home on North 29th Avenue. Lee worked at sodding the yard (it was bare dirt when they moved in) and putting up curtain rods. Maude and Mildred bought and hemmed red draperies for the living room windows.

Mildred knew how proud Gene and Isabel were at being able to purchase a new home so early in their married life. She and John, after almost 30 years of marriage, still rented.

Mildred had a little parakeet, Abner, whom she'd trained to say a few words: "Hello, everybody," "My name's Abner," "I'm a pretty bird," "Hello, Stupid!" Abner always pestered Lee while he was reading by perching on the top of his book and pecking the pages. Isabel said: "We could always tell what Grandpa had been reading."

Abner loved to swing on the end of a yardstick that Mildred held for him. He also liked playing with a miniature plaster doll buggy. It had working wheels and when it was placed on a table, Abner would clamp his beak on the handle and push it to the edge so it would drop. He'd cock his head to one side and wait to hear it hit the floor. Then he'd let out a loud chuckle (very similar to Lee's chuckle).

Mildred and Maude prepared venison one night for dinner after John had bagged a buck. "Don't tell Lee it's deer," Maude said, knowing how finicky he was. The meat looked like pork chops. Lee ate two or three chops with relish. Then Gene, just to see his reaction, told him it was deer. Lee replied, "I thought it tasted kind of funny." He wouldn't eat a bite of it afterwards. Mildred was understandably upset, since she'd planned to use cuts from the deer for several meals while Lee and Maude were there.

During the visit, Mildred and John showed Lee and Maude the tourist sites--the Grand Canyon, Apache Lake, Painted Mountain Park. Maude had a favorite outfit for these excursions--a gaily designed Mexican blouse and long skirt, a gift from Gene and Isabel. Maude enhanced her garb with the silver and turquoise Indian jewelry made and sold in the area. Her white hair was permed and framed her face in soft waves.

Grandson Gene and Isabel took Maude and Lee to the desert town of Butler Valley. Gene wanted his grandparents to see the treeless expanse where he and his Army buddies of the 736 Tank Battalion had trained under General Patton's command.

They had labored in 100-plus degrees in what Gene thought was preparation for Africa or the Mid-East. Instead, his tank battalion wound up in Germany in Europe's coldest weather in years. Isabel wrote to Mardo: "Gene said the abandoned camp, rotting under the Arizona sun, dotted with sagebrush and cacti, was even more desolate-looking than he remembered."

Members of the party sat in what little shade the auto provided--except for Mildred who lay on a cot in the full glare of the sun, wishing its rays would magically penetrate to her lungs and rid her of the asthma that had crippled her since 1929.

She was nut brown from the sun, the skin stretched tightly across her face. Unable to eat when the wheezing and coughing spells were at their worst, she weighed between 70 and 80 pounds.

She, who'd always been vivacious and full of fun, now hated to go places or meet new people. She was so thin and coughed so much, people stared and she said she felt like a freak. The damage to her bronchial tubes and lungs from the kerosene had been irreversible. She and her family had been condemned to 23 years of living hell by the doctor's "cure."

Lee and Maude returned to Ohio in the spring. Soon afterwards, John and Mildred bought an almost new 2-bedroom home, surrounded by grapefruit trees. Mildred was very proud of her new home, the first one she and John had ever owned.

In the autumn of 1952, Mildred told her husband John she had a strong urge to see everyone. In early October, they started the 2,100-mile drive from Phoenix to Ohio.

She saw them all--Bea and Buck Deerwester, Pauline and Sonny Ansley, Geneva and Mardo Williams, her nieces and nephews (even some cousins). Then her asthma worsened. She blamed her relapse on a combination of allergies and the fact that Lee sometimes lighted up a cigarette in her presence. She told John she was afraid she would never make it back to Arizona. The visit was cut short.

Lee and Maude had planned to accompany them on the return trip and stay in Phoenix for the winter. So a mad rush developed--to get the clothing assembled, the canned goods loaded, and to get the group on the road. Mildred and John had planned to stay in Ohio three weeks; they started back home after 10 days.

The mid-size automobile was over-loaded, with four adults, five suitcases, two or three boxes of miscellaneous articles, and all the canned fruits and vegetables Maude had preserved. The springs were almost on the axles. John had to drive carefully although speed was essential.

They took parts of four days to reach the Perry home. "Mildred became so tired that we would have to stop early," Maude remembered. "John would lift her out of the car and carry her into the motel room. She weighed less than 70 pounds. John saw that she got her medicine, inhalants and a heart stimulant. Then we would start early the next morning."

Maude said Mildred had more trouble breathing as the hours passed.

"It seemed as if she was taking only three or four breaths a minute, and every breath was an effort. It was made worse when Lee would forget and light a cigarette within the close quarters of the car. He would shamefacedly crush it out after a puff or two. I never realized until then what an overpowering habit his smoking had become."

Mildred refused to let John stop and put her in a hospital along the way. She just wanted to get back to her new home.

"We made it," Mildred gasped in relief as John carried her into the home she'd despaired of reaching. It had been an ordeal for all--but especially for him. He'd driven the slightly more than 2,100 miles without help; he'd worried ceaselessly about his wife; and he'd been unable to rest at night as she fought for one breath after another.

He called for the doctor. It was Sunday. He was grilling hamburgers for the family dinner but would be there as soon as possible. "If he doesn't come soon, it will be too late," Mildred gasped. Those were her last words. She was gone when the doctor arrived--and the husband and her parents were left to make funeral arrangements. They took little solace from the thought that she wouldn't have to suffer any more.

She weighed under 60 pounds when she died. The undertaker said he'd never seen anyone so emaciated.

The Williamses stayed on with their son-in-law. John Perry had asked his son Gene and his wife Isabel to join him in fulfilling Mildred's last wish--the Golden Wedding Anniversary party for Maude and Lee. The celebration, subdued by the absence of their daughter, was held on February 25, 1953--with the Perrys as hosts and all the Arizona acquaintances of the couple in attendance.

Lee's sister Dawn Ansley flew out for the occasion. John regretted that none of the couple's children could be there, leaving him, his son Gene and family, to do the honors.

During his 29 years of marriage to Mildred, John had become almost a second son to the couple he was honoring on this 25th day of February. Maude watched him with affection as he circulated among the guests. He'd taken his wedding vows seriously--especially the "in sickness and in health" part. When his sprite of a wife became ill, he severed all ties, except to her and their son, and took off for an unknown clime to make a new life for them among strangers.

He'd been considerate, friendly, and helpful; willing to change jobs when necessary and ready to embrace any treatment that might add to his wife's enjoyment of life. "John has been a prince," Maude confided to her husband. "Wherever fortune takes him in the future he will have our best wishes and full support."

After the anniversary celebrants left, John helped Maude and Lee pick up the debris, admire again the gifts left behind, then all retired to dream again of days and times that would never return.

THREE

Not long afterward, Lee and Maude were reading of March winds and April showers, and missing Ohio's greenery. Hot weather already was giving its advance warning to Arizonans. "We might have tried to hitchhike back to the farm if John hadn't completed travel plans when he did," the two agreed.

Son-in-law John and grandson Gene Perry drove them to Yates Center, Kansas, carrying their luggage, Golden Wedding gifts and a living memorial of their daughter Mildred. John had presented them with her pet parakeet, Abner. "Mildred was crazy about that bird," remembered her daughter-in-law Isabel Perry. "She spent much of her time during the last year of her life teaching it to talk."

When the Arizona party met up with Bea and Buck Deerwester in Yates Center, Abner greeted them like old friends--or enemies. "Hello, Stupid," he shrilled, to the amusement of all.

Buck and Bea took her parents home in near record time. All were in a hurry--Lee and Maude to get home, Bea and Buck to return to work.

Lee and Maude arrived in Ohio in late spring 1953, to the singing of birds, the light greenery of new growth on the trees, and the smell of freshly turned earth as farmers prepared for another growing season. To them, it was a pleasing contrast to the palm trees along Phoenix streets and the cactus-riddled landscapes of sand in the outlying areas.

For two years Abner was a welcome reminder of the daughter they had lost. The bird would sing at times but his principal attraction to grandchildren and others who visited was his ability to speak. Maude tried to teach him to say, "Hi, Lee" and other new words but she either lacked patience and know-how or Abner had lost his desire to cooperate.

On a summer day in 1955, Maude left the door to his hanging cage ajar while doing the daily cleaning and feeding. Abner left his prison, flew around the room and, as Lee entered from the porch to help with his capture, darted into the great outdoors.

"We saw Abner with yellow hammers and goldfinches as he sought to establish contacts with other birds," Maude said. "We tried to entice him back throughout the remainder of that summer of 1955 by placing feed in the opened cage on the porch, by calling to him, and by sitting hour after hour in the sun with arms outstretched for convenient landing. Abner never returned."

FOUR

The couple settled in for the most stress-free period of their lives. They could work or loaf, at their convenience. Their income, while small, was sufficient for necessities. And they could visit friends and relatives, attend social events, or simply sit on the roomy porch. The rocking chairs and bench-like swing became grandstand seats for nature's kaleidoscope of colors, the round of bird concerts, the viewing of rare rainbows, and the sudden summer storms with their brilliant flashes of lightning, rolls of thunder, gusts of wind and pelting rain, and sometimes hail.

Maude and Lee said that their lives had been little affected by cataclysmic events in the first half of the century. Some happenings hit closer to home and were lodged in their minds. The sinking of the U.S.S. Maine in the Cuban Harbor (1898) triggered the Spanish-American War and brought the fear of widespread conflict with the chance that 17-year-old Lee might be called for service.

A convict-started fire destroyed a portion of the Ohio Penitentiary in nearby Columbus, Ohio, with a loss of 322 lives on Easter Sunday, 1930. The spectacular mid-air explosion, which destroyed the world's largest dirigible over Lakehurst, New Jersey (May 6, 1937), focused attention on the growing interest in experimental balloons and other kinds of air travel.

The couple discussed the feats of the early fliers. Charles Lindbergh in the first solo flight across the Atlantic landed in Paris to the adulation of people of all nations. "Wrong Way" Corrigan filed a flight plan for a transcontinental flight but ended up in Ireland; aviatrix Amelia Earhart set all kinds of records for women before disappearing in the South Pacific while on a good will mission. The fate of Ms. Earhart (still unsolved in 1995) was of greater interest to them because their newspaperman son Mardo had interviewed her in 1936 when she and her mechanic stopped at a Kenton, Ohio, service station. They were motoring west to east seeking funds to finance the ill-fated trip from which she never returned.

Only the authors of comic books were predicting trips to the moon and inter-planetary flights. "We were thrilled by the idea of television and we thought that the transmission of words and images over the air waves represented the ultimate--that nothing more could be possible," Maude admitted later.

She and Lee had read about the destruction of two Japanese cities by bombs of unbelievable power; the crippling railroad strike, in which President Truman threatened to draft the strikers for after-war peace service, and about the post-World War II's steel and coal strikes--all developments of 1945, the year World War II ended. "They had little effect on our way of life," Maude said. "We still had nothing with which to buy the products that were becoming in short supply."

Each year Lee planted a huge garden--too much for their own use, so they shared tomatoes, cabbages, string beans and potatoes with the children. In fact, Lee was in the garden, hoeing listlessly, on June 12, 1957, when Ross Engle and his wife Ruth drove up the lane for a visit.

They remained only a short time. "Lee looked like death," Ross told Mardo as soon as he could reach a telephone. "He was pale. He was breathing shallowly. He should be in the hospital."

Lee and Maude had not mentioned any problem with the health of either so this message was a shock--a stimulus to action. Lee was rushed to McKitrick Hospital, Kenton, by ambulance. He was resting comfortably on June 17, his 75th birthday. Dr. Louis Black, the attending physician, said he had a chance to regain his health if his heart didn't fail. A combination of emphysema and summer pneumonia had restricted the amount of oxygen in the blood at a time when the heart muscles were being called upon to expend more effort, the doctor explained.

Lee was dismissed from the hospital in late June. Maude took over his care. She prepared his favorite foods, helped him do minor exercises, cleaned his bed clothing when he had an accident, and encouraged him to take a positive outlook. He had no appetite but on that July 16th, he ate all the food she'd prepared for him with the comment: "I'd better start eating if I'm ever going to get out of this bed."

Maude had returned to the living room to resume reading a book when she heard a gasp or a light moan. "What is it, Lee? What do you want?" she called. There was no answer. She found him lying quietly, with eyes closed. He had died without pain even as he was preparing to do what he could to live.

Austin Williams and his wife Edith found her sitting by Lee's side when they arrived a few minutes later. She was confused about what should be done, Austin said. He called the Mt. Victory funeral director, then the children.

As the body rested in the funeral chapel for the last rites, family members gathered to pay their respects to Lee--the husband, the father, grandfather and uncle who had always been the life of every party--and to offer their condolences to the youthful looking widow who was not yet 74.

The family recalled the strengths and weaknesses that had made him so lovable. He chewed tobacco, then smoked heavily. He always tried to convince the children that part of their duties was to clean his cuspidor periodically, but usually ended up doing the filthy job himself. When he finally progressed to the smoking habit, he developed emphysema. Whether or not that caused him to die prematurely was discussed by his survivors.

Sometimes he drank too much liquor. He made a game of telling lewd jokes to the most reserved of people. He made fun of foibles and praised those who stood up for their principles in the face of opposition. He worked hard, bore his setbacks uncomplainingly, and often delayed too long the treatment of his illnesses--as he did in his final summer.

"We loved him for his gaiety and his ability to talk to everyone about anything," said one nephew. "When I was little, he made me feel grown-up," a niece told the gathered mourners. "He kidded me and teased me, but always with a smile. He was never mean."

Maude and the children remembered begging him to sing "The Actor's Boarding House." The subject matter was unusual and exotic to them. Lee sang it in a bawdy style, especially when he'd had a few drinks. Most of the professional singers of the time were very low keyed, but Lee used broad gestures, made his voice expressive and dramatic, walked back and forth as he sang, and overacted at every chance. The family thought it was glorious the way he ended the song, flinging his arms out wide, making his voice deep and raspy, "And the band played Annie Laurie-e-e-e."

Maude's brother Harley said he never could remember when Lee looked as he did in the casket.

The embalmer did not know Lee and had used a photo from early married days to reconstruct his face. The result: a smooth and wrinkle-free visage with no hollows and no sags. Only Maude remembered him as he appeared. She was satisfied and no complaint was made.

She grieved silently, thanked those who had sent floral sprays and arrangements, and told daughter Pauline she would go home with her for a few days. She refused proposals that she share the remainder of her life with the children. She chose instead to go her own way--with their help.

Lee was buried in Hale Cemetery, where Maude would join him more than 36 years later. But in the meantime, she would adapt to an altogether different life and assume responsibilities she'd never undertaken. She would move her residence six times to meet changing conditions and, although more confident, she would retain her air of reticence and the habit of listening that made her so beloved.

Book II
Maude Leaves Rush Creek

Part I: Adjustments

She missed her porch, bowered with honeysuckle, the bird concerts, the colorful sunsets, and the spectacular storms that gave unpredictable drama to the quiet harmony of rural life. But she actually enjoyed one aspect of city living. She no longer had to make the 100-foot trip to the outhouse.

ONE

*F*ollowing Lee's death in 1957, Maude attempted to continue her life on the farm. She had no horse and buggy, and she'd never learned to drive an auto. The farm's drinking water had been condemned after the highest flood waters in years had inundated the well--carrying on its crest a dead muskrat. The inconveniences of living alone there were overwhelming.

Daughters Bea and Pauline suggested that their mother should divide her time between the daughters and son, making her home with each. Maude had heard the rumor and was preparing her arguments when the talk died down.

Mardo's wife, Geneva, with his concurrence, told her sisters-in-law that their mother--at a young 74--should not be compelled to give up her independence. Maude would be lost, Geneva argued, if she had to enter any of their homes, conform to their rules, live her life as the children wanted it. "She loves to cook and bake, but she would never feel free to use our cookware and appliances. She would give up," Geneva insisted.

So Maude, with her children's accord, made arrangements with the Donald Dugans for their daughter, 13-year-old Kathy, to stay with her at night when she might have grown lonesome or afraid. She received permission from another neighbor (the Lauren Ledleys) to obtain drinking water from their well. She relied on neighbors to do her shopping for her-- or drive her to town for that purpose.

Some day, she thought, during the long summer of 1958, "I'll have to move away." But she would put it off as long as she could. The solitude was balm. She awakened to the musical conversation of the robins, the strident call of the blue jays. She could walk along the banks of Rush Creek, where the water rippled softly over the stones in the shallows. She could read or sew--always in the reed rocking chair on the spacious porch. She could do the housework--or put it off.

She could watch the sun rise and set; admire the deep blue of the sky, the shades of white and gray in the clouds, and the flare of colors on the western horizon at dusk. When she had nothing to do, she could think-- about the past with Lee at her side, and about the mysterious future which she would have to explore alone.

She was secluded, but never felt lonely, she said. Neighbors were only a phone call away.

To stay there alone during the winter months was out of the question. The house had no indoor plumbing and no central heating. It was in need of repairs. Winds whipped snow under all the outside doors of the house. She would be isolated if heavy snows buried the lane to the house, or if storm waters caused the creek to overflow. So Maude accepted invitations from her grandson and his wife, Gene and Isabel Perry, to be their guests for the winter in Phoenix, Arizona.

"I loved being with Gene and family," she said. "I baked them their favorite cookies and pies. Isabel made me feel welcome. She was working at Circle K (a convenience store chain) so I felt needed." But when it became spring, Maude grew homesick. She missed the songs of the robins and whippoorwills, the greenery of new grass and fresh leaves, and the soft smell of spring rains on wild flowers and upturned earth.

Maude savored the seclusion of the farmhouse for four summers. Then the day arrived when she could no longer stay in the century-old house to which she had come as a bride. Heavy snows, cold rains, and high winds had taken their toll. The roof was leaking. Window panes had been blown away during the winter's storms. Flood waters had washed out a portion of the lane, making it almost impossible for the neighbors to drive in with groceries they had picked up for her in town. She reluctantly concluded that the isolation, the inconveniences to her, and the demands on her neighbors were just too great.

There were few options. Maude told her daughters and son she didn't want to live in Ridgeway or Mt. Victory. She had no close friends in either place. She preferred Kenton over Bellefontaine. Both were county seat towns. Both were larger, with populations close to 8,000, but she liked Kenton because her friend and sister-in-law, Dawn Ansley, and her niece, Lucille Ansley, lived there.

In 1960, at age 77, Maude, moved to Kenton 12 miles away. She left the sights, sounds and smells of her beloved farm, the freshness of the country air, the morning dews, and the fall flight of swallows. It was a sad moment as she said good-bye to the home she had come to as a bride in 1903.

No longer would she sit on her roomy porch, bowered with honeysuckle, and watch the blackbirds and mocking birds chase marauding crows from an endangered nest, see the sun rise above a field of rippling grain or watch the red ball of a setting sun splash the western heavens.

Her children helped her move. Only the choice belongings were loaded into the rented trailer, for 57 years worth of acquisitions could never be contained in the two-bedroom apartment to which she was moving. The two reed rocking chairs used by her and Lee, the children's hand-carved walnut cradle, Grandma Sarah Williams' spinning wheel, the antique cord bed, were stored in the unfinished rooms under the eaves. They were lost when vandals later raided the vacant house and carried them off.

The sun was shining on that beautiful October day when Maude started her new life. She said farewell to her home and remembered the day as perhaps the gloomiest she had ever known. "This is an adventure," daughter Pauline told her, with little conviction in her voice.

Maude climbed into the car with her youngest daughter. She tried to hide her sadness by promising herself she would return, perhaps for a month or two, the following summer. She picked an imaginary speck from her eye, then took out her handkerchief when she thought no one was looking to wipe away the tears. She never spent another day in that treasured house on the banks of Rush Creek.

Two daughters, the son and their mates helped to get their mother settled into her new home, on South Cherry Street in Kenton, in one side of the Elizabeth Dugan home. (She was an aunt of Donald Dugan, Maude's farmer neighbor.)

Maude had friends in Kenton, as well as her beloved sister-in-law Dawn Ansley, her niece Lucille, and Eunice Ansley Held, Geneva's sister, whom Maude grew to love almost as a fourth daughter.

Lucille, age 55 at that time, still blamed herself for the murder of her father Roy 30 years earlier. She shared the home of her mother Dawn, chauffeuring her and her elderly friends everywhere they wished to go. Maude became one of Lucille's cherished charges.

Maude thrived during that first period as a farmer's widow in a new environment, thanks to her worry-free creed for living. She asked questions at first, before doing the things she'd never done before. She learned to write her own checks, and balance the checkbook. She purchased hospitalization insurance, and insurance on her apartment furnishings.

She made new friends, with the aid of niece Lucille. She purchased a television set, and learned to allocate her time between crafts, socializing, card playing, reading, and the soap operas and news shows. She paid her bills, subscribed to the daily newspaper and established a routine.

Maude and Geneva had a special relationship--a sort of affinity. When her mother-in-law expressed a fear that Bea or Pauline might not approve of a purchase or activity, the daughter-in-law would advise, "Use your judgment--it's your money, your time."

So Maude went her own way, with advice when she asked for it and help when she needed it. One time she talked to Geneva about her need for a new sofa. The old one was frayed badly, and the springs were broken. "But the girls will think I don't need it; that at my age the old one will last."

"What do *you* think? That's what's important," Geneva said. "You have few enough nice things. We'll take you shopping and you can pick out the one you want."

"That's what we did," Maude remembered. "Geneva told Bea and Pauline she thought I deserved a new sofa, so I bought one and I never heard anything more about it."

Maude must have been lonely without Lee but she never talked about it. She went to card games and birthday parties, made friends with Lucille's acquaintances, continued hobbies of bead-stringing and tatting, fashioned cushion covers for friends, activities taught to her by Eunice.

In 1968, Maude made a decision that terminated any possibility of a return to living on the banks of Rush Creek. Lauren Ledley had purchased the Marmon farm and moved his family there, then made overtures to buy the Williams tract. Donald Dugan said he was interested too. And Maude, who at first said the 100-acre farm wasn't for sale, made a trip to the scene and reconsidered.

"The buildings were growing more dilapidated," she said. "Galvanized roofing on the house, granary and barn was rusting out. Granary walls were listing. Some siding had been blown from the west side of the barn. Panes were missing from windows on the house. There was just no way I could pay for the necessary improvements."

She hoped Ledley might restore the buildings, paint the barn red and the house white, and make of it the picture place it once had been--with sprawling buildings on a knoll above Rush Creek and the windmill quietly whirring at its work. So the talks began.

In 1970, she went to Bellefontaine, Ohio, for a meeting with the Ledleys and a representative of the Farmers Home Administration. While she was waiting for the loan to be approved, she received the disquieting news from neighbors that Lee's distant cousin, Herbert Williams (who as a troubled youth had walked home naked after his clothes were stolen from the banks of Rush Creek), was living in her vacant farm house.

Herb had spent several months in a mental institution in Columbus. He'd killed a neighbor's dog by cutting its throat. At the trial, he'd argued his own case, basing his defense on a ruling which he interpreted "imposes the penalty of death for any dog coming onto the highway at you." Maude was concerned about her new "tenant."

A yellowed newspaper clipping, found in one of Maude's picture albums, discussed the dog-killing incident and said: "Although Williams dropped out of high school in his third year, he claims to have read law books since age 14. He appeared quite confident of himself in court but said he will appeal the case should he lose it. 'Besides,' he remarked, 'I'd rather spend my money on an appeal than have my relatives get it.'"

Herb had returned to his home farm, still at odds with the world, and continued to argue with neighbors. He fired at a pickup truck which was passing his house near midnight. A few pellets struck the motorist, a 16-year-old boy, who--according to Mr. Williams--was making undue noise. While Herb was in the Logan County Jail at Bellefontaine, Ohio, awaiting trial, someone burned his house down. He served a short term in jail, then came back to his farm to live in the corn crib!

He blamed the fire on some neighbors with whom he'd been arguing and remained extremely hostile. When the corn crib he was living in burned down too, he sought vainly to get a roof over his head. It was then he located Maude's vacant farm house.

She grew fearful he'd burn the house down. He was heating one room by kindling a blaze in an empty steel barrel. He was also doing his cooking over it. In October, 1970 Mardo, Sonny, and Buck went over to the farm together to tell him to get out. They knew he sometimes carried a gun and were fearful of going alone.

He was in good humor when he greeted Maude's emissaries, invited them into the living room where he was preparing lunch, and laughed out loud after being told the reason for their visit. "Did it take three of you to bring a simple message?" he asked, sensing their uneasiness. He agreed to leave, saying he'd been offered a room in the farm home of widowed Mrs. Donald Dugan.

Maude then sent a note to him: "As the boys told you Sunday, we are considering sale of the timbers in the house and barn, and possible sale of the farm. We will be bringing prospects in from Columbus to look at the property. Your presence there very possibly would spoil the sale. I would consider it a favor if you vacate the house at once. I have no intention of renting it."

Herb left. A few months later, Maude learned he had been admitted to a nursing home in Kenton. He made more friends there than he ever had, simply by cutting his beard, letting his guard down, and ignoring his suspicions. He gave away some of his cash and was preparing to give his truck to a young couple he'd just met when brother Ira intervened. Herb died shortly thereafter.

Once the sale of the farm to Ledley was completed, Maude received a check for $30,000, less some fees, for the buildings, the 100 acres of farm land, creek and woods. It was more money than she'd ever had. That year she paid income taxes for the only time in her life, $1,400 in capital gains. She had been gone from the farm too long to claim it as a residence.

To Maude's great disappointment, Ledley didn't make improvements on the farm. He razed the buildings, leaving only the windmill, grinding away as a landmark to more than a hundred years of Witcraft-Williams custody.

Maude said later she had hoped one of the children might offer to move back, fix up the house and "give me a room for the rest of my life." All remembered the hardships too vividly--were not interested in commuting long distances to work, raising chickens, or returning to a primitive life. None had the finances to paint-up, fix-up, install water service or the septic tank necessary to make farm life attractive.

TWO

After Mrs. Dugan died, the South Cherry Street residence was sold. Maude moved into an apartment in a large, two-story house on North Detroit Street, Kenton, then to another on East Franklin Street (both with the aid of her children and an auto trailer).

Maude aged well. She kept her figure. With the help of daughter Pauline, her silver tresses received the attention they required. Permanents were scheduled when needed, the hair was waved and set, and the farm woman turned city-dweller was the best-coiffed lady in town. She dressed modestly, carried herself with grace and dignity.

In Columbus, Ohio, while visiting with Mardo and Geneva, the three of them went out to eat at a restaurant near the OSU campus. A young college girl stopped by the table, said to Maude, then 82, "You're the most beautiful older person I've ever seen." Maude carried that pride in her appearance all the way through to her 110th birthday--despite frequent moves, broken hips, and the termination of independent living.

In the mid-1960s her estrangement with her brother Waldo came to an end. It had been over 30 years since Waldo, without a word to Maude, had taken the body of their father, Arthur Allen, from the Mt. Victory funeral home to bury him in Toledo. John and James Allen, Waldo's sons, interceded with a plea that harmony be restored. "Dad and Aunt Maude need each other, as they grow older," John Allen insisted. The two reunited happily and enjoyed years of friendly relations before Waldo died at age 88.

Maude visited in Phoenix for eight more winters after Lee died, traveling by auto with her daughter Bea and husband, flying out accompanied by niece Martha Engle or Kenton friends, Carl and Floy Jones. Then, as an experienced traveler, she flew out by herself to meet son-in-law John Perry's new wife, Lucile. He had remarried after Mildred's death. On the way home, Maude's plane was late reaching Chicago and she missed her connecting flight to Columbus.

"It was her first trip alone," Mardo said. "When she didn't show up as scheduled, Geneva and I were scared to death." TWA, the carrier, paged her in Chicago without result. The airline then checked and determined that she had in fact arrived on the flight from Phoenix. They made sure she would be escorted by one of their employees to the next connecting flight to Columbus.

Maude arrived a little more than an hour late, perfectly calm, apparently operating on her old adage, "If you can't fix it, don't worry about it." When the son asked her why she didn't answer the page to her over the loud speaker, she seemed startled he'd even asked and gave the answer that became standard in comparable situations: "I knew it wasn't for me. I didn't know anyone in Chicago."

When Maude visited Phoenix, Isabel said, she made herself loved by her helpful ways, wooed the great-grandchildren Bill and Corine with home-made cookies, pies and egg noodles, was there for the children when they returned from school, and frequently had dinner started when

Gene and Isabel arrived from work.

"Everyone really liked having her with us," Isabel said. "Each year my mom and dad took her to the Bird Show. They (and Corine and sometimes Bill, children of Gene and Isabel) entered birds in the show, so the event was really looked forward to and enjoyed by all."

Maude always went up to Globe for a week or two to visit Lucile and John. She liked John's new wife Lucile, and Lucile liked her, calling her Mother Williams. Maude loved Lucile's children (whom John adopted)-- Vernon, Daisy Lynn (De De), and Jimmy Perry. They called her Grandma.

As much as Maude enjoyed her winters in Arizona, she was always ready to return to Ohio when April arrived. It became a chore for her even to wait for grandson Gene's birthday, April 16. If the temperature climbed into the nineties--as it usually did by then--"she thought it was so hot we'd better go to the store and get some ice cream," Isabel said. She made an exception in 1972 and stayed until May 20, despite the heat, for great-granddaughter Corine's wedding.

Isabel said that Gene's Grandma Maude and her own Grandma Launders always were ready to go shopping. Once, she laughed, "I took them to a nearby department store. I returned two hours later and found them sitting on a bench outside the store. All they'd bought was a spool of thread to mend Corine's dress." They'd both scrimped all their lives and thought long and hard about their purchases.

When John Perry took his mother-in-law on a tour of wholesale jewelry stores, she went on a spending spree (for her), buying pendant and bracelet--each set with a good luck turquoise--for granddaughters Kay and Jerri.

Mardo recalled an incident that revealed his mother's unassuming nature. He and Geneva were accompanied by Maude on a trip to Lebanon, Ohio. Velda Strait, a niece, was to have gone along but made a last-minute cancellation.

The motor tour included dinner and an overnight stay in the Golden Lamb Inn, which had been a stage coach stop on the Columbus-Cincinnati route during colonial times. Maude was assigned to the Lincoln bedroom, with an ornate bedstead and a towering headboard. Her son and daughter-in-law went to another historic suite nearby.

Furnishings were true colonial, Geneva recalled. The only departure was the addition of a telephone to each room. "We got ready to go to the dining room and Mardo thought he would call his mother to tell her to be ready.

"So he did, and she did what I told him she would do. She 'didn't know anyone here,' knew the phone call was a mistake, so didn't answer it. We picked her up for dinner--and talked about what a great time Velda was missing. Mardo told his mother that if Velda had been with her, she would have answered the phone. She just smiled."

THREE

When Maude reached age 89 in October, 1972, she decided she was too old to be gallivanting around and refused invitations either to spend time in Arizona or Florida (with Mardo and Geneva or Pauline and Sonny, who began wintering there in 1972).

In her nineties, her sight and hearing faded. She started to lose weight so Meals on Wheels brought a balanced meal to her Franklin Street apartment, at noon, each Monday through Friday.

One of Maude's frequent visitors was her next door neighbor Eunice Ansley Held. She became a "stand-in" for her sister and brother-in-law, Mardo and Geneva Ansley Williams, who lived 60 miles away in Columbus and often spent time in Florida.

Eunice grew to love Maude for her uncomplaining approach to living. She washed, set and permed her hair, when Pauline was unable to. As Maude's sight faded, Eunice guided her hand so she could sign her checks and helped her balance her checkbook. When Maude said she needed an activity to keep her busy, Eunice taught her to fashion rope necklaces of beads and to make decorative throw pillows. The articles Maude made became gifts, treasured by friends and relatives.

Maude was doing fine until, one windy morning in October, 1974, she opened the storm door of her apartment to pick up a bottle of milk the route man had just delivered. A gust tore the door wide open. She held on to keep it from being ripped from the hinges, was snatched from her doorway and hurled over the concrete stoop into the yard.

Dazed, she lay on the ground for a few minutes. When no one came to help, she crawled up the steps into the kitchen. Eunice, who found her lying on the kitchen floor trying vainly to reach the telephone, called the emergency squad to take her to the hospital. Maude suffered a fracture of the right thigh bone, so close to the hip that the break could be immobilized only by pinning the ends together with a metal plate.

"Due to her age (91)," Dr. N.C. Schroeder, the attending physician, said, "It is doubtful if it will mend." His pessimism was warranted. Three years later, the plate had loosened and the bone ends were grating. As a 94-year-old, she entered Lima Memorial Hospital for hip replacement surgery, came through with flying colors to the amazement of surgeon and anesthetists.

Eunice looked in on her each time Maude returned to her apartment from the hospital and advised the children when nursing attendants were taking advantage. Eunice ran errands for her, baked her cakes and her favorite cookies, and provided the niceties to make her neighbor's existence happier.

"Eunie was always there, during Mom's setbacks--and before and after," Mardo said later. "She contributed a lot to our piece of mind. Words of thanks could never adequately express our appreciation."

The children were thrilled when Maude resumed walking, with the aid of a walker. She went back to living alone, doing everything herself, except for luncheon from Meals on Wheels.

She continued to watch her soaps. She wondered what Lee's reaction would have been to the television shows of the 1980s. He would be startled, then amused, she decided, probably not embarrassed, even though some of the scenes in the soap operas were more risque than anything he'd seen in burlesque shows.

During the 25 or 30 years after his death, Maude said, she'd been shocked by the liberties taken with TV programming--and she was there to watch the changes as they came. The sudden rush to expose all--nudity and near-nudity, rape, child pornography, plus the advertisements for every unmentionable--was extremely distasteful to her.

She questioned the propriety of ads for toilet tissue, sanitary napkins, hemorrhoidal ointments, jock itch, and douches. These areas had always been deemed private, and extremely personal.

FOUR

For Maude's 98th birthday, the children banded together to buy her a new color television set, one with a larger screen, hoping she'd be able to see the image more clearly. Mardo and Geneva were visiting when the dealer called to tell her the new appliance would be delivered early that evening. "Whatever you do," Mardo exhorted his mother as he prepared to drive back to Columbus, "don't try to help the installer. He can handle it alone."

Maude, balanced on her walker, trailed into the living room to watch as the young man--a teenager with little experience, she thought--tried to free the old TV set from the cart on which it sat. The cart was on wheels and the appliance was wedged tightly between handles on the top.

The young man struggled, lifting the cart and its load completely off the floor in his efforts. Maude couldn't resist the impulse to help. She reached for the handle on the cart at the moment the set pulled free. The cart rolled out of the way and Maude, free of her walker, fell heavily against the wall. She fractured her left thigh bone. The installer took the TV set back to the store, fearful she'd never recover enough to enjoy it.

A few days after the bone was set, Maude was on the mend. The day she was to return to her apartment from Hardin Memorial Hospital, Mardo told her, "We all were afraid you'd just give up."

"I couldn't do that," she replied. "You kids are counting on me." Back on her feet with the aid of the walker, Maude celebrated her 99th birthday in the Franklin Street apartment. She got her new TV during her 100th year!

FIVE

Daughters Bea and Pauline and son Mardo visited with their mother more frequently as advancing years made them all aware of life's vulnerabilities. "We talked of things some of us had forgotten or never known," Pauline explained once.

Maude reminisced with amusement about the visit of her mother, Grandmother Allen, during a cold winter in the early 1920s. She said her mother had been to the outhouse and came back sporting "duck bumps" and shivering in every pore. She backed up to the heating stove in the living room, calmly lifted her long petticoats and, with no indication of embarrassment, warmed the vital area.

The children, who never imagined their demure Grandma Allen could be so brazen, were subjected to another shock before she returned to her home in Toledo. They had been smelling smoke in her bedroom after she arose each morning, and sometimes even in the afternoon.

Mildred, Maude recalled, became suspicious. She quietly investigated. But when she told her mother that Grandma had a corncob pipe and was smoking in the privacy of her bedroom, Maude expressed no surprise. "She deserves the satisfaction she gets from smoking," Maude told her daughter. "Keep quiet about it--and, if your brother and sisters know, tell them to keep quiet too."

"Mom said she wasn't superstitious," Mardo remembered. "But she had a saying or warning about many things--not to walk under a ladder, to turn away if a black cat started to cross our path, and prepare to entertain a stranger if a fork or knife fell to the floor."

"An apple a day keeps the doctor away," the woman who never ate raw apples would recite. To her, the fruit was inedible unless prepared in sauce, pie or dumpling.

And she laughed at the "wish" doggerel: "If wishes were horses, beggars would ride; if turnips were watches, I'd wear one by my side."

If Maude spilled the salt, she might throw a pinch of it over her left shoulder to ward off bad luck. A dropped dish towel meant that "an old soak is coming"--presumably a disreputable character who should be afforded little, if any, hospitality.

The children learned that an itchy nose meant "you're going to kiss a fool"; itchy hands--the right: shake hands with a stranger; the left: receive some money; and itchy ears--the right: you're being talked about in a derogatory way; and left: you'll receive a compliment.

Many of the superstitions were relayed by friends and other relatives--

few by Maude and Lee. And some that were popular in high school probably were made up by the students themselves.

The more romantic high schoolers of the early 1920s had a ritual. One finger placed against your cheek asked, "Do you love me?" If your friend put two fingers against the cheek it meant "Yes." Three fingers would ask, "How much?"; and four fingers answered, "With all my heart!" A closed fist against cheek or jawbone meant "no" or "not at all" to the one or three-finger query. It was more of a game than a serious love interchange, and there were no broken hearts.

Maude was amazed at the pace of modern life--how her grown children found time in the 1940s and 1950s to follow the trivia on radio and television, take their children to band and swim practice, to basketball and little league, or participate in the variety of social activities available. "We had none of that while you were growing up," she told her daughters and son. "You had no place to go, no way to get there if you did--unless you went with us in the horse- drawn buggy."

Maude remembered the summer of 1918 as the exception to the everyone-at-home-every-night routine. The son had joined the Boy Scouts and, to attend meetings, he had to be in Ridgeway one Thursday each month. The 13-year-old wasn't permitted to drive the horse after nightfall, so he walked the three-mile distance--passing the isolated farms in the growing dusk on the way, coming back in complete darkness with his heart pounding--fearful of watch dogs that barked as he passed.

Dr. William P. Casto, pastor of the Ridgeway Methodist Church, was the scoutmaster. When he was transferred to another church, the troop was abandoned and Mardo found himself lacking one credit to become "first class." He never made the Eagle Scout ranking to which he aspired.

Maude saved the report cards of the children for all 12 years. One school memory stood out especially in her mind. "Each child returned home at least once a year with the complaint that 'teacher doesn't like me,' or 'teacher is unfair.'"

The children maintained they "didn't know why they were singled out by the teacher," or were sure they "never did a thing," but Maude knew better. She was the teacher's champion; she let the youngsters know the teacher was too busy to spend needless time seeking out innocent victims to punish for uncommitted offenses.

Maude, who never publicly reprimanded a child, was blunt in expressing her opinions about the permissive tactics of later years. "Youngsters lack the knowledge and experience to make their own decisions--they need parental guidance until their teens."

She felt they should be coddled in infancy, guided and directed through childhood so they might be able to walk bravely into early adulthood, willing to seek advice when troubled. They should be taught both the necessities of gainful work and the sense of fulfillment such employment provides. "The best method of teaching," she had maintained throughout her life, "is through the standards lived by the parents."

She would have agreed with William Bennett, the former U.S. Secretary of Education, who challenged the failure of three Presidential candidates to adequately answer a question from a voter in 1992.

The candidates were participating in a public forum when the man, appearing to be in his early 40's and sporting a pony tail, demanded of them: "We are your children. What are you going to do for us?"

They did not answer. The obvious response, Bennett said, should have been: "I am not your father. You are a grown man. If you need help, see a minister, see a priest, see a rabbi, see a counselor." There should be no necessity to use taxpayer money to assist a grown, able-bodied man.

Part II:

More Changes

ONE

*M*aude admitted she was sometimes lonely as she neared the century mark. She thought an activities program might be helpful. So she made plans to move to the Seton Kenton apartment complex in eastern Kenton. Late in the summer of 1983, she found herself supervising two Kenton High School football players as they loaded her treasured corner cupboard onto a half-ton truck.

It was the first time her children had delegated any moving duties to others. The massive piece of walnut furniture--combining both an antique commode and lumber shaped out of boards from the 1854 farm dwelling --was almost too bulky and too weighty for amateurs to wrestle through narrow doors and hallways, or on and off a vehicle.

Maude's new color television, replacement for the one she'd lost in the mishap the previous year, came too.

Busy children and in-laws placed wall hangings and arranged the furnishings in her new apartment at the Seton Kenton on that August day-- just two months before her 100th birthday anniversary. Planning started early for the celebratory occasion--a day, Maude said, she had never dreamed of reaching.The Seton Kenton had no assembly hall large enough to accommodate the group of relatives and friends who planned to honor the century-old woman. The party had to be staged at the nearby Senior Citizens Center, the children decided.

It was not a surprise birthday party. Everyone at Seton Kenton, a federally subsidized, two-story apartment complex, was talking about it. Alice Lingrel, manager, ordered a turn-of-the-century buggy parked on the plaza at the front door of the complex--loaded with corn stalks, pumpkins, and other signs of the fall season. A colorful streamer announced to all that the complex's oldest resident, Maude Williams, was celebrating her 100th birthday on October 23.

Stories were carried in the area newspapers. She received greetings from all over, including the Governor of Ohio and the President of the United States. Maude donned a sedate dress of her favorite blue on the celebratory occasion and expressed amazement at the turnout. Guests came in droves to pay their respects--friends she had made in her early life, the 57 years on the farm, and new friends made from her 23 years in Kenton.

Relatives responded--stayed for the sitdown dinner and the afternoon public reception, at which cake, ice cream, and beverages were served. Her brother, 88-year-old Harley Allen--the practical joker who, 70 years earlier, had stolen the clothes of a swimmer in Rush Creek--sat at her right side. He greeted many of the relatives he had not seen since his teenage years when they were little more than babes in arms. Older friends, like Harry Marmon, were dead. Harley, long retired from his railroad job, was there with his second wife, Norma.

Maude's son-in-law John P. Perry, whom she'd not seen since her trips to Phoenix ended in 1972, came with his wife Lucile. Their three children had paid for their trip. Grandson Gene Perry, who was battling diabetes, also was there--accompanied by his wife Isabel, their daughter Corine Vassel, and their grandchildren Tammy and Jason Vassel.

Nieces and nephews from throughout the region joined with grandchildren, great-grandchildren, and great-great-grandchildren to pay their respects to the grand lady who reigned modestly. She said it was the greatest birthday celebration she had ever experienced. But she revised that opinion later and gave that honor to each of the next nine.

Maude was welcomed at Seton Kenton's own party the day following the family's celebration of her 100th birthday. She met women who became friends, was even reunited with some who'd been acquaintances in her earlier life. Within a few months of moving to the apartment complex, Maude was playing Euchre on an irregular basis and attending Seton's bingo parties.

Three years later, in 1986, Maude welcomed Bonnie Moser as an across-the-hall neighbor. The two had reason to reminisce. During the mid-1940s, Bonnie's late husband Sam had carpentered, assembled and refinished the massive walnut cupboard which dominated one corner of Maude's apartment, in which they sat.

Sam did it primarily because of his affection for Lee and Maude, Bonnie said. The two couples had been playing cards one evening at the farm when Maude bemoaned the lack of cupboard space, Bonnie remembered. The sideboard which had served for 40 years was overloaded. There was no place for the treasured china from Maude's mother and other relatives.

Sam came up with a plan. A little appreciated clothes bureau was stored in a no longer used bedroom. Maybe the drab piece of furniture--itself a collector's item from the 19th century--could be utilized.

Sam took measurements, scratched away some of the lackluster gray paint, and made his proposal to the Williamses. If they would provide the paint remover, hardware, glass panes and the varnish, he would refinish the bureau and use it as a solid walnut base. Then, taking walnut boards from the farmhouse or wood shed, he would fashion a top to display the choice pieces of china.

The only cost would be the meals and the couple's hospitality on weekends when Sam would mix work and play. There was no time limit. The work might extend for weeks. Solid wood had to be found that could be planed, sanded and cut into usable dimensions. The cupboard doors with their inserts of window glass made for slow progress.

The finished product stood before Maude and Bonnie, for both to admire. In the small living room of the apartment at the Seton Kenton, it was almost awesome. It spread five feet across one corner. Treasured heirlooms could be seen through the glassed-in doors. Hidden in the compartment underneath were other mementos.

Maude told Bonnie of another use of walnut from the old house. Guy Dille, a neighboring farmer whose son Roy had married Maude's grand-niece Irene Engle, gathered some boards from the collapsing woodshed and used them in his woodworking hobby.

"Mr. Dille, who died at age 92, dressed each board down to a workable thickness, sanded the strips, and made small souvenir pieces for table or wall. He gave me the cutout of a rooster, glued in parallel sections to make a napkin holder. The children received similar keepsakes to remind them of the house where they were born."

TWO

Maude said that between them she and Lee had a lot of relatives--Lee's parents and grandfather (William I.Witcraft), Lee's brother Herman, and five sisters; Maude's parents and grandfather (Abner Wilson) and her three brothers. There were nieces and nephews. Maude's cousins were scattered and only two, Mrs. Frances Koehn and Mrs. Edna Lucas, became friends in later life when they wrote to Maude about mutual memories.

But in the early years of their marriage, she noted, she and Lee had no joint friends--only his friends and her friends with whom to share the occasional dull evening. Gradually, neighbors became closer, and the couple started meeting people at dances and card parties.

By 1912, with Maude well on the road to recovery from major surgery and no longer susceptible to pregnancy, they started exchanging dinner or card-playing invitations with a dozen couples. Pauline, the couple's youngest, was three then and could be taken on family outings until the late evening. There was no reason for staying home, week in and week out.

Edwin and Lois Clapsaddle of Mt. Victory became close friends. Three of their four daughters were roughly of the age of the Williams' four children. They played amicably--and noisily--when the two families gathered for dinner at one of the two homes, went to sleep without protest when the parents played cards in the evenings.

Maude said Opal was three or four years older than Mildred, and was too involved with school activities to share much time with the younger children. Mabel Clapsaddle was about Mildred's age; Alice was a year older than Bea; and the fourth girl, Geneva, was slightly older than Pauline.

"We were good friends for more than 20 years," Maude recalled. "Then Edwin died and Lois moved in with a daughter. We drifted apart." One time, possibly in the summer of 1919, Edwin hired Mardo to ride a newly purchased horse from near Raymond, Ohio, to Mt. Victory, a distance of about 12 miles. Apparently, Mr. Clapsaddle, who had a reputation as a capable horse trader, became concerned about the welfare of the 14-year-old boy traveling alone for that distance. He met him at Byhalia, about five miles away, and substituted another jockey.

"He gave Mardo a dollar and brought him home," Maude said. "Edwin probably thought it was too far for the teenager to ride a horse bareback."

Neighbors Rob and Mattie Richardson, who were married on the same date as Lee and Maude, became close friends. They raised their six children on a nearby farm before moving to Marion, Ohio. Rob was a cousin of Grant Richardson, whose wife Delpha was 106 years old when she died at her farm home south of Ridgeway.

Hank and Bell Rosebrook, Chet and Bess McMahon, Bill and Nettie Bird, the Jeff Kellers, the Tennants and the Spains, Charles and Lizzie Marmon, and the Beryl Wallaces were part of the inner circle too, Maude remembered fondly. They shared good times and bad with each another.

Everett and Lulu Cronley, who lived south of Mt. Victory, exchanged dinner parties with Lee and Maude, went to card games and neighborhood dances with them. They remained close friends even after the Cronleys moved to Columbus. Lee and Maude grieved when the Cronley's elder son Rolland died, and when Everett himself succumbed.

Maude remembered a visit to the farm by Everett and Lulu in the 1940s. "She was always a big talker and this day proved no exception. She was talking a mile a minute with scarcely a breath between entire paragraphs when 11-year-old Kay entered the room."

"She stood there with her mouth open," Maude said of her granddaughter. "She couldn't believe anyone could talk that fast, and continue so long without encouragement."

THREE

As Maude's sight became even dimmer, she quit fashioning bead necklaces, cushion covers and other articles. She could see the jumbo markings on her playing cards only faintly in bright light.

The optometrist who examined her said she had cataracts but surgery was not an option, since the problem was aggravated by untreatable advanced macular degeneration.

As her hearing worsened, visitors had to shout to make themselves heard. A hearing aid was out of the question at her age. So an amplifier was acquired. The earpiece was attached to a portable control box with a small microphone into which people spoke.

The battery in the control box was charged when not in use by plugging the contact into an electrical outlet. The microphone could be attached to the television speaker, thereby increasing the audio volume reaching the listener. Maude found that impractical and tried it only once.

The telephone presented another problem. The children had an adjustable amplification device installed at the receiver.

FOUR

Pauline was the youngest and probably the most solicitous of the children. She cared deeply for her mother and it showed, especially as the years advanced. Pauline continued to do much of her mother's house cleaning, picked up her laundry each week and brought back the freshly washed and ironed clothes, took the time to talk with her about family, current events and, for years, washed and set her hair.

Pauline had experimented with varied hair stylings for her mother after home permanents made their debut in 1924. She had convinced Maude to cut her hair even shorter, from just below the shoulders to the nape of the neck. This made the task of "perming" simpler--and Maude thereafter was never without a perm.

The most becoming style, Pauline determined, framed her face in tight curls and would remain attractive for a month or more. She and her mother formed an alliance--Maude would let no one else do her hair. For years,

Pauline washed and set her hair every month or six weeks, pampering her with the latest in home permanent grooming at least twice a year.

Pauline's husband was almost as helpful as his wife. Sonny Ansley enjoyed his life and work in Lima, Ohio. He went through the ranks at the Lima Westinghouse plant--from machinist to group leader to foreman, and finally to department superintendent. He was plant superintendent on the night shift when he retired.

He maintained a general workshop in the garage wherever he lived, and he always had time to make a repair or a machinery adjustment for neighbors. In later years, Sonny became a sort of man on call. Maude hoarded the little chores no one else seemed to have the time or the knowledge to do. In some way he would solve the problem--either at her apartment or in his workshop. He never said "no." He did everything from replacing batteries in the wall clock to repairing the motor in the exhaust fan over the stove.

"I'm lost when Pauline and Sonny aren't around," Maude always said, and admitted that her youngest daughter and her husband were spoiling her.

Pauline and Sonny were suited temperamentally. They spent more than 55 years together without a complaint of spousal abuse or a threat to roam in other pastures.

Pauline had an underlying sense of artistry and a desire to try new experiences. She'd learned to water ski when she was 60 years old, and continued until she was almost 75. Her husband piloted the motor boat as she gaily skimmed the waves behind.

She fashioned clothing for her granddaughters and nieces and sewed garments by hand for the dolls of the children in the neighborhood. She did oil paintings by number, crocheted doilies and table covers for friends and relatives.

Pauline slowed down in the mid-1970s after an accident. She and Sonny had just returned from wintering in Florida when he toppled from a ladder while storing empty cartons in a garage cabinet. She tried to break the fall of the now 210-pound man. Her right arm was crushed against the side of the stepladder.

She spent the next seven weeks in Lima Memorial Hospital with her splinted arm hoisted high over her head as the shattered elbow knitted. She became a little quieter, a little less active--but just as indomitable. In 1983, she was stricken with breast cancer, which she battled for five years before she died in 1987.

Maude, who became 104 that year, was devastated, never thinking she'd live to see another of her children die before her.

FIVE

Bonnie Moser and Maude continued to visit back and forth across the hall at the Seton Kenton--and to meet at Maude's birthday parties. The socializing was especially frequent during the summers of 1987 and 1988, when Bea Williams Deerwester stayed with her mother at the apartment complex. Bea had become a widow. Her husband, Buck Deerwester, had died in 1986. Bonnie was her sister-in-law.

Bea hadn't been around as much for Maude as Pauline had. She'd moved from city to city as husband Buck moved from job to job, ending up 2,000 miles away in Phoenix.

Bea's husband, Buck Deerwester, was of a different temperament than Maude's other sons-in-law. He was more ambitious, more single-minded, more self-centered. He never graduated from high school, opting for factory work over an education. He became a department manager at the Acklin Stamping Company in Toledo before abandoning production for sales.

In the late 1940s, in an unusual stroke of luck, he obtained a district sales franchise for Chrysler-Airtemp Corporation at a time when the air conditioning craze was developing. He broke his Acklin ties and moved to Lima, Ohio, near the center of his sales operation.

Buck prospered. He had natural sales ability and he had a good product during a strategic period. His time on the road was minimal--he could handle many of the details by telephone. But his ambition--or the grass on the other side of the fence--beckoned. The Port Clinton Manufacturing Company at Port Clinton, Ohio, dangled a sugar plum for which he reached.

The company, which manufactured duct systems as its principal product, was seeking a profitable way to link their product with the cooling mania. Chrysler Airtemp was a desirable product and Deerwester was its sales manager for the preferred--and most profitable--area, including Port Clinton.

Port Clinton Manufacturing, in the 1960s, offered Wilbert A. Deerwester the position of vice president of sales with his own office, his name inscribed on the door, and a company-purchased car. In addition to his annual salary (more than $12,000 at a time when the average pay was less than $3,000), he would be paid a commission of 15% on all new sales that went into production. There could be no division of his loyalties so he would have to transfer his sales contract with Chrysler Airtemp to Port Clinton Manufacturing.

Buck was overjoyed. He and Bea sold their Lima home and moved to Port Clinton. Bea immediately sought an office job--as she did whenever the home cities changed. They bought a motor boat and took relatives riding on Lake Erie when they visited--with a stop at Lonz Winery for beverage and lunch.

The honeymoon between factory and its new vice president of sales was short-lived. Buck went to New Orleans with the company bigwigs for a corporate conference. He felt important. He made sales contacts. He returned to his private office in an isolated part of the executive wing. He continued to make sales, submit production orders to the plant superintendent, and await the tangible results of his efforts.

At last he was going to get some action, he thought, on the morning he received a memo to proceed to the office of the executive vice president. But that was only to administer the final blow, to complete his disillusionment. Buck was told that his production orders had been countermanded from the first, that the plant was at full production with no move being made to expand facilities, and that there would be no necessity for him to promote future sales.

He went back to his office--the one with his name and title so prominently displayed--placed his feet on the desk and contemplated his future.

He thought about staying in that office year after year, driving his company-owned car from home to plant and back again, and the periodic corporate gatherings at which he would be introduced as vice president of sales. Then he returned to the executive suite and demanded an immediate conference with the president. When they met, Bea told her parents, Buck angrily said that he was hired to promote sales, that he was going to continue selling, and that the company had better make plans to process those orders--or ELSE!

"The company took that as a threat to resign," Bea said. Management told Buck they had no intention of paying him a sales commission for orders that would only create backlogs in their production system. Further, the president said, Mr. Deerwester could continue to use the sales office at the stipulated salary or they could negotiate for his departure.

Buck took the company car and three months' severance pay and was gone after a year and a half. The company took the Chrysler Airtemp franchise, which was the only thing they wanted from the start, Bea said.

The Deerwesters severed their Ohio ties, moved to Arizona, and attempted to start anew. But Buck had lost his touch--and eventually most of his confidence. He lost money in Mesa Steel, bought a janitorial services enterprise which backfired on him and then went back into selling--this time for an insurance firm.

The janitorial services undertaking destroyed his faith in man's word. He bought it, he explained, because he had an implied understanding with the firm's executive vice president. That person would remain and teach him the vagaries of the trade, how to get the best efforts from the Hispanic employees, and how to price the services offered.

Instead, the executive not only left to establish his own competitive enterprise, but he took with him the best customers of the firm he abandoned. Buck struggled for a few months in a business he wasn't qualified to operate. Employees quit due to misunderstandings, and customers broke their contracts when soil marks remained on the floors and windows continued streaked. He sold the firm back to its original owner--at a loss

Buck finally retired after a stint with an insurance company. He found he was unprepared to sell annuity and pension programs to teachers and similar groups. His efforts required monitoring by those with more expertise. His best sales efforts were questioned at insurance headquarters. Before he located in Phoenix, Arizona, to spend the remainder of his life, Buck had lived in Toledo, Lima, Springfield, Port Clinton, Columbus, Magnetic Springs, and Marysville--all in Ohio. Bea had accompanied him, working in office jobs and making a home for him at every stop.

SIX

Daughter Bea thought her mother was settled at the Seton Kenton for the rest of her life when she stayed with Maude during the summer of 1988, sleeping on the couch. "She was getting Meals on Wheels for a balanced meal five days a week. She had a caring helper, Sandie Albert, to do a little housework, prepare an afternoon tea, talk with her and shower her with little attentions an older person appreciates."

Bea's optimism would have faded several months later if she'd been present. But Bea, ending her visit after attending her mother's 105th birthday party at the Seton Kenton, suffered a heart attack the next morning at the home of her niece Jerri Williams Lawrence, in Westerville. Bea was rushed by emergency squad to St. Ann's Hospital.

For two days she rallied enough to talk with the family and apologize to her brother Mardo for having delayed his and Geneva's return trip to Florida. Having done that, she had another heart attack and died on Wednesday, October 26--leaving her brother to carry out her last wishes.

There was no service--only a brief tribute. Her body was cremated and the ashes returned to Phoenix. Nephew Gene Perry and his wife, Isabel, interred the remains at the gravesite of her sister Mildred (Gene's mother) who had died in 1952.

Bea was Maude's last surviving daughter. Maude was torn apart. Only Mardo was left to share with his mother memories of horse and buggy days, mud roads, arduous hard labor dawn-to-dusk, and the almost total lack of conveniences. And the good times--the square dances with Lee, family reunions, churning homemade ice cream on the porch of the old house.

SEVEN

Maude's memories of the old house became selective with advancing years. She remembered an Edison gramophone (circa 1888) with its huge horn and the cylinders which, when spun, made music of a sort. The reed rocking chairs now would be antiques. Lee's cradle, a beautiful structure of knobs and sworls in black walnut, was used for his and Maude's four children.

No one knows what happened to the music box, chairs or cradle--or the Civil War musket. It, with its bayonet, was stored in an upstairs room and was a conversation piece until the early 1940s. A cord bed met the same fate--vanishing mysteriously--as did the spinning wheel which Grandma Sarah Williams and her parents, William I. Witcraft and wife, had used to fashion garments.

Lee's Grandpa Witcraft was the owner once-removed of the Civil War gun. When he was summoned to war duty, he took advantage of the law at that time and hired a resident of the Mt. Victory area to go in his place. The man was pleased with the arrangement, took the $100 offered and served honorably. He returned unharmed and, as a measure of his appreciation, brought to Uncle Billy his rifle and bayonet.

Maude also remembered the upright player piano (a Howard Manuola) that her brother Gene bought for her and the children in 1917, the year before he died. Early models were called a "pushup" and could be used both as a mechanical player piano and standard piano. Maude, instead of taking piano lessons herself, gave them to the children. Imo Clapsaddle drove up in her horse and buggy once a week to give Mildred and Mardo lessons. "Three Blind Mice" was all they learned to play.

But the family used it as a player piano for endless hours. As the operator sat and pumped the foot pedals, a roll of perforated paper moved over a bar with a slot for each note. In the evenings the family gathered around it, pumping out music, and singing along.

Missouri Waltz, You've Gotta See Momma Every Night, and *Indian Love Call* were recalled but names of other popular tunes of the day faded in Maude's memory. "At one time we had 56 music rolls and could mount a concert to meet anyone's taste," she said.

Part III: Maude's Final Move

ONE

*M*aude lived at the Seton Kenton for 6 1/2 years, in the same ground floor apartment, equipped for the convenience and safety of the person who needed wheelchair, walker, or cane to reach bathroom facilities and cooking equipment. She was 106 and expected to die there, when someone complained to health and welfare services that the partially incapacitated resident was sleeping in her electric lift chair some nights, had left the lights burning 24 hours at a time, and had forgotten to turn the water off in the lavatory, flooding the bathroom floor.

Seton Kenton management became fearful she might accidentally set herself or her room on fire. She'd hurt her leg recently, tearing a gash in her calf. She didn't know quite how it happened. The doctor and even the visiting nurse were reluctant to make house calls.

She needed 24-hour supervision, according to the welfare supervisor who said she was prepared to file "willful neglect" charges against Mardo, Maude's last surviving child.

Sandie Albert, Maude's helper and confidante, stormed and ranted about the proposed action. "This will be the final blow. If she goes into the nursing home, she will die within the year," she protested. She'd been doing chores for Maude for more than four years--at first for only two hours a day, then for six hours a day, five days a week. She'd done the essentials--grocery shopping, light cleaning, and errands--even some of the frivolities like manicuring Maude's fingernails and painting them a scarlet red. Maude, who wasn't used to being pampered, loved it. Red was Maude's favorite color. Her dimming sight responded to its brightness.

Granddaughters Kay Williams and Jerri Lawrence, who'd taken off work to help their grandmother over this last hurdle, came to the Seton Kenton on a dreary day in February 1990. When they told their grandma authorities were insisting she move into the Hardin County Nursing Home, she turned her face away so they wouldn't see the tears. "Why won't they leave me alone?" she asked.

Kay stayed with her every night until the move was made. That first night, Kay said, "I woke up on the couch outside her bedroom to what sounded like a roomful of voices. Rising and falling, murmuring, asking questions--waiting for answers. I realized it wasn't a roomful. Only her.

"It was a strange and ghostly music. I strained to catch the words. She was asking her daughters who were dead why they'd left her, why everyone was dead but her. She was crying. I was crying too, wanting to go in and hold her, knowing if I did, she'd ask 'What?' and pretend I'd awakened her."

Kay woke once more to see the light on in her bedroom and watched in trepidation as her grandma, seated on the edge of the bed, grasped the arm of the locked wheelchair close by and pivoted herself into it. She wheeled herself two feet to the portable toilet at bedside, rested for a moment, locked herself in place, shakily stood, grabbed the metal arm of the commode and seated herself.

When she was finished, the backwards progression began, from commode to wheelchair, from wheelchair to bed. She hesitated, she rested, she wavered, she made it--she was sitting on the edge of the bed. She fell back, flinging up her legs, thrashing about as she tried to straighten herself, scooting up with her feet, pumping like a youngster, one long continuous movement, practiced over many years and choreographed. The whole procedure took 45 minutes.

Kay was amazed at how frail and vulnerable her grandma was--and how tough and unstoppable. "She ignored me as if I weren't there," Kay said. "She was able to do it herself and showed no sign of weakness. I vowed that when we reached her new home the attendants would be ordered to let her do things for herself, not lift her from the wheelchair into bed at nights."

During the remaining time--from Thursday to the next Monday--

Jerri, Kay and Sandie attempted to convince Maude that the change from subsidized housing to the modern, well-run Hardin County Home would be to her benefit. "Treat the move as another experience in the long list of things you've witnessed in your lifetime," they requested time after time in different ways.

They sorted the few things she'd be able to take from the many that would go to relatives, to Seton Kenton residents, and to charity. Everyone carefully concealed the tears as one sentimental item after another was discarded.

Maude was able to take the several photo albums, with their record of a lifetime, and the small scrapbook of newspaper clippings she'd gathered over the years--a 1929 story about Rawson and Sarah Williams celebrating their 58th wedding anniversary, a humorous squib about Lee headlined "Had False Molars 18 Years, But Has Toothache Anyway," a moving account of the last rites for slain Roy Ansley, Cousin Herb's brushes with the law, Maude's and Lee's Golden Wedding Anniversary celebration in Phoenix, a 1959 feature about son Mardo, business writer for the *Dispatch*, family obituaries, weddings of nieces, nephews, and grandchildren--landmarks of 60 years. She wanted these albums with her "in case someone stopped by and asked to see them."

She also took an end table, half a dozen dresses, her brightest lamp, her electric lift chair that Sandie had ordered for her, a favorite item once she'd gotten over her fear of the mechanics of using it. She took the windup antique standing clock. "Lee bought that clock when we first were married," she said. "It cost $2.50." She couldn't read the clock face anymore but she could hear the chimes and know the time. The clock had been promised to grandson Joe Ansley, who over the years had put almost $200 into its repairs. The loud tic toc and the chimes brought back many memories for Maude.

She gave the prized corner cupboard (the wood in it 30 years older than herself) to a great-granddaughter, Kathy Israel (Jerri's daughter). An almost new color television set went to Geneva's sister, Eunice Held, who'd lived beside Maude on East Franklin Street and had been more than a helpful neighbor for a score of years. An antique dealer paid $65 for the small bookcase. Sandie got her choice of articles before the charitable agencies were called.

Kay and Jerri were unable to determine from whom the "neglect" complaint originated. They found out, after the move was made and the apartment cleared out, that it may have been Sandie herself who inadvertently brought about the action, with her report to the county nurse about Maude's hurt leg. The nurse felt that Maude was getting so frail she needed full-time supervision, instead of the 30 hours per week Sandie provided, and had passed along her findings to the Hardin County Social Services Agency.

Maude's friends at the Seton Kenton gave her a farewell party. She left on February 23, 1990. "If Lee was alive," she told Kay, "in two days we'd have been married 87 years." The morning was sunny but cold.

Kay wheeled Maude out the front door. She was bundled up in her winter coat, knitted cap, Kay's running pants, mittens of knitted booties. Maude smiled at friends gathered near the front door and waved. "I feel like I'm going to the North Pole!"

When the wheelchair mechanism lifted her into the van and the man locked her in place, she treated it as an adventure. The day was bright with sunshine, bright enough so she could faintly see the snow on the ground from the window of the van. "I haven't been this way in years," she said, gamely smiling, as they drove through the middle of Kenton and turned onto Route 309.

She moved into the Hardin County Home, with Kay holding her hand. With her pictures, her clock, the lift chair and some clothes. Only her granddaughter stood between her and complete panic as she traveled the antiseptic corridors of the Hardin County Home, past strangers who stared and whispered, "That's Maude Williams. She's 106!," marveling at her age and condition. Nearly everyone, it seemed, aides and residents alike, had heard about her.

"I'm going to stay here with you tonight," Kay told her. "We'll meet the nurses and attendants together, we'll break the ice." Before the two got through the evening, they had told the nurse Maude couldn't swallow her pills without a little bread to help them down, explained to the dietitian her preferences in food, and convinced the aides that she was able to make her own way to the portable toilet from the lift chair.

Kay slept in the electric lift chair between Maude and her roommate Lucille Ansley. The Social Services director had been able to talk the Home into a room switch so the 106-year-old aunt and her 86-year-old niece could share. It was thought the arrangement would help Maude feel less homesick and would help Lucille, who'd been failing. The room was spacious enough to accommodate Maude's lift chair and Lucille's television.

The night before Maude arrived, Lucille regrettably had suffered a light stroke. "When she saw us," Kay said, "she didn't seem to be sure who Grandma was, or what was to be her responsibility toward her."

Before Kay fell asleep in the lift chair between them, Lucille said worriedly, "I don't have any money. I can't pay the room rent," thinking they all were in a hotel. So she could sleep, Kay assured her she'd already paid the bill.

Later that night, Kay saw tears on her grandma's cheeks. She stood beside the bed and held her hand. "You promised us, Grandma, that you'd really try, that you wouldn't give up." Maude gave her a wan smile. "I expect I'm too old to change. I used to get so excited about things new. I don't anymore." Kay told her she'd like it there if she'd give it a chance.

When her grandma said, "I feel so useless. I can't see or hear. I can't walk," Kay was ready to cry herself. Then Maude, with her usual pluck, perked up. "You don't suppose they have an exercise program here?" Kay laughed and said she thought they might design a special program just for her.

Maude didn't sleep much that first night. "The bed is too hard," she said the next morning. She'd wanted to bring her own bed, the mattress grooved by her body over decades. But the bed was too large for the space.

The next night Kay didn't stay with her grandma. She came by in the morning. Her grandma, still in her nightgown, was dozing in her lift chair. Her eyes opened. "I told them that bed is too hard," she said. "I slept here in the chair last night."

"They let you?" Kay asked. Maude nodded with a pleased smile. That was when Kay knew her grandma was going to survive in her new home. Kay had breakfast with her--worried that because of her poor sight, she wouldn't be able to find the food on her tray, her glass of milk or coffee by its side. Again, Maude came through with flying colors. With her fork, she tested the sections in the yellow plastic tray, poked and jabbed, came across the eggs. She explored and found her toast, and cereal, milk, and coffee. She ate well, a much more balanced meal than her usual heavily sugared tea and buttered toast.

"Fix my room up real pretty," Maude had asked. And the grandchildren did that, covering the institutional walls with pictures and a vivid embroidery of flowers by daughter Pauline, along with colorful wooden handmade cutouts of geese, and dogs and pigs fashioned by grandson Joe Ansley's wife and her daughter Chrissie.

Before Jerri and Kay returned to their jobs, they said they'd be back in the spring to take their grandma someplace in the car. "I'd like to take a ride by where the folks lived," she said, "when I was a little girl." Her granddaughters promised her that ride.

Kay phoned her grandma every week from New York City. Maude took the calls in the hall on the amplified phone. Kay told her stories about the big city, about her work at Bellevue Hospital, and the latest adventure of her friend Jack O'Connell, independent filmmaker, who'd met Maude for the first time at Christmas, 1989, and had sent her greetings every year thereafter.

The high hopes that niece Lucille would help Maude adjust to living in the County Home never materialized. Lucille remained confused much of the time she shared the room with her Aunt Maude. She confided to cousin Jerri she feared someone was trying to kill her.

Perhaps her several strokes had thrust her back to the time of her father's murder when she'd testified against Jimmy Willis and feared reprisals from his friends and relatives. She also worried that she was responsible for her aunt. If Maude turned on her lamp at night, Lucille would wake up, thinking Maude was lighting candles, terrified the room would catch fire.

Within three months of moving to her new environment, Maude had a bout of pneumonia that landed her in the hospital. Kay called from New York every day, talking with the nurses, who loved Maude, called her a leprechaun, couldn't believe how old she was. Kay was overjoyed the day her grandma was able to take the phone herself. Maude had made a miraculous recovery. But when she returned to the Home, she'd lost what little muscle tone she'd had and could no longer lift herself out of the wheelchair to use the portable john.

"I wouldn't mind not seeing so well," she told her son Mardo, "not hearing. If I could only walk. Sometimes I dream I can walk again."

She was well enough that spring to take her long-awaited trip in the car. Propped up on pillows in the front seat, she guided Kay and Jerri. "It's northwest of Ridgeway, a mile off the road to Kenton. I'll know it when I see it."

Her great-granddaughter Kathy Israel was also in the car. So was Kathy's little girl, Holly, one and one-half years old, almost as excited as her great-great-grandma. They wound up and down the country lanes, looking for the house where Maude lived as a girl, from where she rode her bicycle to Mt. Victory High School each day. The Allen homestead was gone, a trailer in its place, but Maude recognized the big tree to the right of the lane, whose shape she could dimly see.

TWO

Maude, almost deaf and blind, hardly realized her niece Lucille was sharing the room with her. They seldom talked. Maude's impaired hearing and Lucille's soft voice and rambling conversation, unrooted in reality, made communication impossible.

As Maude became accustomed to the monotonous day-to-day routine in the nursing home, her one complaint was that no one greeted her at the dining table or attempted to converse with her. She never knew the common gossip.

That changed in June, 1990, when Julie Hatcher, activities director, put the family in touch with Virginia Brill, a widow living near the Hardin County Home. Virginia, a wonderful, caring woman, agreed to visit Maude in her room an hour each day, Monday through Friday.

She read Maude favorite stories from the *Kenton Times*, discussed the advice of Ann Landers and Dear Abby with her, culled the obits for her for familiar names, and kept her abreast of the doings at the Home. Virginia read Maude's letters to her and wrote her letters for her.

Frances Koehn, a member of the Wilson clan (Maude's mother's family), wrote from her home in El Cerrito, California, seeking Maude's confirmation of the things she remembered--tales of a way of life long since abandoned. She was so eager for an answer that she included with her letters a stamped, self-addressed envelope. Maude, by now nearly blind, was just as eager and sent a reply by almost the next mail. Virginia Brill became the secretarial go-between--a friend who soon knew the thoughts of two strangers attempting to become closer through shared past experiences.

Mrs. Edna Lucas of Centerville, Ohio, another of Maude's cousins, born within 10 miles of Maude's birthplace, also corresponded regularly. Edna, age 89, had visited her at the Seton Kenton on her birthday in 1989, after a gap of 75 years. They hadn't seen each other since Maude's children were small. Edna had been 14 at the time.

Virginia, gentle, kind and thoughtful, kept Maude in communication with friends and relatives, noticed when Maude was out of her favorite butter mints and replenished her supply. Maude could go through a package of mints a week. She'd wheel herself over to the dresser where they sat in their cut glass candy dish, fumble until she found the lid, and reach for a handful. "Now Maudie, you're going to spoil your lunch," the nurses would say. "I get bored," she'd answer.

Virginia Brill became Maude's friend and substitute family when real family wasn't there.

Nurses said the change in Maude's attitude was dramatic. She grew more cheerful, more patient, and more outgoing. Maude's favorite nurse made a point of seeing the family on their next visit. "Maude has regained her interest," she reported. Julie Hatcher, activities director, who'd put the family in touch with Virginia Brill, commented, "I wish other families could do the same for their loved ones here."

Maude became the best loved resident at the Home. She got cards from people she never knew. Nurses and attendants marveled that she was never demanding and never complained. They voted her their favorite resident. Everyone greeted her as "Maudie."

"We thought it was a mark of disrespect when mother was called by her first name by the girls still in their teens," Mardo admitted. "Then they changed it to an affectionate 'Maudie' and included her in every activity they could talk her into."

She survived a second bout of pneumonia and other, less serious illnesses. She presided with grace and elegance at four more birthday parties there, surrounded by relatives and friends. Granddaughter Jerri bought her a new dress for each occasion (sometimes making two or three trips to the store before the "right" one was found), made sure she always had a corsage, and that her hair had been washed and set.

No person, Maude decided, had nicer grandchildren than she. Gene and Isabel Perry had made their Phoenix home available to her all those years she was missing Lee so keenly.

Eddie and Mary Jane Ansley had come to the farm for rifle shooting contests and hikes in the woods, had visited with Maude in every apartment, and had been real friends for over 40 years. Eddie always arranged to have her lift chair repaired when it stopped working. He'd find a technician who'd travel to the Home and fix it there. Maude didn't like to be without her favorite chair, preferring to sleep in it nights because "the bed was too hard."

Joe and Kay Ansley showed their own brand of caring. Joe made sure the antique mantel clock that chimed the hours always worked, replacing parts and reconditioning it. His wife each year had fashioned colorful and cheery wooden novelties to grace the tables and walls of her various homes.

Jerri made frequent visits to her grandma, bringing gifts of mints and clothing, finding robes, nightgowns, and legwarmers when she needed them. Granddaughter Kay called each week from New York City just to talk and say she loved her, and visited as much as she could.

Throughout the years, the grandchildren came often with their children and their children's children, so Maude could get to know the newcomers.

Maude kept track of all her descendants, could call each by name until she passed the century mark. The names started to fade or maybe the "great-greats" became too many.

Mardo wrote in her 108th year to tell his mother how much she'd been admired for her patience, her perseverance, her ability to adjust to change, her uncritical approach to living, and her long history of setting the standards. "If the girls were here," he wrote, "they would want to join me in thanking you for being you, for being there for us, and for sharing those wonderful traits with us."

Mardo couldn't attend her birthday party that year. He was at the bedside of his wife Geneva, who was in a Florida hospital seriously ill from complications due to surgery for a benign brain tumor.

Maude's niece Lucille suffered minor stroke after minor stroke and finally died on March 18, 1992. The two never regained the loving companionship they once shared. During her last few weeks, Lucille, formerly an outgoing person who'd made life worth living for a coterie of older women, rode her wheel chair glumly--a dazed expression on her face as if she were in a perpetual nightmare.

Other roommates came and went. They were old--but none as old as Maude; some were disturbed, and none would take the time or effort to converse. So Maude withdrew into her private reflections. She relied on visits from relatives and the almost daily discussions with companion Virginia Brill to keep her abreast of the times.

At the Home, Maude's picture was taken at every opportunity. She was shown with county commissioners. She was kidded about her political preferences, when she called for a Republican ballot in the general elections. She smiled and conceded that she thought Bill Clinton was too immature to be President.

When asked for her secret of reaching age 100, then 101, then each year through 109, Maude would say, "There is no pat answer. I always ate regularly of whatever we had. There was no concern about eggs, or milk, or cheese, or sweets. My exercise came from the work I did."

The not-to-worry creed she developed during the early part of her marriage helped, she thought, but the genes she inherited may have been more important. As early as the 1700s, the Allens (her father's line) and the Wilsons (her mother's) had compiled records showing that many of their relatives were living to be 80 and 90 when vital statistics gave much lower life expectancies. Both of Maude's grandfathers lived into their late 90s, an uncle died at 96, and her distant cousin Jennings Allen, was 114 years old when he died in Fairfield, South Carolina in 1835.

Members of the family thought two other conditions may have been partially responsible. One was the slow-paced farm living during the first half of the 20th century; another was the place where Maude resided during her first 57 years. Whether it was the latitude, longitude, or the attributes of soil, air, climate and well water, three women who lived most of their lives within three miles of one another each passed the century mark.

Rose Ford of Ridgeway became 104. Delpha Richardson, a half mile south of the Ford home, reached 106, and Maude Allen Williams, whose home until 1960 was barely three miles east of the other two, outlived them to celebrate her 110th birthday in October, 1993. Guy Dille, also in the one-half mile by three-mile area, made it to age 92.

The family thought her alertness may have been prolonged by a vitamin supplement prescribed by Dr. N.C. Schroeder following her first fall in 1974. He'd told her to take niacin--advertised as a dietary supplement to "help maintain a healthy digestive tract and nervous system"--during convalescence from her broken hip.

Religiously, she took one 100 milligram tablet each morning with breakfast--until she moved into the nursing home with its own physician and nurses. It may have been why she continued to remember names, recognize people, and maintain an interest in the everyday happenings about her.

THREE

Maude had entered the Home at 82 pounds, and by her 109th birthday was up to 104 pounds. Maybe the mints were helping. So was Virginia.

Everyone who came to that birthday party marveled at Maude's stamina as she greeted and talked with people. Cousin Edna Lucas, age 92, came, accompanied by her daughter. Maude and Edna reminisced during the party and continued to talk of events that dated back to when both were children near Centerville, Ohio. Maude welcomed her as among the few from her side of the family. Her nephews, John and Jim Allen of Toledo, always came to the birthday parties--accompanied by their wives, Vera and Pat. Most of the other guests, except for Mardo, grandchildren, great-grandchildren, and great-great-grandchildren, were Lee's nieces and nephews.

The Mt. Victory High School Alumni Association honored Maude that year (1992) as their oldest member on the occasion of the 90th anniversary of her graduation. Among signers of the memorial program were Opal Clapsaddle Frye, Mabel Clapsaddle McCall, and Alice Clapsaddle Battles--daughters of the Edwin Clapsaddles, the Mt. Victory friends with whom Maude and Lee had visited during the early 1900s.

Mardo's wife Geneva wasn't at that birthday party. She had died in May. Mardo missed her greatly. For more than 65 years they had listened to each other's gripes, solved every argument before going to sleep, and shared fortune and misfortune. Maude grieved too, feeling as if she'd lost another daughter.

Family members, who took it for granted that their Maude was indestructible, were concerned in early 1993 when Virginia wrote that her 109-year-old friend was becoming forgetful and inclined to doze off during conversations.

Her loved ones banded together to try to revive her interest. The grandchildren and great-grandchildren wrote, called and visited more often. Son Mardo bombarded her with letters filled with questions about her early life on the farm--the good times and the bad. She responded as they hoped she would: she wouldn't give up, not with everyone so desperately wanting her to stick around for a while longer.

With Virginia reading the questions, Maude attempted to recall for Mardo long ago incidents, anecdotes about the family and treasured friends. Within two months, she regained her alertness. In her first letter, dictated to Virginia, she spoke of her love of music (she liked Al Jolson and Eddie Cantor), the beauty of the sunsets on the farm, her addiction to planting a variety of flowers when the garden was cultivated.

Roasting ears were her favorite vegetable, she said, but after she got her false teeth, she had to cut the kernels off the cob. "I used to sew a lot; made nearly all of my own clothes (at first by hand, then using a treadle sewing machine), sewed for the girls, made a lot of comforters."

She spoke lovingly of Pal, her first dog, but couldn't remember any cats. "If we had any, they were kept in the barn. My mother (Lenore Wilson Allen) never let me play with cats when I was young. She said it wasn't healthy."

Another memory was of making a loaf of cornmeal mush for the supper meal, "then in the morning slicing and frying what was left." The children didn't like hot mush in a glass of milk for supper, but loved the fried mush covered with brown sugar syrup for breakfast.

She said she once liked to jump rope, play andy-over with a ball, and hide and seek. Her favorite parlor games, before Lee taught her to play cards, were checkers and dominoes. "I didn't care much for dolls!"

One night in the early years of her marriage, she said she got an unexpected surprise when she started out the kitchen door. A huge man, all in white with a red nose and a corncob pipe in his mouth, silently blocked her way. She almost dropped the pan from her hand and was preparing to shout for help when she realized it was a snowman. Lee had quietly rolled balls of snow from the front yard, across the porch floor and had assembled the creature (complete with a carrot nose) while his wife washed the supper dishes. He was disappointed when there was no scream.

FOUR

On September 16, 1993, Maude slipped from her wheelchair, after being returned from the evening meal. She suffered a minor scratch. Her son and her granddaughter Jerri Lawrence were informed of the accident and went to Kenton immediately. They expressed their concern to the attending nurse about the fall and were assured that Maude had been measured for a restraining belt.

"We left believing such an incident would not be permitted to happen again," Mardo said. "A week later, we were notified she had fallen once more from the wheelchair and had broken her left leg below the knee."

It was a complete break. Bones were separated, with ends grating against each other.

The latest accident occurred as she sat in the wheel chair, much like the first time. No one had taken the time to issue instructions that their oldest resident be placed in bed or lift chair upon being returned to her room from meals or the activity room--that she should not be left unattended.

The head nurse carefully explained to the perturbed family that they did not have the help needed to accompany aged residents to their room for immediate transfer to a more secure place, and that Ohio law did not authorize the placement of a security belt until after the resident had fallen twice from the wheel chair.

Maude was now eligible for the belt!

Doctors and nurses thought the shock of the accident would kill her, or the pain might force the frail woman to conclude that it wasn't worthwhile to live. By sheer willpower, and powerful pain pills, she fought to last through to her October birthday celebration. The plans for it were well underway, she thought, so why abandon them.

"I'll be there," she declared.

Maude had been honored in other years but 1993 became special. After all, she had voiced a wish in a moment of weakness that she could be entered in the Guiness Book of Records as having voted in more consecutive Presidential elections than any other person in history.

She didn't realize the seriousness of her injury--a compound fracture of her porous bones that left the leg dangling helplessly from the knee down. The bones could not be set so the limb was placed carefully in an "immobilizer" to prevent excess movement, and every effort was made to control the excruciating pain.

She made it to her 110th with a month to spare. Nurses and attendants showered her with attention on her birthday, October 23. Family and friends honored her on October 25 (the party day), expressing their appreciation of the woman whose legacy was love, fortitude, patience, and understanding--and who followed a creed of "Don't worry about things over which you have no control."

President and Mrs. Clinton sent their congratulations although Maude wasn't hesitant about announcing she'd voted for George Bush. Her picture appeared on national television when Weatherman Willard Scott gave her the lead-off spot on his program--the fifth year she had been honored.

Seated in the gaily-decked County Home activities room, her hair freshly washed and permed, her lips brushed with lipstick so she wouldn't look so drawn, she greeted every guest, held the babies, and was interviewed by a *Columbus Dispatch* reporter. Between bouts of almost unendurable pain and her pleas for better cushioning of the dangling leg, she told reporter Donna Glenn of her 57 years on Rush Creek, her face smoothing out as she spoke of her and Lee's excitement when the house was wired for electricity in the 1940s.

At one point she smiled weakly and admitted that "a glass of beer would taste good." She wasn't a drinker but at times would share a bottle with one of her children or in-laws. She never wanted more than six ounces--usually settled for four. Granddaughter Kay had shared a beer with her before the move to the Home, and that was Maude's last brew.

Before she moved to Seton Kenton, where any sort of alcoholic beverage was prohibited, "we tried to keep three or four bottles of beer in the refrigerator," Mardo said. "She shared with friends and what was left she offered us. We thought a small glass would be beneficial--a sort of tonic to enhance the Geritol she was taking."

Maude survived what must have been a grueling three hours at the party with only an occasional moan, an infrequent call for rearrangement of pillows around her shattered leg. "It hurts so bad," she said. But the nurses--because of doctor's orders--could not administer the pain medicine before the necessary time had elapsed between doses.

When she was returned to her room, she was transferred gently to her bed. The immobilizing framework was adjusted carefully. Now that there was no necessity for her to be alert, she was given another dose of medication so she could sleep. She had no appetite. She was down to 78 pounds.

The next day when family asked if the celebration had tired her too much, she shook her head. "I can always sleep." She asked that her cards and letters be read to her again. Along with the greetings for the current birthday, the family found in a bureau drawer notes and greeting cards for every occasion--items received over the last several years and retained for the message. She liked Virginia to read and re-read them to her.

In her mementos were greetings from Presidents Ronald Reagan and Bush, recent Ohio Governors, and letters from friends across the nation.

As Maude sat in the lift chair, her leg bound by its brace, Jerri, Kay and Mardo took turns reading her birthday greetings again to her. Their voices seemed to lull her. An occasional smile flickered across her face. Cousin Edna, now age 93, sent a card of regret, saying a severe cold had prevented her from attending the 110th. She wrote: "What a long, exciting life you've had, enjoying all the changes. I only wish I could have been with you more during these years." Everyone in the room knew Maude and Edna would never see each other again.

Nephews John and Jim Allen of Toledo and Austin Williams of Marysville sent messages of cheer, as did grand-nephew Dr. R. Smith of Hilliard, Ohio.

Fern Marmon Smith, in the tradition of her father Harry who had penned poetry to Mildred when they both were ill, sent a rhyme from Phoenix. "I remember fondly and with glee when we lived near you and Uncle Lee." She termed herself Aunt Maude's favorite niece in the West.

Fern's sister, Doris Marmon Barnhart, told Aunt Maude in her birthday note: "You are an example to us all. You took whatever life handed you without complaining."

Grandson Gene Perry, very ill himself with complications due to diabetes, and his wife Isabel sent greetings and fond memories of Maude's Phoenix winters with them.

Corine Perry Vassel, Maude's great-granddaughter, recalled with nostalgia the winters Maude had baked cakes and pies for her while staying with Gene and Isabel. Corine wrote tenderly of the unassuming woman who had helped fashion her own approach to life.

DeDe Perry Farmer, adopted daughter of Maude's late son-in-law John Perry, wrote of the affection she felt for Maude when she visited her parents, John and Lucile Householder Perry in Globe, Arizona.

As these messages were read, Maude seemed briefly to forget her pain. Memories of those Arizona visits--with Lee and in the years without him--were among her most cherished.

Nieces Velda Engle Strait of Columbus and Elizabeth Newell Haddix of Canton, Texas, sent notes of cheer. Irene Engle Dille, a grandniece, remembered the times as a youngster she had stayed with Maude on the farm. She loved to comb Maude's hair, she said, adding: "You're a remarkable lady who never spoke a detrimental word against anyone and, oh, the home-made ice cream you could make."

Niece Ruth Engle of Bellefontaine, Ohio, wrote: "I love you very much. I remember the times we went back and forth, played cards, the Sunday dinners." Maude spoke lovingly of both Irene and Ruth. Irene Engle Dille was the daughter of the late Ralph Engle, Lee's nephew who had worked as his farm hand in the second decade of the 1900s. Ruth was the widow of Ross Engle, Ralph's brother, who--while working as a farm hand for his Uncle Lee--talked young Mardo into raiding the melon patch with him.

Kay's New York friend, filmmaker Jack O'Connell, gave Maude a chuckle by writing that she was the most beautiful woman in Ohio and could have been a movie star. She liked his blarney, always told the nurses Jack was her big city boy friend, and proudly displayed his every communication. Jack's photo of Maude, taken in 1989, accompanied her front page obituary in the *Kenton Times*.

Maude, in those final days, missed communications from Mary Jane Ansley, wife of Grandson Eddie Ansley. Mary Jane was the most ardent card-sender in the family. She mailed cards for every occasion--even for New Year's, Memorial Day, and the Fourth of July. Maude joked with Mary once that she had forgotten to send her a card on Groundhog Day. When Mary Jane died of cancer in March 1991, the card-sending stopped. Eddie admitted he was no communicator.

Mardo read a birthday greeting from one well-wisher, who, in an effort to make Maude smile, had sent her a poem about "Grandmother's Outhouse"--a tale recapturing the era of the "luxury three-seater," with a size for everyone and the Sears Roebuck catalog for toilet paper. It always was located at least 100 feet from civilization, had a "unique smell, that wasn't very pleasin'," and had one admirable trait, according to a citified cousin. "Not once did I hear my mother say, 'Don't forget to flush.'"

Bonnie Deerwester Moser, sister of Maude's late son-in-law Buck, sent a note in a similar vein--but with no intent to embarrass this imperturbable woman (who, so far as could be determined, never told a smutty story). Bonnie spoke of the old man who went to his doctor with the complaint that he was having a bowel movement each morning at nine o'clock. "Why, that's wonderful--that's stupendous," the doctor congratulated. "I wish I could be that regular."

"But doctor," he protested, "I don't get up until ten o'clock."

Maude appreciated every message and asked that they be read and re-read to her, but the announcement from great-granddaughter, Corine Perry Vassel, that she herself had become a grandmother impressed her the most. Kelsea Jean Ramirez, born April 1, 1993, in Mesa, a suburb of Phoenix, to Tammy and Tommy Ramirez, gained fame among the Williamses as Maude's only sixth generation descendant during her lifetime, a great-great-great-granddaughter.

The young family moved to Oregon--even farther away from Ohio than Phoenix--so Maude never got to meet Kelsea.

As she listened to the reading of her cards, Maude drank coffee, heavily sugared the way she liked it, and nibbled at buttered toast. The pain in her leg grew worse. The nurses gave her medication and carried her wasted body to the bed. She didn't complain.

Mardo covered her with the quilt she had sewn by hand 70 years ago. He smoothed back her hair and leaned down to kiss her good-bye. She raised her head in alarm. "Are you leaving so soon?" That was the last time Kay saw her grandma, but she will always keep that picture of her in her mind. Despite her pain and weakness, her grandma had so much life in her. Kay wished she could have stayed and held her hand that night and all the days and nights to come.

FIVE

The doctor said Maude's pain would decrease if the ends of the bone began to heal. But after the birthday party, her suffering increased because of deep blackened sores that developed on the immobilized leg and the heel of her foot. It was feared they would become gangrenous.

Jerri and her husband Fred became Maude's advocate, going with her to the doctor's office, insisting the doctor change the medication to a stronger one and give the nurses at the Home permission to increase her dosage as needed. There was no concern about drug addiction, only about making the few weeks she had left less painful.

Nurses and attendants greeted her cheerfully, calling out to "Maudie" to see this, listen to that. She was their favorite patient. She smiled at them through her misery, asked nothing except to have her broken leg adjusted or a cushion added. They worked with faces averted, even though they knew she couldn't see the tears in their eyes or hear the choke in their voices.

Sometimes she was in a dreamlike state during the weeks following her 110th birthday. She thought often of her three daughters--Mildred, the sprightly one with a sense of humor more like her dad; Bea, perhaps the prettiest of the three, who overcame an early physical handicap and fashioned a happy future for herself; and Pauline, the youngest, who expressed her love tangibly by routinely coming home to help with house cleaning and other duties.

She thought of Sonny, a favorite son-in-law, who'd died of a heart attack in July 1989 (and who'd maintained for years that Maude would outlive them all); she remembered Geneva, a good friend--younger than her by 20 years, who'd died in May 1992; niece Lucille also died that year as did Mildred's husband John.

With so many friends and family dead, she must have wondered many times, "Why not me, instead of them?" Especially sad was the death of her great-grandson, Brad Ansley, at the young age of 23. Brad, son of Kay and Joe, died of leukemia May 19, 1993.

Although gravely ill herself, she continued to express concern for grandson Gene Perry. Critical circulatory problems were repeatedly closing the veins in his legs. Maude didn't realize it, but he was dying, even as one day in her life faded into the confused outline of another. He would survive her by little more than a month.

Maude began welcoming the hugs passed along by every nurse, every attendant who came in contact with her. The hugging was triggered by a poem sent by grand-niece, Roberta Yoder--a poetic reminder to its readers, advocating "giving a hug" today and advising Maude the message was accompanied by a special hug from Roberta on her 110th birthday.

The poem had been enlarged and hung prominently for all to read at Maude's final birthday celebration. The cake's decoration had read "To a

Remarkable Lady" and that lady, who'd been so shy throughout her life and so reluctant to make a public display of affection, got more hugs in those last days of her life than she'd received in all her prior existence.

Semi-conscious part of the time, her thinking blurred by pain killer and a failing heart, attendants said she sometimes called them by her dead daughters' names--Mildred, Bea or Pauline. Mildred had been dead for more than 41 years.

Perhaps her dreams, distorted as they were, centered on the hope that she soon would be joining her loved ones.

She might have panicked at the last, thinking, *What if, when I get there, they aren't there to greet me?* If so, with her next breath, she must have decided, *I can't do anything about it--so, why worry?*--calling on her lifelong creed of solving what problems she could, erasing from her mind those things over which she had no control.

She was in a deep coma when nurses brought medication to her the morning of November 26, 1993. She died with a half-smile on her face, perhaps picturing the faces she wanted to see, or savoring release from the continuous excruciating pain.

A young nurse's aide approached the family after her death and tearfully asked for some memento that she could cherish and show to her children, from not only the oldest woman she'd ever known but also the one who'd inspired high principles of love, kindness and courage by the way she lived.

There was little show of grief at the quiet funeral service. Some wiped away a tear, but it was for their own loss in the passing of a woman who for six generations had set the standards for living and now had set the standards for uncomplaining death.

Good-bye, Mother, Grandmother, Aunt, and Cousin. We miss you.

You will be with us as long as we can see and hear the things you loved--the rustle of standing corn in the hot August breezes or the guttural croaking of frogs, which once graced the farm creek by the hundreds, the plaintive call of the whippoorwill in the gathering dusk, and the setting sun as it paints low-hanging clouds in reds and golds and purples.

Ancestors of Maude Allen

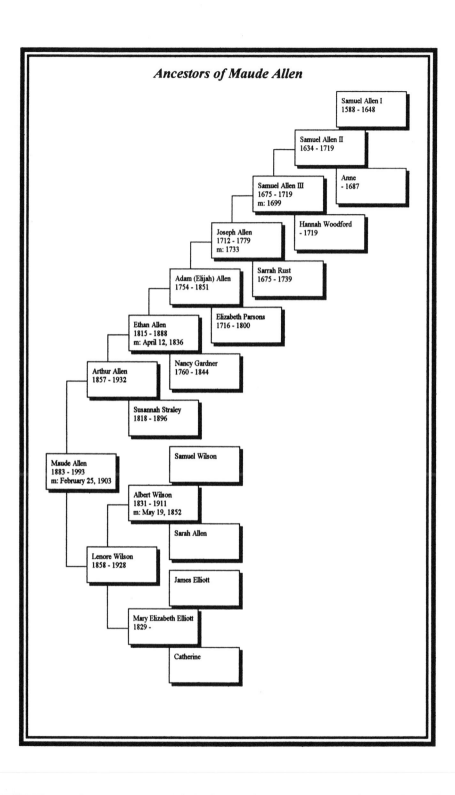

Samuel Allen I
1588 - 1648

Samuel Allen II
1634 - 1719

Anne
- 1687

Samuel Allen III
1675 - 1719
m: 1699

Hannah Woodford
- 1719

Joseph Allen
1712 - 1779
m: 1733

Sarrah Rust
1675 - 1739

Adam (Elijah) Allen
1754 - 1851

Elizabeth Parsons
1716 - 1800

Ethan Allen
1815 - 1888
m: April 12, 1836

Nancy Gardner
1760 - 1844

Arthur Allen
1857 - 1932

Susannah Straley
1818 - 1896

Maude Allen
1883 - 1993
m: February 25, 1903

Samuel Wilson

Albert Wilson
1831 - 1911
m: May 19, 1852

Sarah Allen

Lenore Wilson
1858 - 1928

James Elliott

Mary Elizabeth Elliott
1829 -

Catherine

Ancestors of Lee Williams

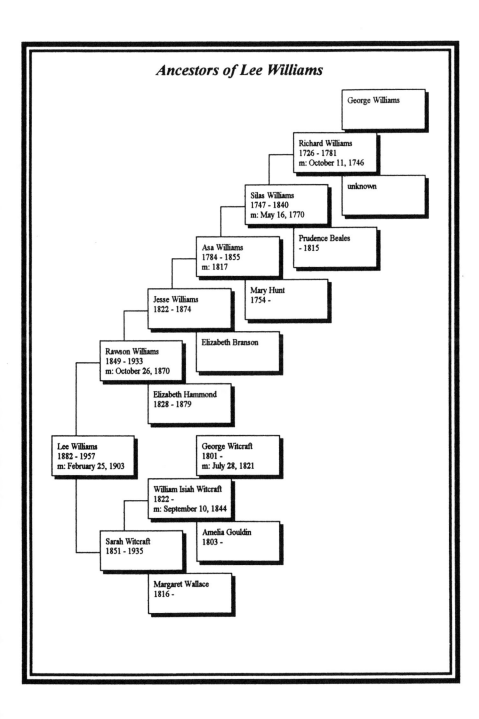

George Williams

Richard Williams
1726 - 1781
m: October 11, 1746

unknown

Silas Williams
1747 - 1840
m: May 16, 1770

Prudence Beales
- 1815

Asa Williams
1784 - 1855
m: 1817

Mary Hunt
1754 -

Jesse Williams
1822 - 1874

Elizabeth Branson

Rawson Williams
1849 - 1933
m: October 26, 1870

Elizabeth Hammond
1828 - 1879

Lee Williams
1882 - 1957
m: February 25, 1903

George Witcraft
1801 -
m: July 28, 1821

William Isiah Witcraft
1822 -
m: September 10, 1844

Amelia Gouldin
1803 -

Sarah Witcraft
1851 - 1935

Margaret Wallace
1816 -

Ancestors of Mardo Williams

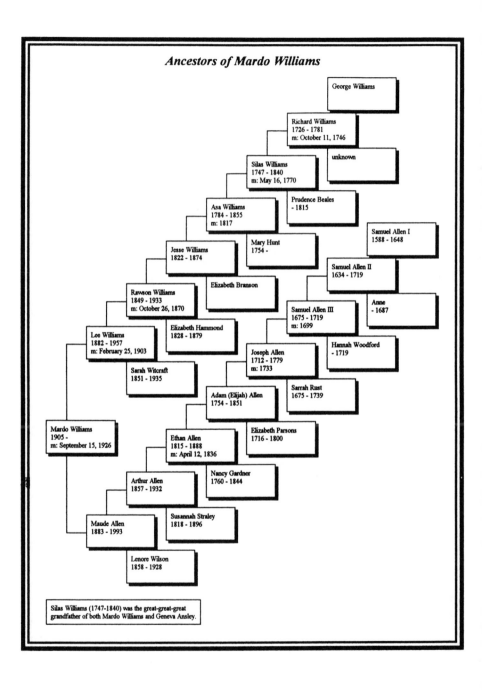

George Williams

Richard Williams
1726 - 1781
m: October 11, 1746

unknown

Silas Williams
1747 - 1840
m: May 16, 1770

Prudence Beales
- 1815

Asa Williams
1784 - 1855
m: 1817

Mary Hunt
1754 -

Samuel Allen I
1588 - 1648

Jesse Williams
1822 - 1874

Elizabeth Branson

Samuel Allen II
1634 - 1719

Rawson Williams
1849 - 1933
m: October 26, 1870

Samuel Allen III
1675 - 1719
m: 1699

Anne
- 1687

Lee Williams
1882 - 1957
m: February 25, 1903

Elizabeth Hammond
1828 - 1879

Hannah Woodford
- 1719

Joseph Allen
1712 - 1779
m: 1733

Sarah Witcraft
1851 - 1935

Sarrah Rust
1675 - 1739

Adam (Elijah) Allen
1754 - 1851

Mardo Williams
1905 -
m: September 15, 1926

Elizabeth Parsons
1716 - 1800

Ethan Allen
1815 - 1888
m: April 12, 1836

Nancy Gardner
1760 - 1844

Arthur Allen
1857 - 1932

Susannah Straley
1818 - 1896

Maude Allen
1883 - 1993

Lenore Wilson
1858 - 1928

Silas Williams (1747-1840) was the great-great-great grandfather of both Mardo Williams and Geneva Ansley.

Ancestors of Geneva Ansley

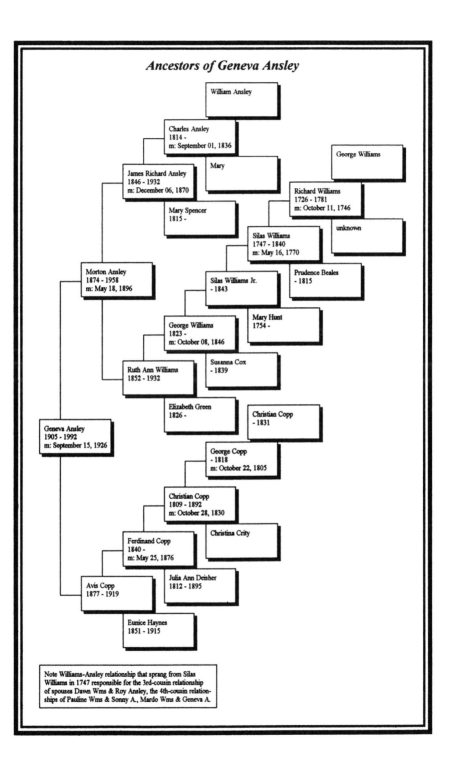

William Ansley

Charles Ansley
1814 -
m: September 01, 1836

Mary

George Williams

James Richard Ansley
1846 - 1932
m: December 06, 1870

Richard Williams
1726 - 1781
m: October 11, 1746

Mary Spencer
1815 -

unknown

Silas Williams
1747 - 1840
m: May 16, 1770

Morton Ansley
1874 - 1958
m: May 18, 1896

Silas Williams Jr.
- 1843

Prudence Beales
- 1815

Mary Hunt
1754 -

George Williams
1823 -
m: October 08, 1846

Ruth Ann Williams
1852 - 1932

Susanna Cox
- 1839

Elizabeth Green
1826 -

Christian Copp
- 1831

Geneva Ansley
1905 - 1992
m: September 15, 1926

George Copp
- 1818
m: October 22, 1805

Christian Copp
1809 - 1892
m: October 28, 1830

Ferdinand Copp
1840 -
m: May 25, 1876

Christina Crity

Avis Copp
1877 - 1919

Julia Ann Deisher
1812 - 1895

Eunice Haynes
1851 - 1915

Note Williams-Ansley relationship that sprang from Silas
Williams in 1747 responsible for the 3rd-cousin relationship
of spouses Dawn Wms & Roy Ansley, the 4th-cousin relationships of Pauline Wms & Sonny A., Mardo Wms & Geneva A.

INDEX

TO ORDER MORE BOOKS, WRITE:

CALLIOPE PRESS
POST OFFICE BOX 2408
NEW YORK, NEW YORK 10108-2408